RTI
Success in Secondary Schools

A Toolkit for Middle & High Schools

by
Jim Wright

DUDE PUBLISHING
A Division of
National Professional Resources, Inc.
Port Chester, New York

Publisher's Cataloging-in-Publication
(Provided by Quality Books, Inc.)

Wright, Jim, 1959-
 RTI success in secondary schools : a toolkit for
middle & high schools / by Jim Wright.
 p. cm.
 Includes bibliographical references.
 ISBN-13: 978-1-934032-99-2
 ISBN-10: 1-934032-99-9

 1. Inclusive education--Handbooks, manuals, etc.
2. Children with disabilities--Education--Handbooks,
manuals, etc. 3. Middle school education.
4. Education, Secondary.   I. Title.

 LC1200.W76 2011   371.9'046
                        QBI11-600192

Acquisitions Editor: Helene M. Hanson
Production Editor, Cover Design: Andrea Cerone,
National Professional Resources, Inc., Port Chester, NY

© 2012 Jim Wright

Dude Publishing
A Division of National Professional Resources, Inc.
25 South Regent Street
Port Chester, New York 10573
Toll free: (800) 453-7461
Phone: (914) 937-8879

Visit our web site: www.NPRinc.com

All rights reserved. Materials in the Exhibits and Appendices may be reproduced/photocopied by the purchaser of this book, for educational purposes only. Commercial use of any of the contents of this book is forbidden without prior written permission from the publisher. Other than for the aforementioned sentence, no part of this may be reproduced or transmitted in any form or by any means, electronic or mechanical, including photocopying, recording, or by any information storage and retrieval system, without permission in writing from the publisher. Not for resale.

Printed in the United States of America

ISBN 978-1-934032-99-2

To Lucy, who brought us light.

Contents

Acknowledgements iv

Preface v

Chapter 1: RTI: A Model to Help Struggling Learners in Middle & High Schools..1

   • Exhibit 1-A—Middle & High Schools: Top Tasks for Implementing RTI........ 12

Chapter 2: Launching RTI in Your Secondary School: Assess Readiness and Create a Plan............................17

   • Frequently Asked Questions About…RTI at the Middle & High School Level 25

   • Exhibit 2-A—Establishing and Running a District-Level RTI Leadership Team: Frequently Asked Questions................................32
   • Exhibit 2-B—Engaging the Reluctant Teacher: Seven Reasons Why Middle and High School Instructors May Resist Implementing Classroom RTI Interventions 35
   • Exhibit 2-C—Ideas to Build Teacher Understanding and Support for RTI....37
   • Exhibit 2-D—Conducting a Response-to-Intervention 'SWOT' Analysis......38
   • Exhibit 2-E—RTI Goals Planning Sheet: A 4-Stage Implementation Process..41
   • Exhibit 2-F—Conducting an RTI School or District Resource Inventory 44

Chapter 3: Establishing a Strong RTI Problem-Solving Team 47

   • Frequently Asked Questions About…Middle & High School RTI Problem-Solving Teams...58

   • Exhibit 3-A—Secondary Level: Teacher Referral to RTI Problem-Solving Team 63
   • Exhibit 3-B—RTI Team Introductory Script (Share With Referring Teacher at the Start of the Initial Meeting).....................................64
   • Exhibit 3-C—RTI Problem-Solving Team Roles & Responsibilities.............65
   • Exhibit 3-D—RTI Team: Initial Meeting 'Companion Guide'........................66
   • Exhibit 3-E—RTI Team: Initial Meeting Minutes Form, Secondary Grades..76
   • Exhibit 3-F—RTI Problem-Solving Team Effectiveness Self-Rating Scale ..81
   • Exhibit 3-G—Creating a 'Multiple-Source' Process to Initiate Middle or High School Student Referrals to the RTI Problem-Solving Team 82

- Exhibit 3-H—The Case Manager-Teacher 'Pre-Meeting': Creating a More Efficient RTI Team Process 83
- Exhibit 3-I—Engaging the Student as an Active RTI Partner in the Intervention Planning Process 85

Chapter 4: Developing Student Intervention Plans 89

- Frequently Asked Questions About...Middle & High School Interventions 100

- Exhibit 4-A—Developing Shared Guidelines for Determining 'Evidence-Based': Recommendations for Schools 106
- Exhibit 4-B—Intervention & Related RTI Terms: Definitions 111
- Exhibit 4-C—Defining Academic Problems: The First Step in Effective Intervention Planning 112
- Exhibit 4-D—Defining Problem Student Behaviors and Matching to Appropriate Interventions: A 5-Step Process 116
- Exhibit 4-E—Academic Interventions 'Critical Components' Checklist 121
- Exhibit 4-F—Intervention Integrity: Methods to Track the Quality with Which Interventions Are Carried Out 127
- Exhibit 4-G—Scheduling RTI Supplemental Services in Middle and High Schools: Five Ideas 136
- Exhibit 4-H—Tier 1 (Classroom) Interventions: Building Your School's Capacity 138
- Exhibit 4-I—Documenting Tier 1 (Classroom) Interventions: A Sample Form 147
- Exhibit 4-J—Reading Comprehension 'Fix-Up' Skills: A Toolkit 150
- Exhibit 4-K—'Defensive Behavior Management': Advance Planning, Connecting With the Student, and Defusing Crisis Situations 154

Chapter 5: Using Data to Guide RTI—Screening, Instructional Assessment, and Progress-Monitoring 157

- Frequently Asked Questions About...Middle & High School Assessment & Progress-Monitoring 167

- Exhibit 5-A—Finding Students At-Risk: How to Create a Comprehensive Middle or High School-Wide Screening Plan 173
- Exhibit 5-B—The RIOT/ICEL Matrix: Organizing Data to Answer Questions About Student Academic Performance & Behavior 181
- Exhibit 5-C—'Academic Enabler' Observational Checklists: Measuring Students' Ability to Manage Their Own Learning 187

- Exhibit 5-D—Teacher-Friendly Methods to Monitor Tier 1 (Classroom) Interventions 192
- Exhibit 5-E—RTI Classroom Progress-Monitoring Worksheet: Guidelines... 195

Chapter 6: The 'RTI Tipping Point'—Making the First Positive Steps Toward Systems-Level Change 199

- Exhibit 6-A—RTI and Secondary Schools: Planning to Implement 5 Key Elements 206
- Exhibit 6-B—Evaluating a Student's 'Non-Responder' Status: An RTI Checklist 213

Addendum
- Core Instructional Ideas to Promote Literacy Skills in Secondary Classrooms 221

Resources 234

Acknowledgements

Although the topic of Response to Intervention (RTI) has been prominent nationally since at least 2004, the prospect of bringing the RTI problem-solving model to middle and high schools is still a daunting, unexplored frontier for many school districts. This book, *RTI Success in Secondary Schools: A Toolkit for Middle & High Schools,* grew out of the extensive training and consultation that I have done with school districts in New York State and other parts of the country to help them to tailor RTI to match the realities of secondary schools.

I would like to thank all of the secondary-level educators whom I have worked with over the past five years whose questions, experimentation, and willingness to share both their successes and failures have greatly expanded my understanding of how RTI can be effectively implemented in middle and high schools. Their contributions are reflected throughout the book.

I would also like to express my deep appreciation to Bob Hanson and Helene Hanson of National Professional Resources, Inc. (NPR, Inc.), my publisher. Both have been extremely supportive of (and patient with!) this project.

I also am indebted to Andrea Cerone at NPR, Inc., who tirelessly translated the many RTI forms that I created into a format compatible with my publisher's book compositing software.

And finally, I owe a special thank you to my wife Mimi, who encouraged me to put time into completing the book when our personal time was in short supply.

Preface

This book is an in-depth manual on how to bring Response to Intervention (RTI) to middle and high schools. RTI is a comprehensive model that has been adopted by schools across the nation to identify and support at-risk students. In theory, RTI can be applied at any grade level. However, RTI has up to the present been primarily an initiative adopted within the elementary grades—with good reason. While large-scale change is never easy, schools usually find it most manageable in the early grades to implement the key RTI elements, including teaching (or reteaching) deficient skills during core instruction, scheduling time for supplemental interventions, and motivating students to apply their best efforts.

The challenge, however, is to effectively adapt RTI to work in secondary-level settings, where implementation issues are considerably greater (Duffy, 2007). By middle and high school, the yawning gap in academic skills that separates the struggling learner from peers can appear to the content-area teacher to be almost unbridgeable; finding the time for supplemental interventions in the already-packed master schedule may seem impossible; and the students who most need academic intervention can look to the observer as if they have lost all motivation to try.

Then why attempt to bring the RTI model to middle and high schools? RTI is worth the investment in secondary education because it benefits students, teachers, and school districts. First, RTI benefits the at-risk student. There are many factors that can interfere with a student's academic success in the higher grades, including deficits in basic skills; lack of higher-level problem-solving strategies; a failure of the student to be motivated by traditional pay-offs to learning such as good grades; negative peer pressure that devalues academic success; emotional issues; and problems with substance abuse, to name just a few. The RTI model is designed proactively to find the struggling learner, analyze his or her learning needs, and blockers to success, and provide a plan tailored to address those needs and overcome those blockers. As schools become more flexible and personalized in their response to their most marginal students through RTI, the strong likelihood is that they will retain more of these students through to graduation. And graduation is key to students' future well-being. For example recent government statistics indicate that a high school graduate earns at least 18% more per year on average than a student who has dropped out of school (U.S. Bureau of the Census, 2011).

Second, RTI helps teachers. Educators in the secondary grades regularly complain—with justification—that they lack the tools to motivate their marginal students and to remediate those students' academic skill deficits. At the same time, through such initiatives as Race to the Top, state and federal education departments are increasingly holding middle and high school teachers directly accountable for the academic performance of the students who they teach. RTI gives teachers a problem-solving framework to accurately identify the factors interfering with a struggling student's success and to put into place the classroom strategies that can help the student to succeed.

Third, RTI helps school districts. In most states, just a handful of high-visibility, high-stakes statistics are used to summarily judge the quality of middle and high schools, such as student attendance; performance on state tests; number of violent incidents occurring in the school; and graduation rate. With its school-wide screening of students for academic risk; multiple tiers of student intervention; use of research-based intervention strategies; and regular monitoring of student progress on intervention, RTI gives schools a coherent and unified process to find and fix student problems. If done right, RTI holds the promise of improving the crucial statistics on student performance and building climate on which these secondary schools are evaluated.

This manual is intended for those building and district change agents—administrators, support staff, teachers, and others— whose goal is to bring Response to Intervention to their middle and high schools. The focus of this book is on action, and it is designed specifically as a step-by-step blueprint for rolling out RTI at the building level.

Lao Tzu, the Chinese sage, noted some 2500 years ago, "A journey of a thousand miles must begin with a single step." As educators embark on the quest to bring RTI to their middle and high schools, it is worth remembering that systemic, school-wide change does not happen overnight. While some benefits of RTI will often be noticeable immediately (e.g., improved communication and problem-solving among staff; use of more effective intervention strategies with at-risk students), schools should also have the long view in mind and be prepared to commit a minimum of three to five years to fully implement the RTI model. But readers who are ready to plunge into the chapters of this book have already accomplished the most important RTI task of all: taking the first step.

References

Duffy, H. (August 2007). *Meeting the needs of significantly struggling learners in high school.* Washington, DC: National High School Center. Retrieved from http://www.betterhighschools.org/pubs/

U.S. Bureau of the Census. (2011). *Education and synthetic work-life earnings estimates.* Retrieved on September 23, 2011, from http://www.census.gov/prod/2011pubs/acs-14.pdf.

Chapter 1
RTI: A Model to Help Struggling Learners in Middle & High Schools

> *Zach is a 10th-grade student attending a large high school in a suburban school district. Zach presents a host of concerns to his teachers. He appears to put limited effort into class assignments and homework, and is failing both English and Social Studies after the second marking period. Zach also skips classes occasionally—and lately has begun to miss whole days of school. His teachers assume that Zach's problems stem from a lack of motivation, apathy about school, and perhaps laziness.*
>
> *Unbeknown to his teachers, however, Zach's school difficulties stem primarily from deficits in academic skills. He has a long history of reading difficulties and even now reads much less fluently than do his peers. Zach also has limited capacities in reading comprehension: if he reads a passage that he does not fully grasp, he lacks the necessary comprehension 'fix up' strategies to understand the content. And there are a number of common academic vocabulary terms that Zach never really learned. When teachers use words in class like 'hypothesis' and 'integration', Zach nods along with the other students but misses the meaning.*
>
> *Encumbered by specific skill deficits—lack of reading fluency, limited reading comprehension fix-up skills, gaps in general academic vocabulary—Zach finds the reading-intensive curriculum in his high school to be overwhelming and punishing. Zach would never approach his teachers for help, both because he cannot clearly articulate what specific assistance he needs and because he senses that his teachers are annoyed with him for not turning in work and believe that he is choosing not to try. Zach cannot name one adult in school who he thinks would miss him if he dropped out. He is now just counting the days until he turns 16 and is no longer required to attend school.*

Scenarios similar to this are not unusual in America's middle and high schools. Faced with large class sizes and demanding courses to instruct, teachers often feel that they are overburdened and have little time to individualize instruction to support students with delays. Struggling learners come into classrooms with a cascade of problems—academic skill deficits, behavioral problems, poor study and organizational skills—that interfere with their learning and school motivation. And there is often no systematic process in these schools to provide teachers and other school staff with the necessary tools and resources to clearly and specifically identify student problems, match those students to evidence-based interventions, and monitor their progress to judge whether the interventions are effective. Instead, schools are often quick to oversimplify the nature of the problem and to pin blame for academic failure or behavioral problems mostly or solely on the student (e.g., the student is unmotivated or apathetic or lazy). The true explanation—that student failure is most frequently a result of the learner being mismatched in a significant way to the demands of the instructional setting—is often overlooked (e.g., Foorman & Torgesen, 2001).

This book is written to give middle and high school staff the tools to break out of the negative, self-perpetuating cycle of student failure through adoption of the Response to Intervention (RTI) model. Under RTI, a school assumes at the outset that a student in a general education classroom with academic delays has typical abilities and that it is the school's responsibility to find the appropriate instructional practices to close the achievement gap between that student and his peers. This initial assumption that the student is 'typical' changes only at the point when the school has clear evidence that the student has failed to improve despite a series of well-selected, well-implemented intervention plans. With evidence of 'non-response' in hand, the school then has grounds to investigate the possibility of a learning disability or other within-child explanation for the student learning problem.

RTI & Secondary Schools: Preventing Student Disengagement & Dropout

A primary goal of public schools is to provide students with the essential social and academic skills to prepare them for college, gainful employment, and active civic involvement. Yet, in a given school year, about 3.5 percent of students attending public high schools will leave those schools without graduating—a rate that has not changed appreciably in the past two decades (Cataldi, Laird, & KewalRamani, 2009). Nationally, in fact, nearly 9 percent of individuals age 16-24 no longer attend school and have failed to earn a high school diploma. The negative economic and social impact on students who leave high school without graduating is enormous. Adults who leave school without a diploma earn an average yearly income that is 40 percent lower than those who graduate from high school or obtain a GED. Individuals who drop out also are more likely to be unemployed and to become incarcerated (Cataldi, Laird, & KewalRamani, 2009).

Too often, secondary schools actively intervene to prevent a student from dropping out only when the problem has become severe and virtually impossible to turn around (Jimerson, Reschly, & Hess, 2008). However, evidence suggests that the pattern of underperformance and social and academic disengagement that can lead to dropping out can often be discerned years before the student ultimately exits the school system. For example, one recent study found that, using only available data on grades, attendance, and behavior, schools can reliably identify by sixth grade which students are high-risk candidates for dropping out (Balfanz, Herzog, & MacIver, 2007).

Proactive identification of struggling students allows the school to flag student problems at an earlier stage, when those problems will typically require less intensive intervention resources and have a greater probability of a positive outcome. To provide at-risk students with appropriate interventions, however, schools must often change their own culture and restructure their educational services. Research into optimal elements of effective high schools, for example, suggests that marginal students are most likely to attain success in settings that can offer a range of learning options matched to individual learners, employ strategies to engage parents as educational partners, use screening data to identify students at risk of school failure, establish a continuum of academic and behavioral intervention programs developed to address common student concerns, and connect caring adults as mentors to work with disengaged students (Bridgeland, DiIulio, & Morison, 2006).

Response to Intervention (RTI) is a comprehensive model of school-wide student support (Glover & DiPerna, 2007) that can give middle and high schools a roadmap for developing a process to identify and help students with emerging academic and behavioral problems. The RTI model at the secondary grade levels capitalizes on established best practices in middle and high school dropout prevention. In the RTI school, student services are arranged in a multi-tier system and students are provided with appropriate interventions calibrated to their risk status and needs. Additionally, RTI interventions are evidence-based and the school is able to measure the integrity with which those interventions are carried out. The RTI process is data-driven. Academic or behavioral data is first collected to assess the student's starting point and to set a goal for improvement. Then additional formative data is collected on an ongoing basis to determine whether the student has actually benefited from the intervention plan and attained the pre-set goal.

Details of the RTI Model

The RTI model gives schools the capacity to identify struggling students who require more intensive academic assistance, to match those students to appropriate evidence-based intervention strategies, to measure students' progress during intervention plans, and –ultimately—to judge whether the intervention plans are effective. There are some variations in RTI implementation across the nation (U.S. Department of Education, 2006). However, researchers are in general agreement on the most important components of the RTI model, which are described below (e.g., Burns & Gibbons, 2008; Vaughn, 2003).

Supporting Students through a Continuum of Intervention Services

Schools that successfully implement RTI organize their intervention supports for students along a continuum. This continuum of student supports is typically divided into levels, or tiers, with students who have more significant academic needs receiving more intensive support. While there is some variation across states, a version of the RTI continuum that is widely used divides intervention support into three tiers: Tier 1: Classroom Instruction and Interventions; Tier 2: Supplemental Group-Based Interventions; and Tier 3: Intensive, Individualized Intervention

Plans. All interventions used in RTI are 'evidence-based': that is, they have been demonstrated to be effective through research studies of high quality.

Tier 1: Classroom Instruction and Interventions. Tier 1 supports are those instructional and intervention strategies that are universally available across the school to all learners and in every classroom. For any content area, the elements of Tier 1 instruction and interventions are all-encompassing in scope. They include the curriculum, commercial and teacher-made instructional materials, whole-group instructional strategies that benefit a diverse group of learners, and any intervention assistance that teachers can feasibly give to individual students who need it. Tier 1 can be thought of as the toolkit of instructional strategies and interventions that general education teachers independently and routinely employ to increase the 'carrying capacity' of their classrooms to address a wide range of student academic needs. As a general rule, Tier 1 support is judged to be successful if, as a result, at least 80 percent of students in any academic or content area experience success in the general education setting and do not require more intensive RTI intervention help.

Tier 2: Supplemental Group-Based Interventions: Standard Treatment Protocol. Because of variability in skills, ability, and learning history, a certain number of students in every school, in order to master new instructional content or to remediate deficits in basic academic skills, will require additional intervention assistance beyond what the classroom teacher alone can provide. It is estimated that, in a typical secondary school, perhaps up to 15 percent of students may benefit from supplemental intervention support. When possible, Tier 2 supplemental intervention occurs in small-group format, because groups are an economical means to deliver intervention services. Group-based Tier 2 interventions are sometimes referred to as a 'standard treatment protocol' approach because a single, standard intervention program can be provided to all students participating in a given group. To ensure effectiveness, Tier 2 groups should be limited to no more than 7 students. Also, those students selected for any Tier 2 group should have a shared profile of intervention need (e.g., reading comprehension, study and organizational skills, etc.) that will reasonably allow a teacher to provide group interventions that benefit all group members.

Because scheduling of group interventions can be so challenging in middle and high schools, secondary schools are increasingly exploring computer-based supplemental instruction as an alternate means to provide Tier 2 intervention support.

Tier 3: Intensive, Individualized Intervention Plan: Problem-Solving Protocol. Tier 3 intervention support is the most intensive that a school can provide to students in general education. It is estimated that about 5 percent of students in a middle or high school may require Tier 3 assistance at any one time. A student is usually referred for intensive Tier 3 support because he or she has not previously achieved academic success despite having received classroom (Tier 1) and supplemental small-group (Tier 2) interventions. At the Tier 3 level, a trained multidisciplinary RTI Problem-Solving Team at the school typically meets with the general education teacher or members of the teaching team that work with the student. Together, they create a customized intervention plan matched to the student's academic needs. This team-based exploratory method for creating an optimal student intervention plan is commonly referred to as the 'problem-solving protocol'—because it requires that the RTI multidisciplinary team collect data on the student's academic functioning and follow a structured set of steps to select the best intervention for the student. By their very nature, Tier 3 intervention plans in secondary schools are highly varied and matched to students' individual needs. For instance, a single Tier 3 intervention plan might include strategies that content-area teachers will apply in the classroom, group or individual supplemental instruction provided in the classroom or in a separate setting, and even interventions that require the student to assume primary responsibility (e.g., seeking tutorial help from a teacher during a free period, if needed).

Using Data for Student Screening, Intervention Placement, and Progress-Monitoring

Middle and high schools that follow the RTI model collect and use existing data to identify struggling students at the earliest possible moment. Additionally, these schools have assembled an array of curriculum-based measures to identify and track basic academic skills, as well as commercial or teacher-made assessments to evaluate more complex student academic skills. To flag and provide intervention assistance to at-risk students, these schools regularly monitor 'early warning indicators' such as grades, disciplinary office referrals, and attendance. Additionally, these schools use appropriate grade-wide academic screening tools to locate those students in the general population who are performing significantly below academic expectations but might otherwise have been overlooked. Students who receive Tier 2 or Tier 3 services are monitored periodically using brief academic measures to determine whether their intervention plans are helping them close the gap with their more academically able peers.

RTI & Secondary Schools: Origins & Need for Further Research

The precipitating event that brought RTI to the public schools was the reauthorization by Congress in 2004 of the Individuals With Disabilities Education Improvement Act (IDEIA 2004). Language included in that legislation encouraged schools to view a student's response to appropriately matched, well-delivered instruction as crucial information in determining whether that student might require special education services. Soon after, the US Department of Education created new regulations based on IDEIA 2004 that pressed states to "permit the use of a process based on the child's response to scientific, research-based intervention" (34 C.F.R. 300 & 301, 2006; p. 46786). Additionally, the federal regulations put the responsibility squarely on schools to "ensure that underachievement in a child suspected of having a specific learning disability is not due to lack of appropriate instruction" (34 C.F.R. 300 & 301, 2006; p. 46787). However, the federal government also made clear that, across the nation, there are variations in the RTI model and that each state must decide on the RTI model to be used by its schools (U.S. Department of Education, 2006).

The RTI model has been implemented most quickly at the elementary level, with middle and high schools lagging several years behind (Duffy, 2007). One reason for the delay in bringing RTI to the higher grades is that secondary schools are structured quite differently than elementary buildings and present their own systemic barriers to change. In middle and high schools, instruction is compartmentalized. Teachers at this level are seen traditionally as content-area experts (Kamil et al., 2008) rather than as interventionists with the resources and skills to target the specific needs of struggling students. In fact, most secondary schools have yet even to determine what are the essential elements of 'high-quality universal instruction across content areas' (Duffy, 2007; p. 9). Yet there is broad agreement among RTI researchers and practitioners that the RTI model can be a highly effective framework to find marginal students and help them become successful.

Implementing RTI Step-by-Step: Key Objectives for Schools and an Overview of the Book

Specific details about how to make the RTI model work at middle and high schools are presented in the remainder of this book which consists of three major parts:

1. *Chapters.* First, there are the chapters themselves, which are written to be brief, concise reviews of important RTI topics. A listing of those chapter topics appears below.
2. *Frequently Asked Questions (FAQs).* Appearing at the end of chapters 2-5 are questions and answers about each chapter topic, written in a style and format to be accessible to educators and parents. These 'frequently asked questions' can be used as handouts for presentations or shared as RTI information resources for stakeholders in the school community.
3. *Exhibits.* These materials associated with each chapter are designed to be stand-alone, step-by-step implementation guides that schools can use to accomplish key RTI tasks. Some are straight text while others include forms that can become working documents.

By following the recommendations presented herein, secondary schools will be able to:

- *Create an RTI Leadership Team & build staff understanding and support for RTI (Chapter 2).* As a first step, districts should move quickly to assemble an RTI Leadership Team to develop and implement their RTI model consistently across all schools. Additionally, middle and high schools should work systematically to build understanding and support for RTI among their teachers and other stakeholder groups.

- *Assemble an RTI Problem-Solving Team (Chapter 3).* The building RTI Problem-Solving Team (RTI Team) meets to create customized intervention plans for students with the most intensive needs. Because it deals with high-stakes, high-visibility student cases, the RTI Team should follow a highly structured problem-solving meeting format.

- *Select and document evidence-based interventions (Chapter 4).* A central expectation in the RTI model is that middle and high schools will use intervention strategies that are 'evidence-based'. Schools should assemble collections of evidence-based interventions to share with teachers, as well as provide teachers with coaching and support in the use and documentation of these interventions.

- *Assess students and use data to monitor the impact of intervention plans (Chapter 5).* RTI is driven by data. Schools should proactively screen all students for behavioral and academic concerns periodically through the school year. Any student on an intervention plan should have baseline data collected, goals set for improvement and ongoing progress-monitoring to determine if the intervention plans are effective.

- *Move the school actively toward an positive RTI 'tipping point' (Chapter 6).* In many middle and high school settings, RTI will require comprehensive changes in staff responsibilities throughout the school. This concluding chapter discusses the concept of a 'tipping point' at which staff attitudes can suddenly crystallize in favor of— or in opposition to—RTI. It offers recommendations for key first steps that can promote the success of RTI in your school.

Before advancing to the next chapter, readers should complete the informal RTI readiness survey *Middle & High Schools: Top Tasks for Implementing RTI* that appears as Exhibit 1-A.

References

Balfanz, R., Herzog, L., & MacIver, D. J. (2007). Preventing student disengagement and keeping students on the graduation path in urban middle grades schools: Early identification and effective interventions. *Educational Psychologist, 42,* 223–235.

Bridgeland, J. M., Dilulio, J. J., & Morison, K. B. (2006). *The silent epidemic: Perspectives of high school dropouts.* Seattle, WA: Gates Foundation. Retrieved from http://www.gatesfoundation.org/nr/downloads/ed/TheSilentEpidemic3-06FINAL.pdf

Burns, M. K., & Gibbons, K. A. (2008). *Implementing response-to-intervention in elementary and secondary schools.* Routledge: New York.

Cataldi, E.F., Laird, J., & KewalRamani, A. (2009). *High school dropout and completion rates in the United States: 2007* (NCES 2009-064). National Center for Education Statistics, Institute of Education Sciences, U.S. Department of Education. Washington, DC. Retrieved from http://nces.ed.gov/pubsearch/pubsinfo.asp?pubid=2009064

Duffy, H. (2007). *Meeting the needs of significantly struggling learners in high school.* Washington, DC: National High School Center. Retrieved from http://www.betterhighschools.org/pubs/

Foorman, B. R., & Torgesen, J. (2001). Critical elements of classroom and small-group instruction promote reading success in all children. *Learning Disabilities Research & Practice, 16,* 203-212.

Glover, T. A., & DiPerna, J. C. (2007). Service delivery for response to intervention: Core components and directions for future research. *School Psychology Review, 36,* 526-540.

Jimerson, S., Reschly, A.L., & Hess, R. (2008). *Best practices in increasing the likelihood of school completion.* In A. Thomas & J. Grimes (Eds). *Best Practices in School Psychology - 5th Ed* (pp. 1085-1097). Bethesda, MD: National Association of School Psychologists.

Kamil, M. L., Borman, G. D., Dole, J., Kral, C. C., Salinger, T., & Torgesen, J. (2008). *Improving adolescent literacy: Effective classroom and intervention practices: A practice guide* (NCEE #2008-4027). Washington, DC: National Center for Education Evaluation and Regional Assistance, Institute of Education Sciences, U.S. Department of Education. Retrieved from http://ies.ed.gov/ncee/wwc

U.S. Department of Education. (2006). *Assistance to States for the education of children with disabilities and preschool grants for children with disabilities; final rule.* 71 Fed. Reg. (August 14, 2006) 34 CFR Parts 300 and 301.

Vaughn, S. (2003). *How many tiers are needed for Response to Intervention to achieve acceptable prevention outcomes?* Paper presented at the National Research Center on Learning Disabilities Responsiveness-to-Intervention Symposium, Kansas City, MO.

Exhibit 1-A
Middle & High Schools: Top Tasks for Implementing RTI

Middle & High Schools: Top Tasks for Implementing RTI	0 Work has not yet begun toward the goal	1 Work toward the goal has begun (Beginning Phase)	2 Progress has been made but the goal has not yet been attained (Intermediate Phase)	3 This goal has been accomplished (Advanced Phase)
My middle or high school has:	0	1	2	3
Screening procedures in place to locate students at risk. The school has procedures and decision rules to identify students who should be referred to the RTI Problem-Solving Team for academic or behavioral concerns. For example, the school may: • Monitor 5- and 10-week grade reports and refer any student who receives two or more failing grades. • Track office disciplinary referrals and refer students with repeated referrals who have not responded positively to lesser forms of intervention such as an administrator/parent conference. • Monitor student attendance and tardiness rates. • Maintain a 'watch list' of at-risk students from year to year, including students transitioning into the school from lower grades. • Screen the student population with academic measures—e.g., Oral Reading Fluency, CBM Reading Comprehension Maze Passages, CBM Math Computation, Measures of Academic Progress (MAP) from www.nwea.org.				
Reached a shared understanding among faculty about how to provide Tier 1 interventions in a consistent manner across classrooms. Standardizing Tier 1 interventions across the school requires: • Consensus regarding the minimum effort that is reasonable for teachers to expend in Tier 1 (classroom) interventions. • Creation of a menu of feasible classroom strategies to address common student concerns such as lack of organization skills or limited reading comprehension. • Provision of staff development, coaching and other support to teachers initially to encourage their adoption of an expanded range of Tier 1 interventions.				

Exhibit 1-A, continued

Middle & High Schools: Top Tasks for Implementing RTI	**0** Work has not yet begun toward the goal	**1** Work toward the goal has begun (Beginning Phase)	**2** Progress has been made but the goal has not yet been attained (Intermediate Phase)	**3** This goal has been accomplished (Advanced Phase)
My middle or high school has:	0	1	2	3
Made supplemental academic interventions available for students found at-risk through school-wide screenings. The school has established supplemental (Tier 2) services for students struggling with academic skills. Those services may be delivered through small-group instruction or computer-assisted instruction. • Tier 2 groups should be capped at 7 students. All students enrolled in a given group should have a similar set of academic needs so that they can benefit from the same group intervention procedures. Instruction/interventions should be evidence-based. • Tier 2 computer-assisted instruction should be evidence-based.				
Put into place a formal process for Tier 3 (RTI Team) referrals. The school has a defined process in place for referring students to the RTI Team. That referral process includes these elements: • Student referrals can originate from a number of sources (e.g., classroom teachers, school social workers, school psychologists, guidance counselor, administration, parent, etc.). • People who can refer students understand the profile of academic or behavioral concerns that warrant referring a student to the RTI Team. • The school designates a small number of contact staff (e.g., school social worker, school psychologist, guidance counselors, school administration) through whom student referrals are channeled.				

Exhibit 1-A, continued

Middle & High Schools: Top Tasks for Implementing RTI	**0** Work has not yet begun toward the goal	**1** Work toward the goal has begun (Beginning Phase)	**2** Progress has been made but the goal has not yet been attained (Intermediate Phase)	**3** This goal has been accomplished (Advanced Phase)
My middle or high school has:	0	1	2	3
Created consistent and fair policies throughout the school for homework assignments and acceptance of late work. Ideas to be considered for a schoolwide homework/late work policy include: • Setting a reasonable cap on the amount that homework counts toward the course grade (e.g., 10-20 percent). • Establishing guidelines across classrooms for the acceptance of late work, including penalties and conditions (such as illness) under which those penalties are to be waived. • Requiring that all teachers hand out periodic (e.g., weekly) outlines detailing all upcoming classwork and homework assignments. • Allowing the RTI Team latitude on a case-by-case basis to modify a student's homework expectations or allow an extension in acceptance of late student work if evidence shows that the student has otherwise mastered essential course concepts (e.g., the student is passing quizzes and tests).				
Adopted an efficient problem-solving model. The problem-solving team is a multi-disciplinary team that meets regularly to discuss student referrals. This RTI Team: • Follows a consistent, structured problem-solving model. • Schedules initial meetings to discuss student concerns and follow-up meetings to review student progress and judge whether the intervention plan was effective. • Develops written intervention plans with sufficient detail to ensure that the intervention is implemented with fidelity across settings and people. • Builds an 'intervention bank' of research-based intervention ideas for common student academic and behavioral concerns.				

Exhibit 1-A, continued

Middle & High Schools: Top Tasks for Implementing RTI	0 Work has not yet begun toward the goal	1 Work toward the goal has begun (Beginning Phase)	2 Progress has been made but the goal has not yet been attained (Intermediate Phase)	3 This goal has been accomplished (Advanced Phase)
My middle or high school has:	0	1	2	3
Identified RTI-relevant existing (archival) data to be routinely brought to RTI Team meetings. The RTI Team surveys the data already collected and stored by the school (existing or 'archival' data) and decides: (1) what specific data should routinely be brought to RTI Team meetings and; (2) who is responsible for bringing it. Examples of data that would be useful at initial intervention team meetings include: • Attendance records. • Current quiz, test, and homework grades. • Office disciplinary referral information.				
Inventoried intervention resources available in the building or district for use by the RTI Team. The inventory should include: • Formal programs or services available to at-risk students. • Specific personnel with specialized training in academic or behavioral interventions (who can serve as consultants or coaches to teachers). • Curriculum materials—including computer-assisted instructional or remedial programs—that can be included in student intervention plans when appropriate. Once inventoried, intervention resources should be organized into a list by presenting student concerns, with information about how each resource can be accessed by the RTI Team.				

Exhibit 1-A, continued

Middle & High Schools: Top Tasks for Implementing RTI	**0** Work has not yet begun toward the goal	**1** Work toward the goal has begun (Beginning Phase)	**2** Progress has been made but the goal has not yet been attained (Intermediate Phase)	**3** This goal has been accomplished (Advanced Phase)
My middle or high school has:	0	1	2	3
Mapped adolescent and family services offered by local human-services agencies. Through the RTI Team or other vehicle, the school has: • Surveyed the range of relevant agency services or programs offered in the community that target adolescents or families. • Identified referral procedures and key contacts in local agencies to access their programs or services. • Developed the capability (with agency and family/student agreement) to invite agency representatives to join the RTI Team in 'wrap-around' intervention-planning meetings.				
Developed a process to train students to be self-advocating, self-managing learners. The school recognizes that students have important responsibilities in middle and high school interventions. To accomplish this goal, the school: • Provides training to students in how to analyze their learning needs and advocate for those needs. • Creates the expectation that students will be invited to RTI Team meetings when appropriate. • Develops a student 'intervention contract' listing those elements of the intervention plan that require student participation—to ensure understanding and motivation for compliance.				
The capacity to monitor student progress during interventions. The RTI Team has the capacity to use reliable, valid measures to track student progress in response to intervention plans and can make data-based decisions within several weeks about the effectiveness of those plans.				

Chapter 2
Launching RTI in Your Secondary School: Assess Readiness and Create a Plan

While the general elements of RTI can be implemented at any grade level, researchers have not yet arrived at a consensus on a single RTI model that is ideal for all middle and high schools (Duffy, 2007). Indeed, it is unlikely that a single "one-size-fits-all" RTI approach will ever be developed that will work for every secondary school across the country—because these schools have diverse student populations and are also faced with varying levels of available instructional resources, different state academic standards, and other important local factors that directly impact student achievement. For the foreseeable future, then, secondary schools must adopt an exploratory approach as they roll out RTI in their building. They must be prepared to implement the RTI model, evaluate success on an ongoing basis, and make mid-course corrections as needed.

Nonetheless, the initial steps will be the most crucial in implementing RTI in any middle or high school, as those first efforts help to determine whether a school embarks on a pathway of eventual success with RTI or instead encounters failure. With so much at stake, school leaders cannot rely on chance when introducing the RTI model to a building. Rather, careful, methodical planning is essential to ensure that the school has a multi-year roadmap for RTI implementation, anticipates and proactively responds to possible sources of stakeholder resistance, and lines up the resources necessary to support RTI. This chapter outlines exactly what first steps a secondary school should take when it launches RTI.

The RTI Leadership Team: A Vehicle for Oversight and Planning (District level)

Secondary schools should expect that RTI will take several years to fully implement (Burns & Riley-Tillman, 2009), that this initiative will include a sizable number of components, and that it will impact instruction and behavior management across the entire building. Because of its complexity and large scope, RTI requires careful planning. It is therefore recommended as the first step in RTI implementation that a district-level team—referred to hereafter as the 'RTI Leadership Team'—be created. For detailed instructions on how to set up an RTI Leadership Team and what that team's functions are, review Exhibit 2-A, *Establishing and Running a District-Level RTI Leadership Team: Frequently Asked Questions*. This form can be used to track progress.

The RTI Leadership Team's primary responsibilities are to develop a multi-year plan for rolling out RTI in a coordinated manner across all campuses in the district (including secondary schools) and to monitor and guide the district-wide RTI roll-out. The RTI Leadership Team should be multi-disciplinary. Its membership must include those district leaders who control resources and personnel that can be allocated to RTI. Additionally, the RTI Leadership Team should include representatives from elementary, middle, and high schools.

Laying the RTI Foundation: Key Steps

The RTI Leadership Team can assist secondary schools in their quest to adopt an RTI model by:

1. assessing possible staff reluctance or resistance to RTI;
2. educating stakeholders in the school community about the RTI model;
3. identifying those strengths and challenges from both within and outside of the school or district that could affect implementation of RTI;

4. generating a comprehensive, multi-year RTI roll-out plan;
5. inventorying resources throughout the school or district that can be used to support student intervention planning and progress-monitoring.

These RTI Leadership Team responsibilities are explained more fully below:

- *Assessing Stakeholder Resistance.* Because RTI requires restructuring the way in which student instruction and interventions are delivered at the classroom level and across the school, implementation of this model requires comprehensive, systems-level change. But change does not come easily to any institution, particularly one so ingrained in traditional practices as is the typical middle or high school. Before introducing an RTI model, educational leaders should first fully understand what sources of stakeholder resistance might be present that could interfere with the adoption of RTI.

  For example, Walker (2004) notes that general education teachers are less likely to support individualized student interventions and more likely to favor group-based instructional and behavior management strategies. Additionally, individual teachers vary in their ability to instruct and manage behaviors effectively (Gerber, 2003; Kamil et al., 2008), suggesting that some instructors in a school may be less "tolerant" of struggling students simply because they lack the teaching skills to appropriately accommodate them. There are other possible reasons that content-area teachers at the secondary level may resist the expectation that they provide intervention support in the classroom. Teachers may be concerned that they will lose control of classroom behaviors if they attempt new intervention strategies (Kamil et al., 2008), or they may be reluctant to provide RTI intervention support to apparently unmotivated students (Walker, 2004). Furthermore, there is often confusion and disagreement at the secondary level about what quality practices should be considered essential 'core instruction' and used routinely in every content-area classroom (Duffy, 2007).

A useful activity for the RTI Leadership Team as it prepares to implement RTI is to identify possible common reasons why content-area teachers may be reluctant to engage in classroom intervention efforts. By fully understanding the degree of RTI resistance and its possible sources, of course, a school will find itself in a much better position to tailor its RTI rollout to address and overcome that resistance. For a structured activity that can assist in uncovering potential reasons that teachers might be reluctant to implement interventions in the classroom, see Exhibit 2–B, *Engaging the Reluctant Teacher: Seven Reasons Why Middle and High School Instructors May Resist Implementing Classroom RTI Interventions.*

- *Building Teacher Understanding and Support for RTI.* Teacher support for the RTI model is essential for its success. When seeking to enlist faculty support, schools should offer RTI information in short, teacher-friendly presentations or discussion forums; emphasize the benefits of RTI in addressing chronic concerns about struggling students; solicit teacher input in the development of the RTI model; and demonstrate that RTI is a flexible, comprehensive problem-solving framework rather than an isolated, stand-alone program. Review the guide appearing as Exhibit 2-C, *Ideas to Build Teacher Understanding and Support for RTI,* for advice on promoting staff buy-in for the RTI model.

- *Identifying RTI Strengths and Potential Problems Through a SWOT Analysis.* A significant hazard facing schools that implement RTI is the sudden emergence of an unknown or unexpected challenge that can stall or even undermine the initiative. Such challenges can arise from within the school organization or outside of it. An additional concern for schools is the possibility that they might overlook possible strengths or enabling factors either within or outside of the organization that could promote the success of RTI. One structured heuristic, or guide to problem-solving, that the RTI Leadership Team may wish to use to identify both positive and negative factors that could impact RTI implementation is the SWOT ("Strengths-Weaknesses-Opportunities-Threats") analysis (SWOT analysis, 2009). A SWOT analysis is a structured inquiry tool often used by corporations, non-profit agencies, and other entities that first examines strengths and weaknesses within an organization that may affect the success of an initiative. The SWOT analysis then looks beyond the organization at possible opportunities and threats on the horizon that could also impact an initiative. The results of an RTI SWOT analysis can be very useful in guiding the RTI Leadership Team to develop a more realistic multi-year plan for RTI implementation. Review Exhibit 2-D, *Conducting a Response-to-Intervention 'SWOT' Analysis,* for detailed instructions in carrying out a SWOT analysis.

- *Developing a Multi-Year RTI Implementation Plan.* Because rolling out RTI is an ambitious undertaking that requires changes through a school, the RTI Leadership Team must draft a multi-year plan to coordinate the many tasks required for success. Such a plan should focus on four major elements: (1) building staff understanding and support for the RTI model; (2) creating a continuum of effective student academic and behavioral interventions in Tiers 1 through 3; (3) developing the proactive capacity to screen all students in the school for emerging academic or behavioral concerns and the ability to monitor the progress of selected students who receive supplemental (Tier 2 or 3) interventions to determine whether they are benefiting from those interventions; and (4) establishing an RTI Problem-Solving Team that can create individualized intervention plans matched to those students with the most intensive intervention needs. Specific guidelines for how to carry out each of these RTI elements are presented in subsequent chapters of this book.

When generating the multi-year RTI plan, the RTI Leadership Team can plan more realistically if it observes a 4-step process to promote effective systems change (Ervin & Schaughency, 2008). The team first selects a major RTI goal (e.g., "To build the capacity of content-area teachers to implement classroom literacy interventions."). The team then considers the natural stages of RTI implementation that unfold over time (and the tasks appropriate for each stage). Those 4 stages include: Preparation; Initial Implementation; Institutionalization; and Ongoing Development/Updating. For a more detailed description of the 4-stage systems-change framework described here, review exhibit 2-E, *RTI Goals Planning Sheet: A 4-Stage Implementation Process,* which provides a convenient planning form.

- *Inventorying District or School Resources to Support RTI.* It is unlikely in the current difficult funding climate that schools will be given additional federal or state money to implement RTI. In an era of tight budgets, then, schools must look to their existing resources to support their RTI initiatives. So an important function of the RTI Leadership Team is to inventory current district and school resources that can possibly be reallocated toward RTI implementation—and then to make sure that those resources are made available and accessible to staff. Among resources that the team might inventory at the school or district level are: (1) staff members who have flexible job descriptions or schedules that would allow them to assist with interventions, assessment, or other RTI tasks; (2) personnel with specialized training and skills that would recommend them as consultants, coaches, or trainers on RTI topics;(3) commercial academic and behavioral intervention resources or published training materials previously purchased by the district or school; and (4) screening and progress-monitoring tools available to track student academic and behavioral performance. (An important question to be answered for each RTI resource indentified through this inventory is whether the resource can be easily accessed by schools. If unsure, the Leadership Team should clarify the process for accessing that resource.) Once a master inventory of RTI resources has been compiled, the RTI Leadership Team can share the inventory with schools to aid them in their RTI implementation. For an example of a form that can be used to complete a district- or schoolwide resource inventory, review Exhibit 2-F, *Conducting an RTI School or District Resource Inventory.*

From RTI Launch to Full Implementation: Next Steps

Introducing RTI to a middle or high school is a bold but necessary venture that will ultimately help those struggling students who concern educators the most. But schools cannot hope to stumble into success with RTI by accident. Rather, they must carefully lay the groundwork in the early stages to ensure that RTI has the greatest chance to be fully accepted and integrated both into the day-to-day operation of classrooms and throughout the building. This chapter has presented a series of tangible steps that any school can follow to clear a path for RTI, even on those campuses with demanding curricula, limited resources, and challenging student populations.

The recipe for an effective RTI launch is for secondary schools to establish a strong RTI Leadership Team and then use that team to assess their baseline 'RTI readiness', assess possible staff resistance to RTI, work hard to overcome that resistance and educate stakeholders in how RTI can improve student academic performance and behaviors, create a comprehensive multi-year plan to roll RTI out in the building, and inventory resources to fully use what schools already have to support the RTI project. With those initial and essential steps accomplished, a district is ready to more deeply investigate the key components that make up RTI: Problem-Solving Teams, intervention plans, and assessment/progress-monitoring.

References

Burns, M., & Riley-Tillman, T. C. (2009). Response to intervention and eligibility decisions: We need to wait to succeed. *NASP Communique,* 38(1), pp. 1, 10, 11.

Duffy, H. (August 2007). *Meeting the needs of significantly struggling learners in high school.* Washington, DC: National High School Center. Retrieved from http://www.betterhighschools.org/pubs/

Ervin, R. A., & Schaughency, E. (2008). Best practices in accessing the systems change literature. In A. Thomas & J. Grimes (Eds.), *Best practices in school psychology V* (pp. 853-873). Bethesda, MD: National Association of School Psychologists.

Gerber, M. M. (2003). *Teachers are still the test: Limitations of response to instruction strategies for identifying children with learning disabilities.* Paper presented at the National Research Center on Learning Disabilities Responsiveness-to-Intervention Symposium, Kansas City, MO.

Kamil, M. L., Borman, G. D., Dole, J., Kral, C. C., Salinger, T., & Torgesen, J. (2008). *Improving adolescent literacy: Effective classroom and intervention practices: A practice guide* (NCEE #2008-4027). Washington, DC: National Center for Education Evaluation and Regional Assistance, Institute of Education Sciences, U.S. Department of Education. Retrieved from http://ies.ed.gov/ncee/wwc.

SWOT analysis. (2009, September 1). In *Wikipedia, the free encyclopedia.* Retrieved September 1, 2009, from http://en.wikipedia.org/w/index.php?title=SWOT_analysis&oldid=311362911

Walker, H. M. (2004). Use of evidence-based interventions in schools: Where we've been, where we are, and where we need to go. *School Psychology Review*, 33, 398-407. pp. 400-401.

Frequently Asked Questions About...
...RTI at the Middle & High School Level

1. **What is Response to Intervention (RTI)?** RTI is a school-wide model of student support. While all students can benefit from the RTI model, a primary focus is students in general education classrooms who are struggling with academic and/or behavior problems. The foundation of RTI in any school is strong core instruction in every classroom. The school also uses screening data such as brief academic assessments, disciplinary office referrals, attendance, and grades to identify students who need additional intervention assistance. The school then designs individualized intervention plans for those at-risk students to help them meet their learning needs. All interventions used under RTI should be 'evidence-based': that is, they have been shown through rigorous research to be effective in school settings. When the school puts students on intervention plans, the school collects baseline data to estimate the student's current performance in the area(s) of academic or behavioral difficulty and sets goals for improvement. During the intervention, the student is monitored periodically so that the school can judge in a short amount of time (e.g., 6-8 instructional weeks) whether a particular intervention plan is effective.

2. **What type of student is RTI designed to help?** The RTI model benefits all students. The first area of focus for RTI is on high-quality universal instruction. In a typical school, however, it is estimated that about 20 percent of the general education student population may not be successful even when receiving high-quality classroom instruction. These 'difficult-to-teach' students require more specialized intervention plans to supplement their core instruction. Schools can also see benefits in applying the standards of the RTI model to special education students. Schools should expect, for example, that the Individualized Education Programs (IEPs) of students with special needs will contain evidence-based instructional and behavior management strategies, identify student baseline and performance goal levels, and require the collection of progress-monitoring data to determine if those students are in fact reaching their performance goals.

3. **How does RTI organize a school's intervention services?**
RTI intervention services are set up in a multi-tier system, with intervention plans becoming increasingly intensive as students face a higher risk of school failure. The first tier of RTI support, Tier 1, is universal instruction/intervention and is available to all students. Tier 1 is the responsibility of the classroom teacher, who delivers strong core instruction and also employs a range of feasible, practical strategies to provide additional academic or behavioral support for struggling students. It should be noted that a classroom Tier 1 intervention plan continues as a required foundation even for those students who may eventually go on to receive more intensive intervention assistance at Tiers 2 and 3.

In a typical school, up to 20 percent of students will need additional interventions to address academic delays beyond what is available in the classroom. Most of these students would receive supplemental Tier 2 intervention services. When setting up Tier 2 services, a school will typically adopt what is referred to as the 'standard treatment protocol' approach. That is, the school identifies common areas of student concern (e.g., deficits in general academic vocabulary, limited reading comprehension 'fix up' skills) and purchases or creates an evidence-based 'standard treatment' program to target these students' academic deficits. Tier 2 services are most often delivered in small groups (capped at 6-7 students) or via computer-based learning.

Approximately 5 percent of general-education students in a typical school receive Tier 3 intervention support in a given year. The profile of a Tier 3 student is one who has not responded to lesser interventions and who is facing a potentially negative, high-stakes outcome such as course failure if that student cannot significantly improve his or her academic or behavioral performance. Most schools adopt a 'problem solving protocol' when planning intensive, Tier 3 interventions. The school establishes an RTI Problem-Solving Team that meets with the referring teacher(s) and efficiently uses the intervention resources of the building to develop a customized intervention plan that matches the unique needs of the student.

4. **What role do assessment and data collection play in the RTI process?** Student assessment is a necessary part of RTI, as data allows the school to locate students who need intervention support and to judge in 'real time' whether specific interventions are actually helping those students. At Tier 1, the teacher who has a student on classroom intervention collects information from the instructional environment to show if the student is benefiting from that intervention plan. Because teachers typically intervene proactively at Tier 1 to address emerging student deficits before they become major, the stakes are lower. Therefore, the kinds of data collected by teachers to document their classroom interventions can be varied and may not be as time-intensive or rigorous as data collection at the higher-stakes Tiers 2 and 3. At Tier 1, for example, a high school English teacher may document a student's classroom writing intervention through work samples of student writing assignments, grades, occasional scoring of writing assignments using a rubric, and a weekly administration of a Curriculum-Based Measurement writing probe.

RTI schools also adopt a proactive approach to identifying struggling learners by selecting several methods to screen the entire student population at several points per year. Middle and high schools may use a mix of data sources in their screenings, including brief, timed academic measures (e.g., Curriculum-Based Measures such as oral reading fluency probes and Maze Reading Comprehension passages); disciplinary office referrals; grades; attendance; recent state test results; etc. Individuals who are flagged in these universal screenings as needing additional intervention support are placed in supplemental (Tier 2 or 3) intervention services.

Academic measures selected to monitor the progress of students at Tiers 2 and 3 should possess 'technical adequacy': that is, they should be valid, reliable, have multiple alternate forms to allow repeated administration, and be sensitive to short-term student academic gains. Examples of CBMs that can be useful for assessing academic skills for secondary students include oral reading fluency, reading comprehension (Maze passage), math computation, and writing probes.

Students who receive Tier 2 'standard treatment protocol' interventions should have their progress monitored at least 1-2 times per month. Students on high-stakes Tier 3 interventions overseen by the RTI Problem-Solving Team should be assessed at least weekly.

5. **What is the role of the classroom teacher in the RTI model?** The classroom teacher is responsible under RTI for providing high-quality core instruction to effectively reach the widest possible range of learners. Additionally, the teacher notes any struggling students who need additional 'differentiated' instructional or behavioral support and provides that support in the form of a Tier 1 (classroom) intervention plan. Of course, the teacher should document Tier 1 interventions. The teacher should also be prepared to refer any students who do not respond sufficiently to classroom Tier 1 interventions for higher levels of RTI support—while continuing to use RTI classroom strategies with those students. The classroom teacher should also contact parents of struggling students to share concerns about these students and to encourage open, positive and regular communication between school and home.

6. **What are student responsibilities under RTI?** Teachers and administrators in secondary schools rightly expect that students receiving RTI support will follow through with their part of the intervention plan. After all, schools are accountable for teaching students to become self-advocates for their learning needs. However, many struggling students are disengaged learners who lack the skills or motivation to seek tutorial help from their teachers or take part in other commonly offered RTI supports. Middle and high schools should consider routinely inviting students who are on intensive, Tier 3 interventions to RTI Problem-Solving Team meetings and having those students and their parents sign a 'school success intervention plan' to signify that they understand and agree to participate in all intervention strategies. Additionally, school staff should ensure that they communicate with struggling students and their parents in a manner that clearly details the school's concerns about student performance but also conveys the message that they value these students, welcome them in their classrooms, and are

optimistic that—if the student, home and school work together—student academic or behavioral goals can be achieved. Finally, in the school setting, marginal students benefit from having mentor figures to whom they can turn when they encounter problems with their RTI plan or need encouragement and guidance.

7. **What is the parent's role in the RTI model?** The school is responsible for finding ways for struggling students to be successful—whether or not parents choose to actively participate in their children's educational program. Nonetheless, there is wide agreement that parents play a crucial role in guiding and motivating their children toward academic success. For example, parents can serve as influential role models for work and study skills, set up and supervise homework sessions, stay in close communication with the school about their child's academic performance and behaviors, and dispense home privileges contingent on the effort that their child makes in school. There is no question that the protective factors offered by parents who are positively involved in their children's schooling directly promote academic success and support the mission of RTI. Schools must, however, also recognize that, for a variety of reasons, not all parents find it easy to be involved in their child's education. Schools can most fully engage the power of parent participation by expecting that teachers will contact parents when a student begins to experience difficulties in school, inviting parents to attend RTI Problem-Solving Team meetings, taking care that staff adopt respectful language and tone when speaking with parents about their children, and consistently treating parents as respected colleagues in the RTI process.

8. **How can RTI information assist schools in identifying students who need special education services?** When a student is being considered for possible special education services, the school must first answer a fundamental question: Are that student's academic problems primarily a result of educational factors such as a mismatch between student and instruction, or do they stem instead from a chronic, within-child condition such as a learning disability? The RTI model provides evidence that helps schools to rule out

instructional explanations for underperformance by clearly defining a student's problems, matching those problems to evidence-based interventions, verifying that all interventions are fully carried out as designed, and collecting formative assessment data to judge whether the student has made adequate progress in moving from baseline to goal levels. In other words, when a general education student is ultimately found to be a 'non-responder' to appropriate evidence-based interventions, that failure to respond can be viewed as one diagnostic marker that serves as partial evidence for a possible underlying learning disability or other special education condition.

9. **Why must schools use 'evidence-based' interventions in RTI?** Schools have limited resources and time to put effective interventions in place for struggling students. That is simply a reality of our public education system. Therefore, the RTI model requires that schools be able to justify the intervention strategies that they select by showing that they are 'evidence-based,' i.e., that there is sufficient research to support these strategies. Most researchers agree that evidence-based interventions are those whose effectiveness has been demonstrated through well-crafted studies that use rigorous research methodologies. Ideally, too, these studies should have been published in reputable research journals that have a blind peer-review process to ensure that only studies of the highest quality are published.

10. **Is RTI required by law?** RTI was first introduced to public schools across the nation with the reauthorization by Congress in 2004 of the Individuals With Disabilities Education Improvement Act (IDEIA 2004). This federal legislation encourages the spread of RTI in public education by directing states to allow any of their schools to adopt an RTI model if they so choose and by explicitly preventing states from mandating the continuing use of a test score discrepancy formula in diagnosing learning disabilities. However, IDEIA 2004 also lets states decide whether to require that their schools adopt RTI and, if so, what the particulars of each state's RTI model might look like. At present, then, the U.S. Department of Education strongly supports schools' efforts to restructure their student support

according to RTI guidelines. However, schools should contact their state education departments for guidance in determining whether RTI is mandated statewide and for specifics about what RTI model(s) their state supports.

Exhibit 2-A
Establishing and Running a District-Level RTI Leadership Team: Frequently Asked Questions

Frequently Asked Questions	Action Steps
What is the purpose of the RTI Leadership Team? The RTI Leadership Team has several functions: (1) to draft and update a district RTI implementation plan; (2) to keep all schools throughout the district in compliance with good RTI practices; and (3) to identify and make available to schools the resources required to implement RTI successfully: • *Drafting a multi-year plan.* This will guide the district in the implementation of RTI while using existing resources. The team's RTI Plan should encompass a three-year rollout schedule. Each year, that plan is updated to accommodate changes in district funds and resources, changes in state and federal guidelines and regulations, and new findings in RTI research. • *Supervising RTI implementation.* The RTI Leadership Team oversees that RTI is implemented in a uniform manner throughout the school district. For example, the team ensures that the same procedures and measures are used to complete universal screenings in literacy across all classrooms or schools at each elementary grade, that RTI Problem-Solving Teams in each building use a similar meeting process, and that each school observes the same decision rules in determining if a general-education student on intervention is a 'non-responder'. One caution: Be sure not to overlook 'dissident' voices when selecting RTI Leadership Team members. Members who may have some reservations about RTI but also possess experience and knowledge may be valuable to the team.	☐ *Determine the team's scope and responsibilities.* At the district level, decide on what the scope, authority, and responsibilities of the RTI Leadership Team are to be. Be sure to confront potentially difficult questions such as 'Will the RTI Leadership Team's RTI recommendations be binding on individual schools or merely advisory?' ☐ *Review state guidelines that may impact your RTI Leadership Team.* Review any relevant guidelines or regulations from your state department of education to determine whether the state offers guidance on the makeup and functioning of the RTI Leadership Team or content of an RTI district plan.
Who should serve on the RTI Leadership Team? Your district should assemble a multi-disciplinary team to serve as your RTI Leadership Team. The team should include influential district administrators such as those who control resources (e.g., staff development funds; instructional budgets) or supervise staff (e.g., school psychologists, reading teachers) across the district. Additionally, the team should have representatives from school buildings to help the team to keep lines of communication open with its campuses. Finally, the membership on the team should be balanced to include representatives from important stakeholder groups (e.g., building administrators, general education teachers, etc.).	☐ *Generate a recruitment list.* Create a list of positions and/or personnel from school buildings and at the district level to be recruited for the RTI Leadership Team. Review the list to ensure that no important district department, school/ program, or stakeholder group has been overlooked.

Exhibit 2-A, continued

Frequently Asked Questions	Action Steps
How should RTI Leadership Team meetings be organized? Team meetings should follow a fixed schedule, with a standard set of meeting agenda items regularly brought up for team discussion: • *Regularly scheduled meetings.* The RTI Leadership Team should meet at least monthly to allow it to effectively oversee the RTI implementation process across the district—and to respond to problems or challenges as they emerge. • *Standing meeting agenda.* In addition to those topics brought up for discussion by team members, the RTI Leadership Team should establish a small set of standing agenda items—key discussion topics that are revisited at each meeting. Examples of topics that might be included on a team's standing meeting agenda might include school-wide literacy screenings, resources for classroom interventions, and update in state RTI guidelines and regulations. • *Subcommittees.* If the RTI Leadership Team is so large that frequent meetings are difficult to schedule and unwieldy to run, consider dividing the team's work among subcommittees (e.g., Assessment, Academic Interventions, Behavioral Interventions, District RTI Plan). Each subcommittee would meet as frequently as needed to complete its work. The full RTI Leadership Team may then meet less often (e.g., on a quarterly basis) to review and approve subcommittee recommendations.	☐ *Schedule meetings.* Create a schedule of RTI Leadership Team meetings for the full school year—and ensure that those meeting dates are shared with all team members. ☐ *Draft a standing meeting agenda.* Select topics to be put onto a standing meeting agenda for the RTI Leadership Team. Set time aside occasionally at team meetings to discuss items that should be removed from or added to the agenda. ☐ [Optional] *Develop a list of subcommittees.* Divide the duties of the full RTI Leadership Team into subcommittees. For each subcommittee, select a descriptive name, define its duties, and recruit members from the larger team.
What are structured forms of planning that can benefit the RTI Leadership Team? No RTI Leadership Team is likely to think of all necessary steps or to avoid all pitfalls when implementing RTI. However, there are structured planning formats that teams can follow to increase the probability that they have considered the most important issues when preparing a district RTI Plan: • *SWOT analysis.* In the complex RTI planning process, it can be helpful to perform a SWOT ('strengths-weaknesses-opportunities-threats') analysis to determine those enabling and hindering forces within and outside of the school district that could affect RTI implementation. (Directions and a form for conducting an SWOT analysis appear as Exhibit 2-D. • *Stages of RTI implementation.* When introducing any significant changes, the RTI Leadership Team should plan for that systems change by using a four-stage process: (1) Preparation; (2) Initial Implementation; (3) Institutionalization; (4) Ongoing Development/Updating. (A form that includes this four-stage planning process appears as Exhibit 2-E.)	☐ *Conduct a SWOT analysis.* Reserve time at an RTI Leadership Team meeting to conduct a SWOT analysis, using the forms provided in this chapter. ☐ *Follow the four-stage systems change framework for all RTI initiatives.* Make it a habit when creating and updating the district RTI plan to subject each major component of the plan to the four-stage systems-change framework that appears elsewhere in this chapter.

Exhibit 2-A, continued

Frequently Asked Questions	Action Steps
How can the RTI Leadership Team find resources to support RTI? The great majority of school districts that implement RTI will do so largely by using their existing resources. The RTI Leadership Team can help the school district adopt an RTI model by systematically inventorying district and building resources (personnel, instructional and assessment materials, staff development funds, etc.) that can be made available to support RTI. (See *Conducting an RTI School or District Resource Inventory* as appears in Exhibit 2-F.)	☐ *Conduct an inventory of RTI resources.* As one of its first acts, the RTI Leadership Team should conduct a thorough inventory of resources available to support RTI at the district level and at each school. This inventory should be updated yearly.

Exhibit 2-B
Engaging the Reluctant Teacher: Seven Reasons Why Middle and High School Instructors May Resist Implementing Classroom RTI Interventions

Directions: Read through each of the possible reasons listed below for why a teacher may be 'reluctant' to use classroom RTI interventions and select the **top 3** reasons that MOST apply to your school. Number those selected items in descending order of importance. For each of the explanations that you select, generate ideas to overcome teacher reluctance.

	1. **Lack of Skills.** Teachers lack the skills necessary to successfully implement academic or behavioral interventions in their content-area classrooms (Fisher, 2007; Kamil et al., 2008).
	2. **Not My Job.** Teachers define their job as providing content-area instruction. They do not believe that providing classwide or individual academic and behavioral interventions falls within their job description (Kamil et al., 2008).
	3. **No Time.** Teachers do not believe that they have sufficient time available in classroom instruction to implement academic or behavioral interventions (Kamil et al., 2008; Walker, 2004).
	4. **No Payoff.** Teachers lack confidence that there will be an adequate instructional pay-off if they put classwide or individual academic or behavioral interventions into place in their content-area classroom (Kamil et al., 2008).
	5. **Loss of Classroom Control.** Teachers worry that if they depart from their standard instructional practices to adopt new classwide or individual academic or behavior intervention strategies, they may lose behavioral control of the classroom (Kamil et al., 2008).
	6. **Not Deserving.** Teachers are unwilling to invest the required effort to provide academic or behavioral interventions for unmotivated students (Walker, 2004) because they would rather put that time into providing additional attention to well-behaved, motivated students who are 'more deserving'.
	7. **The Magic of Special Education.** Content-area teachers regard special education services as 'magic' (Martens, 1993). According to this view, interventions provided to struggling students in the general education classroom alone will be inadequate, and only special education services have the power to truly benefit those students.
	Other: _____ _____ _____

Exhibit 2-B, continued

Brainstorm Ideas to Overcome Teacher 'Reluctance'...

Reason 1
- _____
- _____
- _____
- _____

Reason 2
- _____
- _____
- _____

Reason 3
- _____
- _____
- _____
- _____

References

Fisher, D. (2007). Creating a schoolwide vocabulary initiative in an urban high school. *Journal of Education for Students Placed at Risk,* 12, 337-351.

Kamil, M. L., Borman, G. D., Dole, J., Kral, C. C., Salinger, T., & Torgesen, J. (2008). *Improving adolescent literacy: Effective classroom and intervention practices: A practice guide* (NCEE #2008-4027). Washington, DC: National Center for Education Evaluation and Regional Assistance, Institute of Education Sciences, U.S. Department of Education. Retrieved from http://ies.ed.gov/ncee/wwc.

Martens, B. K. (1993). A case against magical thinking in school-based intervention. *Journal of Educational and Psychological Consultation,* 4(2), 185-189.

Walker, H. M. (2004). Use of evidence-based interventions in schools: Where we've been, where we are, and where we need to go. *School Psychology Review,* 33, 398-407.

Exhibit 2-C
Ideas to Build Teacher Understanding and Support for RTI

Teacher support for the RTI model is crucial for its success. When seeking to enlist faculty support, schools should offer RTI information in short, teacher-friendly presentations or discussion forums; emphasize the benefits of RTI in addressing chronic concerns about struggling students; solicit teacher input in the development of the RTI model; and demonstrate that RTI is a comprehensive problem-solving framework rather than an isolated, stand-alone program.

	Goal	Possible Action Steps
1.	**Offer RTI information to teachers in a series of short presentations or discussion** forums. A common mistake that schools make in rolling out RTI is to present their teachers with RTI information in a single, long presentation—with little opportunity for questions or discussion. Instead, schools should plan a series of RTI information-sharing sessions with teachers throughout the school year. Any large-group RTI training sessions (e.g., at faculty meetings) should be kept short, to ensure that the audience is not overwhelmed with large volumes of information. Consider using smaller instructional team or department meetings as a vehicle for follow-up presentations, discussion, and teacher questions about RTI.	☐ *Create a year-long RTI information-sharing plan.* Determine what RTI information your school would like to present to staff, as well as the degree of faculty input and discussion needed. Then draft a year-long plan to communicate with staff about RTI. Each year, update the plan to keep faculty updated about implementation of the RTI model.
2.	**Present RTI as a coordinated, schoolwide approach to address long-standing teacher concerns about struggling students.** The fact that many states now strongly encourage or mandate RTI may not be enough to convince teachers that they should support RTI. Instead, schools should consider framing RTI as a broad, schoolwide solution to help teachers to better instruct, motivate, and manage the behaviors of struggling learners. Teachers want fewer class disruptions, more uninterrupted instructional time, higher performing students, targeted supplemental academic help for students who need it, and better communication among educators about the needs of all students. As schools make the case for RTI, they should demonstrate how it will help teachers to manage the day-to-day challenges that they face in their classrooms.	☐ *Get feedback from teachers about their classroom concerns.* Find opportunities to engage teachers in productive discussions about what they see as the greatest challenges facing them as instructors. Note the teacher concerns that surface most often. For each teacher concern, generate ideas for how an RTI model in your school might help teachers with that issue. Craft these ideas for instructor support into 'talking points' and include them in your school's RTI presentations.
3.	**Solicit teacher input when building your school's RTI model.** Teachers are a valuable resource that schools should tap when implementing RTI. When schools solicit teacher questions about RTI, include teachers on planning teams to help to develop the RTI process, and treat teacher objections or concerns about RTI as helpful feedback rather than stubborn resistance, those schools send the message that teachers are full partners in the RTI planning process.	☐ *Include teachers on the RTI Leadership Team.* One of the best ways to ensure that teachers have input into the RTI development process is to include teacher representatives on the RTI Leadership Team, the group that oversees the district's implementation of RTI.
4.	**Link all significant school and district initiatives to RTI.** RTI is a comprehensive, proactive model to identify and assist struggling students. Yet teachers may erroneously perceive RTI as just another program that is likely to last for only a short time and then disappear. Any RTI training for staff should make the point that RTI is not a single-self contained program but is actually an all-inclusive and flexible framework for student support that encompasses all existing student support programs and strategies.	☐ *Organize all school programs under the RTI framework.* A useful workshop exercise that can help a school to correct the possible tendency of staff to underestimate and dismiss RTI is to present it as an elastic multi-tier problem-solving framework. First, the school lists all of its significant current programs or initiatives intended to assess or intervene with students with academic or behavioral needs. The school then assigns each of the programs or initiatives to Tier 1, 2, or 3 in the RTI framework. The message for staff is that, while specific programs may come and go, the overarching RTI model is both adaptable and durable--and that much of the power of RTI rests on its potential to integrate a series of isolated programs into a larger unified and coordinated continuum of student support.

Exhibit 2-D
Conducting a Response-to-Intervention 'SWOT' Analysis

Introduction: The RTI SWOT (Strengths-Weaknesses-Opportunities-Threats) form is designed to assist members of the RTI Leadership Team undertake a structured review of positive and negative factors both within and outside of their school or district that can influence the success of RTI. Directions for completing an RTI SWOT analysis appear below. A brief sample SWOT analysis appears on the next page. Form 1 provides format for conducting this analysis.

How to Complete the RTI SWOT Analysis. The RTI Leadership Team reserves sufficient, uninterrupted time to complete the SWOT analysis.

List Key RTI Objectives: The Leadership Team first generates a list of important RTI objectives which becomes the basis for a SWOT analysis. Each RTI objective is framed as a goal statement. Examples of RTI objectives include "to promote teacher understanding & support for RTI" and "to adopt a core set of school-wide classroom (Tier 1) evidence-based literacy strategies across all content areas".

Consider Factors Within the Organization: For each RTI objective, the Leadership Team considers strengths and weaknesses within the organization that might impact the success of the objective.
- *Strengths* are factors within the school or district that may help to achieve the RTI goal.
- *Weaknesses* are factors within the school or district that may hinder efforts to achieve the RTI goal.

Consider Factors Outside the Organization: For each RTI objective, the Leadership Team considers opportunities and threats that lie outside the organization that might impact the success of the objective.
- *Opportunities* are factors outside of the school or district (e.g., state or federal guidelines, mandates, and regulations; funding; emerging research; public opinion) that may support attainment of its RTI goal.
- *Threats* are factors outside of the school or district (e.g., state or federal guidelines, mandates, and regulations; funding; emerging research; public opinion) that may interfere with attainment of its RTI goal.

Sample Response to Intervention 'SWOT' (Strengths-Weaknesses-Opportunities-Threats) Analysis Form

School / District: Smithtown Middle School   Date: September 23, 2009

Person(s) Completing 'SWOT' Analysis: Smithtown Central School District RTI Leadership Team: All members attending

RTI Objective	Inside the Organization		Outside the Organization	
	Strengths	Weaknesses	Opportunities	Threats
To Promote Teacher Understanding & Support for RTI	• There is a general awareness of RTI among faculty due to past trainings. • Staff at our school are open to new ways of organizing services, resources to better meet needs of struggling students.	• We have a lack of understanding among staff about how RTI will impact teachers' instructional role and job description. • There has been poor coordination to date in efforts across school district to deliver single, unified message about RTI and teacher practice.	• An increasing number of teacher training programs now include RTI content in their coursework. • Teachers' unions and other 'teacher-friendly' organizations are making more RTI information available to members.	• Different government-sponsored state & national initiatives (e.g., No Child Left Behind) are proliferating that compete with RTI for teacher awareness.
To Adopt a Core Set of School-Wide Classroom (Tier 1) Evidence-Based Literacy Strategies Across All Content Areas	• The school has put considerable effort into professional development for secondary school faculty on differentiated instruction over the past 3 years. • Teachers in our school express a genuine interest & willingness to provide individualized support for struggling students in the general education classroom.	• There is a great deal of variation across content-area classrooms in what strategies are used to support literacy skills. • Teachers from different instructional departments do not regularly communicate about good general education practices to boost student literacy skills.	• The What Works Clearinghouse, sponsored by the US Department of Education, has published a series of 'practice guides' detailing evidence-based classroom intervention ideas. These guides are a good source for Tier 1 (classroom) intervention ideas. They also offer direction in how to evaluate research supporting classroom interventions.	• The emphasis by government and the public on standardized test results may increase teacher pressure to cover course content quickly in group presentation format and to not use additional literacy strategies to promote deeper understanding for struggling students. • No universal definition of 'evidence-based' yet exists in the research community for schools to use.

Chapter 2 • Launching RTI in Your Secondary School: Assess Readiness and Create a Plan   39

Exhibit 2-D, Form 1

Response to Intervention 'SWOT' (Strengths-Weaknesses-Opportunities-Threats) Analysis Form

School / District: _____ Date: _____

Person(s) Completing 'SWOT' Analysis: _____

RTI Objective	Inside the Organization		Outside the Organization	
	Strengths	Weaknesses	Opportunities	Threats

Exhibit 2-E
RTI Goals Planning Sheet: A 4-Stage Implementation Process

Description: The *RTI Goals Planning Sheet,* Form 1 of this Exhibit, is intended to help the RTI Leadership Team effectively manage the complexity of a comprehensive RTI plan. The *Planning Sheet* lists major RTI components and then further divides each component into a series of specific implementation tasks. Each specific task can then be linked to the appropriate stage in the RTI roll-out: *preparation; initial implementation; institutionalization; ongoing development/updating.* These stages are drawn from research into effective systems change (Ervin & Schaughency, 2008).

General Guidelines: The *RTI Goals Planning Sheet* should be used by the district's RTI Leadership Team as it develops a plan for developing and rolling out an RTI model over multiple school years.

First, the RTI Leadership Team generates a series of 'RTI Implementation Goals.' These goals should be more general, global goals that will require attention through all stages of the RTI implementation process. An example of an RTI Implementation Goal for a secondary school might be: "To build the capacity of content-area teachers to implement classroom literacy interventions." Each goal should hav its own Form 1.

The RTI Leadership Team next takes each of the general RTI Implementation Goals and breaks that global goal into a series of specific subtasks. Subtasks are then sorted by stage of implementation. A listing of the 4 stages of RTI implementation appears below, with sample items.

Stage 1: Preparation: List any preparatory steps such as development of materials or staff training.

Examples of Preparation Tasks:
- "Review the past year's teacher referrals to the building RTI Problem-Solving Team. Based on those referrals, create a list of the top 8 reasons that classroom teachers refer students for additional intervention support."
- "Create a menu of Tier 1 (classroom- & teacher-friendly) interventions that match the top 8 reasons that teachers refer students for more intervention support."
- "Inventory those building and district personnel who are available to serve as intervention consultants and coaches for secondary classroom teachers."

Stage 2: Initial Implementation: Describe the tasks required to actually implement the goal.

Examples of Initial Implementation Tasks:
- "Provide training to content-area teachers to help them to define student behavioral and academic problems in specific, measureable terms."
- "Distribute the Tier 1 intervention menu to teachers and provide training in the use of the strategies."
- "Distribute the list of building and district consultants/coaches available to assist classroom teachers in the effective use of Tier 1 interventions."

Exhibit 2-E, continued

Stage 3: Institutionalization: Once the goal is initially carried out successfully, devise a plan to weave various activities that support the goal into the day-to-day institutional routine of the school.

Examples of Institutionalization Tasks:
- "Set guidelines for classroom teachers on use of Tier 1 (classroom) interventions for targeted students: e.g., how many interventions should be attempted the format to use to document interventions, the length of time that Tier 1 interventions should be attempted before referring for higher levels of RTI support."
- "Encourage teachers routinely to use weekly instructional team or department meetings as an opportunity to develop classroom intervention plans for struggling students."

Stage 4: Ongoing Development/Updating: The RTI model is steadily evolving as new research indicates better methods for data collection, intervention planning, etc. The RTI Implementation Plan should include Ongoing Development/Updating tasks—ongoing activities to ensure that the district's practices confirm to best practices over time.

Examples of Ongoing Development/Updating Tasks:
- "Monitor the What Works Clearinghouse website (http://ies.ed.gov/ncee/wwc/publications/practiceguides/) for new 'practice guides' detailing effective classroom interventions suitable for secondary schools."
- "Appoint knowledge brokers in the district who will keep current on new interventions that are effective for use in secondary classrooms and add those new intervention ideas to the school's Tier 1 intervention menu."

Reference
Ervin, R. A., & Schaughency, E. (2008). Best practices in accessing the systems change literature. In A. Thomas & J. Grimes (Eds.), *Best practices in school psychology V* (pp. 853-873). Bethesda, MD: National Association of School Psychologists.

Exhibit 2-E, Form 1
RTI Goals Planning Sheet: A 4-Stage Implementation Process

RTI Implementation Goal: _____ School Year: _____

Rollout Stage?	Task Title	Task Description	Person(s) Responsible	Target Date	Date Done
☐ *Preparation* ☐ *Initial Implementation* ☐ *Institutionalization* ☐ *Ongoing Development/ Updating*					
☐ *Preparation* ☐ *Initial Implementation* ☐ *Institutionalization* ☐ *Ongoing Development/ Updating*					
☐ *Preparation* ☐ *Initial Implementation* ☐ *Institutionalization* ☐ *Ongoing Development/ Updating*					
☐ *Preparation* ☐ *Initial Implementation* ☐ *Institutionalization* ☐ *Ongoing Development/ Updating*					
☐ *Preparation* ☐ *Initial Implementation* ☐ *Institutionalization* ☐ *Ongoing Development/ Updating*					
☐ *Preparation* ☐ *Initial Implementation* ☐ *Institutionalization* ☐ *Ongoing Development/ Updating*					
☐ *Preparation* ☐ *Initial Implementation* ☐ *Institutionalization* ☐ *Ongoing Development/ Updating*					

Exhibit 2-F
Conducting an RTI School or District Resource Inventory

Directions: In your district or school, inventory the resources available to support RTI (personnel, academic and behavioral intervention, assessment and progress-monitoring). Once you have compiled a list of RTI resources throughout your district or school, organize them in an easy-to-access list (e.g., to be used by your RTI Leadership Team or building RTI Problem-Solving Team).

1. Personnel Resources

Personnel/Flexible Time. List the names of any personnel available in your school/district with flexibility in their schedule that may allow them—with appropriate training—to support RTI in various ways (e.g., delivering selected student interventions; assisting with school-wide student academic screenings, etc.) Check the 'Availability/Access?' box next to any name if you are unsure of how to access the person for RTI support. After completing the survey, follow up to answer your availability or access questions.

Availability/ Access?	Name	Position
☐	•	
☐	•	
☐	•	
☐	•	
☐	•	

Personnel/Expert Knowledge. List the names of those personnel in your school/district with formal training or experience in academic or behavioral interventions, assessment, or other RTI topics who can serve as consultants, coaches, or trainers to other staff. Check the 'Availability/Access?' box next to any name for which you are unsure of the availability of that person or of how to access the person for RTI support. After completing the survey, follow up to answer your availability or access questions.

Availability/ Access?	Name	Position	Area(s) of Expertise
☐	•		
☐	•		
☐	•		
☐	•		
☐	•		

Exhibit 2-F, continued

2. Intervention Resources

Academic Intervention Resources. List any resources available in your school/district that could be used to support academic interventions at any level (Tiers 1-3). Check the 'Availability/Access?' box next to any item for which you are unsure of the availability of the resource or of how to access it. After completing the survey, follow up to answer your availability or access questions.

Availability/ Access?	Academic Intervention Resource	Availability/ Access?	Academic Intervention Resource
☐	•	☐	•
☐	•	☐	•
☐	•	☐	•
☐	•	☐	•
☐	•	☐	•

Behavior Intervention Resources. List any resources available in your school/district that could be used to support behavioral interventions at any level (Tiers 1-3). Check the 'Availability/Access?' box next to any item for which you are unsure of the availability of the resource or of how to access it. After completing the survey, follow up to answer your availability or access questions.

Availability/ Access?	Behavior Intervention Resource	Availability/ Access?	Behavior Intervention Resource
☐	•	☐	•
☐	•	☐	•
☐	•	☐	•
☐	•	☐	•

3. Assessment/Progress-Monitoring Resources

Student Assessment/Progress-Monitoring Resources. List any resources available in your school/district that could be used to conduct school-wide screenings or to monitor the academic or behavioral progress of students at any level (Tiers 1-3). Check the 'Availability/Access?' box next to any item for which you are unsure of the availability of the resource or of how to access it. After completing the survey, follow up to answer your availability or access questions.

Availability/ Access?	Assessment/Progress- Monitoring Resource	Availability/ Access?	Assessment/Progress- Monitoring Resource
☐	•	☐	•
☐	•	☐	•
☐	•	☐	•
☐	•	☐	•

Chapter 3
Establishing a Strong RTI Problem-Solving Team

Middle and high school students sometimes experience significant problems that can threaten to derail their progress and even lead to their eventual dropping out. Students in crisis are not an anomaly: It is estimated that—in a typical school—perhaps as many as 5% of a general school population may require intensive RTI intervention supports each year (Christ, 2008). When such problems occur, schools require the capacity to quickly identify the specific academic or behavioral issues interfering with these students' success and then to design a feasible and effective evidence-based intervention plan matched to their specific needs. The RTI Problem-Solving Team (or RTI Team) is the vehicle for assembling customized intervention plans for those students who display the most intensive and serious problems.

The RTI Team is composed of a multidisciplinary group of educators who participate in an investigative process to collect data about the student, discern from that data a profile of need, and then select appropriate interventions likely to lead to the desired improvements in student academic performance or behavior. The RTI Team follows a research-validated structured approach known as the 'problem-solving model' (Bergan, 1995) to understand and analyze student challenges. Distilled to its essence, the problem-solving model requires that a consultant (in this case, the entire RTI Team) work with the referring teacher(s) to: (1) identify the student problem in specific, measureable, observable terms; (2) analyze the student problem to uncover underlying functions or reasons to explain why the problem is occurring; (3) implement an evidence-based intervention plan whose elements are logically selected to assist the student; and (4) evaluate student performance on an ongoing basis to determine if the plan does in fact help the student to reach academic or behavioral goals.

An Overview of the RTI Problem-Solving Team Meeting Process

The RTI Team follows a structured problem-solving process that makes the most efficient use of time to achieve the goal of developing effective student intervention plans. (The material in this section was originally presented in Wright, 2007). The RTI Team problem-solving process is triggered when a teacher who wants to refer a student completes the *Secondary Level: Teacher Referral to RTI Problem-Solving Team Form* (Exhibit 3-A). When the RTI Team receives this completed form, it schedules an initial meeting with that referring teacher. Prior to the initial meeting, the case manager meets with the referring teacher to review the referral form, answer any questions that the teacher may have about the RTI Team process, and decide what additional background and baseline information should be collected before the meeting.

At the start of the initial RTI Team meeting, the facilitator explains to the referring teacher the purpose and structure of the problem-solving meeting. RTI Teams can use the sample *RTI Team Introductory Script,* as in Exhibit 3-B, as a guide for their opening comments. The RTI Team meeting then moves to a general review of the teacher's referral concerns. The team and referring teacher quickly narrow those concerns to a manageable number, set goals for student improvement, create intervention plans matched to the student concerns, and identify methods for monitoring the student's response to the intervention strategies. The referring teacher leaves the initial meeting with a detailed intervention plan. A follow-up meeting is scheduled (typically within 6 to 8 weeks of the initial meeting), at which the team will reconvene with the teacher to judge whether the intervention plan was successful or needs to be modified or replaced.

Roles of RTI Team Members. For each meeting, RTI Team members are assigned to one of four rotating roles: facilitator, timekeeper, recorder, and case manager (Wright, 2007). Each role is essential to the team process, and, therefore, the team should ensure that there are at least four members attending each meeting (not counting the referring teacher). RTI Team members are trained so that they are able to assume any of the four roles. In addition, the RTI Team Coordinator is an important non-rotating role, which helps to ensure that the team's day-to-day operations are maintained. Consult Exhibit 3-C, *RTI Problem-Solving Team Roles & Responsibilities,* for specific descriptions of each of the RTI Team roles.

Steps in the Initial RTI Team Meeting. Experienced RTI Teams can be expected to complete initial student referral meetings in about 30 minutes. Below is a brief explanation of the 8 steps of the RTI Team meeting process (as originally presented in Wright, 2007). (For more in-depth description of these meeting steps, refer to Exhibit 3-D, *RTI Team: Initial Meeting 'Companion Guide'* and Exhibit 3-E, *RTI Team: Initial Meeting Minutes Form: Secondary Grades.* Also, schools that wish to determine the 'RTI readiness' of their present problem-solving team can use the form *RTI Problem-Solving Team Effectiveness Self-Rating Scale* that appears as Exhibit 3-F).

- *Step 1: Assess Teacher Concerns.* At the opening of the RTI Team meeting, the referring teacher presents his or her primary concerns about the student's behavioral or academic difficulties. Team members ask questions as needed to clarify their understanding of the teacher's concerns.

- *Step 2: Inventory Student Strengths/Talents.* The teacher and team list the student's strengths, talents, and interests. This information about the student's strengths is often used later in the meeting to design interventions that are motivating to the student.

- *Step 3: Review Baseline or Background Data.* Information that had been collected on the student prior to the meeting is presented to assist the team in understanding the nature of the referral concern. Examples of baseline or background information that teams often find useful are highlights from the student's cumulative folder, Curriculum-Based Measurement data in Oral Reading Fluency, attendance and office disciplinary records, and classroom observation data.

- *Step 4: Select Target Teacher Concerns.* The RTI Team has limited time available, so realistically it can expect to create intervention plans for no more than one or two teacher concerns during a typical problem-solving meeting. If at the start of the meeting the referring teacher has brought up more than two concerns, the team takes a moment at this stage to assist the teacher in trimming the list to the top 1 or 2 concerns that will be the focus of the remainder of the meeting. These key concerns should be stated in measurable, observable terms.

- *Step 5: Set Academic and/or Behavioral Outcome Goals and Methods for Progress-Monitoring.* The RTI Team is able to judge whether an intervention is successful if, at the conclusion of the intervention, the student has attained a pre-selected goal of improvement. In this stage of the initial meeting, the team and referring teacher set a specific goal that the student is expected to reach in several weeks when the follow-up RTI Team meeting is held. The team also selects at least two methods for monitoring the student's 'response to intervention' for each of the 1 or 2 referral concerns. The team decides who will be responsible to collect and chart the progress-monitoring data to bring to the follow-up RTI Team meeting.

- *Step 6: Design an Intervention Plan.* The team generates a list of research-based intervention ideas that match the student's referral concern(s). The referring teacher selects those ideas that seem most feasible to use in the classroom. The team and teacher fill in all of the relevant details of each intervention strategy and identify any staff members who will assist the teacher in putting the intervention in place.

- *Step 7: Plan How to Share Meeting Information with the Student's Parent(s).* If the parent cannot attend the RTI

Team meeting, a staff member (usually the classroom teacher) is delegated to contact the parent after the problem-solving meeting to communicate the main details of the intervention plan. This can be most effectively accomplished by sharing a copy of the meeting minutes.

- *Step 8: Review Intervention & Monitoring Plans.* The team thoroughly reviews details of the intervention and progress-monitoring plans at the close of the meeting as a final check that the teacher and other team members understand the elements of these plans and that each person with a role in carrying out the plans knows his or her responsibilities.

Developing Uniform Guidelines for RTI Team Referrals

In order to guarantee under RTI that all staff are held accountable for their role in RTI and all students have equal access to intervention support, the RTI Team should define early on: (1) what constitutes an appropriate RTI Team referral; and (2) who is empowered to refer a student to the team. By formulating, writing down, and sharing these expectations with all staff, the RTI Team will make its referral process more transparent while also weaving that referral process into the routine practice of school staff.

Creating Uniform Expectations for Teacher Referrals to the RTI Team. The RTI Team attempts to strike a balance in accepting teacher referrals. On the one hand, the team should be proactive in meeting on students who are having difficulties before those students' academic or behavioral problems have a chance to spiral out of control. On the other hand, teachers should first make a good-faith effort to provide individualized interventions in the classroom and to document interventions attempted before referring students to the RTI Team. To give classroom teachers clarity about their intervention responsibilities, the RTI Team should develop specific guidelines for those teachers on expectations for classroom interventions. A detailed discussion on teacher responsibilities for Tier 1 classroom interventions appears in Chapter 4 of this book. At minimum, though, the RTI Team should include in its guidelines:

- Information about how teachers can access a listing or collection of evidence-based interventions appropriate for classroom use.
- A form to be used by teachers to document Tier 1/classroom interventions.
- An expected minimum length of time that classroom interventions should be attempted before a student is referred to the RTI Team.

Once classroom intervention guidelines have been created and shared with faculty, the Team should develop a process to screen each incoming RTI Team referral to verify that the referring teacher has in fact followed the guidelines and provided adequate classroom interventions to a student before seeking to bring that student to the RTI Team. If any RTI Team referrals are judged to be premature, a building administrator or designee should meet with the classroom teacher to review the established classroom intervention guidelines, to point out what additional classroom interventions might be tried before bringing the student to the RTI Team, and to offer coaching or other support to the teacher as needed to aid in carrying out those classroom interventions.

Mapping Out Possible Sources for RTI Team Referrals. The classroom teacher is obviously an important source for RTI Team referrals. However, schools are setting themselves up for failure if they leave sole discretion to teachers about whether to refer a student to the RTI Team. Such an arrangement creates the very real possibility that a teacher reluctant to meet with the RTI Team will not refer a student who desperately needs RTI assistance or at least might delay making that referral until the student's presenting challenges are much more difficult to solve. The most direct means for the RTI Team to guarantee that any student needing RTI support will get it is to develop guidelines for soliciting RTI Team referrals from multiple sources. For example, a school may adopt an RTI Team referral policy that makes clear that teachers, counselors and other support staff, and school administrators are each empowered to refer students to the RTI Team if they have information that warrants such an action. An RTI Team referral policy should also include a process by which parents who are concerned about their child's poor academic or behavioral performance can contact the school and have their child referred to the RTI Team. Because middle and high schools routinely collect data on student grades, office disciplinary referrals, and attendance, an RTI Team referral policy may also include procedures to review these archival data periodically (e.g., every five weeks). For recommendations on how to document an appropriate range of referral sources, consult Exhibit 3-G, *Creating a 'Multiple-Source' Process to Initiate Middle or High School Student Referrals to the RTI Problem-Solving Team*.

Input from Teacher and Student: Preparation before the Initial Problem-Solving Meeting

Many RTI Team referrals come from classroom teachers who are concerned about particular students. The important preparatory stage of the RTI Team process, then, begins with the referral from the classroom teacher and ends just before the RTI Team holds its initial meeting on the student. It is recommended that two key 'pre-meetings' occur in this opening phase. First, a representative of the RTI Team—the case manager—checks with the referring teacher to prepare the student case for the actual RTI Team initial meeting. Second, a school representative meets with the referred middle or high school student to collect information and to invite the student to participate in the RTI Team meeting.

Agreeing on the Student Problem and Data to Be Collected: Case Manager and Teacher Pre-Meeting. A common problem noted by RTI Teams at the secondary level is that a substantial portion of their meeting time is inefficiently spent attempting to shape teacher concerns into actionable student problem-identification statements and deciding what data need to be collected to allow the team to adequately understand the functions or reasons for the identified student problem(s). One recommendation that RTI Teams should strongly consider is to build in a brief 'pre-meeting' between an RTI Team representative (known as the 'case manager') and the referring teacher.

The purpose of this pre-meeting is for the case manager to share with the teacher the purpose of the upcoming full RTI Team meeting, to clarify student referral concerns, and to decide what data should be collected and brought to the RTI Team meeting. Consult Exhibit 3-H, *The Case Manager-Teacher 'Pre-Meeting': Creating a More Efficient RTI Team Process,* for a convenient two-page guide for conducting a structured and effective pre-meeting. Taken from that guide is this suggested agenda for conducting the case manager-teacher pre-meeting:

1. *Explain the purpose of the upcoming RTI Problem-Solving Team meeting.* The case manager explains that the RTI Team meeting goals are to: (a) fully understand the nature of the student's academic and/or behavioral problems; (b) develop an evidence-based intervention plan for the student; and (c) set a goal for student improvement and select means to monitor the student's response to the intervention plan.

2. *Define the student referral concern(s) in clear, specific terms.* The case manager reviews with the teacher the most important student referral concern(s), helping the teacher to define the concern(s) in clear, specific, observable terms. The teacher is also prompted to prioritize his top 1-2 student concerns.

3. *Decide what data should be brought to the RTI Team meeting.* The case manager and teacher decide what student data should be collected and brought to the RTI Team meeting to provide insight into the nature of the student's presenting concern(s).

Given the difficulty that staff in middle and high school settings often have in finding times to meet, schools may be tempted to conclude that pre-meetings between case managers and teachers are simply too much work. That conclusion would be a mistake. RTI demands that an RTI Team have in hand an accurate and specific definition of the student's problem(s) and the data to fully understand the problem(s) before it develops an intervention plan. It is obviously much more efficient for a case manager and teacher to accomplish these goals at a brief pre-meeting than waiting for the full RTI Team to convene and devote an equivalent amount of time to reach the same objectives with six people or more sitting around the table.

Encouraging Student Participation in the RTI Team Meeting. Unlike at the elementary school level, students at middle and high schools often attend their own RTI Team meetings. Secondary schools should strongly consider having students attend and take part in their own RTI Problem-Solving Team meetings for two reasons. First, as students mature, their teachers expect that they will assume increased responsibility in advocating for their own learning needs. Second, students are more likely to fully commit to RTI intervention plans if they attend the RTI Team meeting and have a voice in the creation of those plans. The recommendations offered below for engaging the student as an active participant in the RTI Team meeting are taken from Exhibit 3-I, *Engaging the Student as an Active RTI Partner in the Intervention Planning Process*.

The student should be adequately prepared to attend the RTI Team meeting by first engaging in a 'pre-meeting' with a school staff member whom the student knows and trusts (e.g., school counselor, teacher, administrator). By connecting the student with a trusted mentor figure who can help that student navigate the RTI process, the school improves the odds that the disengaged or unmotivated student will feel an increased sense of connection and commitment to his/her own school performance (Bridgeland, DiIulio, & Morison, 2006). A student RTI 'pre-meeting' can be quite brief, lasting perhaps 15-20 minutes. At this meeting, the school staff member will share information about the student's academic or behavioral problems that resulted in an RTI Team referral, describe the purpose and steps of the RTI Problem-Solving Team meeting, stress the student's importance in the intervention plan, have the student describe his/her own learning needs, and—finally—invite the student to take part in the upcoming RTI Team meeting.

If the student agrees to attend the actual RTI Problem-Solving Team meeting, he/she participates fully in the meeting. Teachers and other staff attending the meeting make an effort to keep the atmosphere positive and focused on finding solutions to the student's presenting concern(s). At the end of the RTI Team meeting, the student signs off on his/her intervention plan. Form 1 of Exhibit 3-I provides a format for this. After the meeting, the RTI Team monitors to ensure that all parties, including the student, follow through with their part of the intervention plan.

RTI Teams: A Critical Component of RTI That is Built to Last

The focus of this chapter has been on the role of the RTI Problem-Solving Team in creating customized Tier 3 intervention plans of sufficient power to bring about significant improvements in the school success of students who present with intensive academic or behavioral challenges. The RTI Team typically meets on only relatively small numbers of students, perhaps 5% of a school's population. Nonetheless, the RTI Team is of great importance in the Response to Intervention model because it is often the last hope for precisely those students who are at greatest risk for significant underperformance or dropping out. The success of the RTI Team is to be measured not in its good intentions. Rather, that success can be seen in the team's demonstrated ability to identify struggling students, to intervene effectively in a timely manner, to formatively track students on intervention to determine whether they adequately respond to selected interventions, and to document the full range of intervention efforts to help the school to decide whether a student requires more educational or behavioral assistance than can be provided using general education RTI resources alone. Given the critical function that the RTI Team plays in supporting students who require the most intensive intervention support, schools should construct their RTI Teams with care to ensure that that they are up to the task.

References

Bergan, J. R. (1995). Evolution of a problem-solving model of consultation. *Journal of Educational and Psychological Consultation,* 6(2), 111-123.

Bridgeland, J. M., DiIulio, J. J., & Morison, K. B. (2006). *The silent epidemic: Perspectives of high school dropouts.* Seattle, WA: Gates Foundation. Retrieved on May 4, 2008, from http://www.gatesfoundation.org/nr/downloads/ed/TheSilentEpidemic3-06FINAL.pdf

Christ, T. (2008). *Best practices in problem analysis.* In A. Thomas & J. Grimes (Eds.), Best practices in school psychology V (pp. 159-176). Bethesda, MD: National Association of School Psychologists.

Wright, J. (2007). *The RTI toolkit: A practical guide for schools.* Port Chester, NY: National Professional Resources, Inc.

Frequently Asked Questions About...
...Middle & High School RTI Problem-Solving Teams

1. **How frequently should the RTI Team meet?** It is recommended that the RTI Team reserve a standing block of time each week for student problem-solving meetings. Many schools set aside 2-3 hours per week, although the amount of time scheduled for meetings will depend on the number of students typically referred in a week to the RTI Team.

2. **Who should serve on the RTI Team?** RTI Teams can be flexible in their membership but should be multidisciplinary (e.g., school counselor, special or general education teachers, etc.). RTI Teams should make a special effort to recruit teachers to increase the team's credibility with classroom teachers. One useful idea is for teams to enlist a larger number of teachers and support staff and to rotate the members who sit on the team each week. By rotating its members, the RTI Team can reduce the weekly commitment required of any single member and increase the willingness of teachers and support staff to serve on the team.

3. **How much RTI Team time should be set aside for a student RTI case?** An initial student RTI case should typically not exceed 30 minutes. Follow-up RTI Team meetings often do not exceed 20 minutes. Streamlined, efficient RTI Team meetings are possible provided that the team has done its necessary advance work (e.g., meeting with the classroom teacher(s) to clarify referral concerns; ensuring that important data on the student is collected prior to the initial student) to prepare for the actual meetings.

4. **What is a reasonable number of student RTI cases that can be handled by an RTI Team in a school year?** A single RTI Team can comfortably manage between 25 and 40 Tier 3 cases in the course of a typical school year. There are several factors that influence the actual numbers of students referred to the team, including the overall success of core instruction in the school and expectations for Tier 1 (classroom) interventions that would precede an RTI Team referral.

Schools can estimate the number of students likely to be referred to the team in one of two ways. First, the school can simply look at past rates of referral to the RTI Team in its own building. For example, if 29 students were referred to the RTI Team in the previous year, it is likely that a similar number of students will be referred in the present school year. Second, the school can look at RTI research, which suggests that as many as 5 percent of a building's student population may require a Tier 3 (RTI Team) intervention plan in a given school year. In a middle school with 1000 students, this prevalence rate of Tier 3 cases predicts that as many as 50 students may be referred to the RTI Team across the academic year—indicating that the school should consider creating at least two separate RTI Teams (e.g., one at each grade level) to manage the referral load.

5. **When should the RTI Team decide to accept student referrals from classroom teachers?** At the middle and high school level, a substantial number of students are referred directly by teachers to the RTI Team. A basic expectation of RTI, however, is that content-area teachers will serve as RTI 'first responders' who can proactively identify students with emerging academic or behavioral concerns, provide reasonable individualized (Tier 1) intervention support, and document those classroom intervention efforts. The RTI Team should develop guidelines for classroom teachers about when a struggling student should be considered for referral to the RTI Team. Such guidelines would include a standard form that teachers would use to document their Tier 1 intervention efforts, as well as a minimum timespan that Tier 1 interventions would be tried (e.g., 4 to 6 instructional weeks) before an RTI Team referral is considered. RTI Teams should also ensure that teachers receive the support necessary to implement Tier 1 interventions, including having access to a range of evidence-based intervention ideas, as well as coaches and consultants on staff that can help teachers to select appropriate interventions and use them correctly.

6. **Should an administrator sit on the RTI Team?** A school can run an effective RTI Team with or without administrators serving on the team. Advantages of an administrator serving

on the RTI Team are both that the team has the high-profile backing and support of building leadership and that the team can get quick clarification at meetings about whether they can access any school intervention resources that are controlled by administration. A possible disadvantage of an administrator sitting on the RTI Team is that the leader's presence at meetings might reduce the comfort level of referring teachers and make them reluctant in the presence of their supervisor to speak candidly about their inability to address the needs of a struggling student. Even if an administrator does not sit on the team, the RTI Team should keep building leadership regularly updated on upcoming and current RTI cases and be able to count on administrators to enforce teacher expectations for compliance with the building's RTI guidelines.

7. **Once an intervention plan has been designed by the RTI Team, how long should that intervention last before the team meets again to evaluate its effectiveness?** An intervention plan should be in place long enough to judge with confidence whether it is working. It is recommended that RTI Teams set a reasonable default length of time that intervention plans will be in effect (e.g., 6 to 8 instructional weeks). However, teams should also have the latitude to set longer or shorter intervention timespans based on the facts of the specific student case. For example, a high school may allow 6 instructional weeks to pass before holding a follow-up RTI Team meeting on a student whose intervention targets content-area vocabulary but may schedule a follow-up meeting in only 3 weeks for a student whose intervention addresses highly disruptive classroom behaviors.

8. **How many intervention plans should the RTI Team implement before deciding that a student has failed to adequately respond to general education interventions?** Each school district must develop its own decision rules for judging when a series of general education intervention plans have failed to work and for deciding that a student is not responding adequately to intervention. The foundation assumption of RTI is that students who begin to experience academic or behavioral problems are typical and that it is the school's responsibility to find strategies will allow those

students to experience success. A district's decision rules should require evidence beyond a reasonable doubt that a student is not responding to general education RTI interventions. For many districts, these decision rules require that at least 3 separate intervention plans be attempted—with each intervention plan being tried for at least 6 to 8 instructional weeks—before the school can adequately judge whether a given student has or has not responded to intervention.

9. **How can the RTI Team find the resources necessary to implement intensive student intervention plans?** It is a reality that most schools will need to rechannel existing resources to support RTI. The middle or high school RTI Team should inventory those resources in the building or district that can be used to support student interventions and assessment. Resources to be canvassed include staff whose schedule permits them to assist with student interventions or assessment (e.g., reading teacher, school psychologist, paraprofessionals); staff with specialized expertise in such areas as reading instruction or behavior management who can serve as consultants or intervention coaches; commercial materials for academic instruction or intervention; commercial professional development materials for academic or behavioral intervention or assessment, etc. RTI Teams should consult this inventory of intervention and assessment resources at problem-solving meetings when putting together plans for student intervention and assessment.

10. **How can the RTI Team convey the message to faculty and parents that it is not simply a preliminary step to a special education referral?** As schools make the transition to the RTI model, teachers and parents may initially be reluctant to embrace the focus of RTI on supporting struggling students in the general education setting. The most effective means for the RTI Team to convince teachers and parents that it is not a conduit for special education referrals is by creating strong and useful intervention plans that are effective in general education classrooms. Schools may also consider requiring that any student who is referred for a special education evaluation based on a parent request is simultaneously referred to the building's RTI Team. This 'fast

track' RTI Team referral process for any parent-initiated referrals to special education reinforces the message that information about students' response to intervention in the general education setting is critical in determining their possible special education status.

Exhibit 3-A
Secondary Level: Teacher Referral to RTI Problem-Solving Team

Student:_____ Teacher: _____ Date: _____

Course/Subject: _____ Number of Absences This Year: _____

Period(s) or Day(s) of Week/Time(s) When Course Meets:_____

Global Skills Rating. Rate the student's standing relative to other students in his or her class on the skills listed below. (If you are unsure of the student's abilities on a particular skill, leave it blank.)

Skill	1	2	3	4
Reading Skills	1	2	3	4
Mathematics Skills	1	2	3	4
Written Expression Skills	1	2	3	4
Study & Organizational Skills	1	2	3	4
Classroom Conduct	1	2	3	4

1 = Significantly/Severely Below Grade Level
2 = Somewhat Below Grade Level
3 = At Grade Level
4 = Above Grade Level

Test/Quiz Grades. Chart the most recent test and/or quiz grades for this student.

For each of 6 columns (1-6):
Test___ Quiz___
Scale: 0, 20, 40, 60, 80, 100
Date: ___/___/___
Grade: _____

Concerns. List up to **3** primary concerns that you have with this student in your classroom:

1. _____
2. _____
3. _____

Strategies. List specific strategies that you have tried in the classroom to support this student in area(s) of concern.

1. _____
2. _____
3. _____
4. _____
5. _____

Exhibit 3-B
RTI Team Introductory Script
(Share With Referring Teacher at the Start of the Initial Meeting)

"Welcome to this initial RTI Team meeting. We are meeting with you today to discuss concerns that you have about a student, _____.

The purpose of this meeting is for us all to work together to come up with practical ideas to help this student to be more successful in school. I am the facilitator for today's meeting. The person taking notes during the meeting will be _____. The case manager for this student is _____. The time-keeper for the meeting is _____.

You can expect this meeting to last about ____ minutes. By the time you leave, we should have a complete student intervention plan put together to help address your concerns.

Our team and you have a lot to do today and only limited time in which to do it. To help us to work efficiently and not waste your time, we will follow a structured problem-solving model that goes through several stages. Together, our team and you will:

- Assess your major concerns about the student
- Help you to pick the one or two most important student concerns for us to work on today
- Set specific student goals for improvement
- Design an intervention plan with strategies to help that student improve, and
- Decide how to share information about this plan with the student's parent(s)

As the student's teacher, you are the most important participant in this meeting. Please let us know at any time if you disagree with, or have questions about, our suggestions. Our meeting will not be a success unless *you* feel that the intervention ideas that we offer will address the student's difficulties and are feasible for you to do.

Our meeting notes will document your referral concerns for the student and the intervention plan that we come up with. These notes may be shared with others who are not here today, including child's parent(s) and the building administrator. However, we ask that everyone here keep the *conversations* that take place at this meeting confidential.

Do you have any questions?"

Adapted from the School-Based RTI Team Project Complete Forms & Related Resources, available at: http://www.interventioncentral.org/htmdocs/interventions/sbit.php. Used with permission.

Exhibit 3-C
RTI Problem-Solving Team Roles & Responsibilities

RTI Team Role	Responsibilities	Tips for RTI Teams
Facilitator	☐ Opens the meeting by welcoming the referring teacher(s), parents, and student; describing what is to be accomplished at the meeting, and how long the meeting will last. ☐ Guides the Team through the stages of the problem-solving process. ☐ Checks for agreement between Team members at important discussion points during the meeting. ☐ Maintains control of the meeting (e.g., requesting that participants not engage in side-bar conversations, reminding the team to focus its problem-solving discussion on those factors over which it has control—e.g., classroom instruction).	• Write a short introductory 'script' to ensure that important points are always reviewed at the start of the meeting. • Create a poster listing the steps of the meeting problem-solving process as a visual guide to keep Team members on task and to transition from one step to another.
Recorder	☐ Creates a record of the intervention meeting, including a detailed plan for intervention and progress-monitoring. ☐ Asks the Team for clarification as needed about key discussion points, including phrasing of teacher 'problem-identification' statements and intervention descriptions.	• Sit next to the facilitator for ease of communication during the meeting. • When the Team is engaged in exploratory discussion, use 'scratch paper' to capture the main points. When the Team reaches agreement, recopy only the essential information onto the formal meeting forms.
Time-Keeper	☐ Monitors the time allocated to each stage of the meeting and informs members when that time has expired.	• Give the Team a 'two-minute warning' whenever time is running low during a stage of the meeting. • If time runs out during a meeting stage, announce the fact clearly. However, let the facilitator be responsible for transitioning the team to the next meeting stage.
Case Manager	☐ Meets with the referring teacher(s) briefly prior to the initial RTI Team meeting to review the teacher referral form, clarify teacher concerns, decide what additional data should be collected on the student. ☐ Touches base briefly with the referring teacher(s) after the RTI Team meeting to check that the intervention plan is running smoothly.	• If, when you meet with a referring teacher prior to the RTI Team meeting, you discover that his or her concern is vaguely worded, help the teacher to clarify the concern with the question "What does [teacher concern] look like in the classroom?" • After the RTI Team meeting, consider sending periodic emails to the referring teacher(s) asking how the intervention is going and inviting them to inform you if they require assistance.
Coordinator	☐ Handles the logistics of RTI Team meetings, including scheduling meetings, reserving a meeting location, arranging coverage when necessary to allow teachers to attend meetings, and notifying Team members and referring teachers of scheduled meetings.	• During the time set aside for weekly RTI Team meetings, reserve time for the Team to review new student referrals and to schedule them in the meeting calendar. • Define those coordinator duties that are clerical in nature (e.g., scheduling meeting rooms, emailing meeting invitations, etc.) and assign them to clerical staff.

Exhibit 3-D
RTI Team: Initial Meeting 'Companion Guide'

Step 1: Assess Teacher Concerns	Allotted Time: 5 Minutes

GOALS:
- The case manager or facilitator reviews information from the referral form.
- The referring teacher is encouraged to discuss his or her major referral concerns.

SAMPLE QUESTIONS:
- *Given the information that you wrote down on the referral form, what are the specific difficulties that you would like to have us address today?*
- *How is this student problem interfering with the student's school performance?*
- *What concern(s) led you to refer the student to this team?*

The RTI Team is ready to move on to the next meeting step when…
- Team members have a good knowledge of teacher concerns.

TIP:
To save time, the case manager or meeting facilitator can:
- Open with a short script about how the meeting will be conducted.
- Review information from the *RTI Team Teacher Referral Form*.
- Ask the teacher if there are any additional concerns or questions not documented on the *Referral Form*.

Step 2: Inventory Student Strengths & Talents	Allotted Time: 5 Minutes

GOALS:
- Discuss and record the student's strengths and talents, as well as those incentives that motivate the student. This information can be valuable during intervention planning to identify strategies that will motivate the student to participate.

SAMPLE QUESTIONS:
- *Please tell us a few of the student's strengths, talents, or positive qualities that might be useful in designing interventions for him or her.*
- *What rewards or incentives have you noted in school that this child seems to look forward to?*
- *What are classroom activities in which the student does well or seems to enjoy?*
- *What are hobbies or topics that interest this student?*

The RTI Team is ready to move on to the next meeting step when…
- The team has identified personal strengths, talents, and/or rewards that are likely to motivate the student if integrated into an intervention plan.

TIP:
- The referring teacher may want to meet with the child *prior* to the RTI Team meeting to collect information about those incentives or activities that the student finds motivating.

Exhibit 3-D, continued

| Step 3: Review Background/Baseline Data | Allotted Time: 5 Minutes |

GOALS:
- Review background or baseline data to better understand the student's abilities and potential deficits.
- Determine the student's current level(s) of performance in areas of academic or behavioral concern.

SAMPLE QUESTIONS:
- What information has been collected to document the student's current level of functioning in the academic or behavioral area of concern?
- What is student's frequency of absences and tardies this year?
- What number and type of disciplinary office referrals has the student received this year?
- What information from the student's cumulative folder (e.g., test results, teacher comments, past report card grades) might give insight into the student's academic or behavioral difficulties?

The RTI Team is ready to move on to the next meeting step when...
- The team has reviewed and discussed all pertinent background and baseline data.

TIP:
The student's classroom teacher knows that student best. Set the expectation that the referring teacher be responsible for pulling together essential archival information about the student for the initial meeting (for example, attendance and office disciplinary data, key highlights from the student's cumulative folder).

| Step 4: Select Target Teacher Concerns | Allotted Time: 5-10 Minutes |

GOALS:
- Define the top 1-2 teacher concerns in easily observable, measurable terms.
- For behavioral concerns, understand the dimensions of the problem (e.g., the frequency, duration, and/or intensity of the challenging behavior).
- For academic concerns, identify any underlying skill deficits, note whether the student is appropriately matched to the level of difficulty of classroom instruction, and estimate the current rate of student work completion.
- For each teacher concern, decide what underlying reasons, or functions, best explain the student's difficulties.

SAMPLE QUESTIONS:
- *From the list of concerns that you have shared with our team, what are the top ONE or TWO problems that you would like us to concentrate on today?*
- *(Academic) What can you tell us about the student's current skill levels, rate of homework and classwork completion, attention to task, general level of motivation?*
- *(Behavioral) How long does each behavioral outburst last? About how frequently do episodes occur?*

Exhibit 3-D, continued

- *(Behavioral) What kinds of events happen in the room just before the student has an outburst or displays problem behavior? How do adults react to the student's problem behavior? How do classmates react to the problem behavior? What is the outcome or consequence for the student after he or she engages in the problem behavior?*
- *What do you think is a reason that the student shows the behavior(s) of concern? How does this behavior help the student to get his or her needs met?*

The RTI Team is ready to move on to the next meeting step when…
- The team has selected one or two primary teacher concerns.
- Everyone on the team can visualize the target concerns because they are stated in specific, observable, measurable terms.
- The referring teacher and team agree on possible underlying reasons ('functions') for the student's academic or behavioral concerns.

TIP:
- The team can save time and run a more efficient meeting if team members list all teacher concerns at the start of the meeting but postpone engaging in an extended discussion about any particular concern until the teacher selects that problem as a TOP concern.

Step 5: Set Academic and/or Behavioral Outcome Goals and Methods for Progress-Monitoring	**Allotted Time: 5 Minutes**

GOALS:
- For each of the academic or behavioral referral concerns, set ambitious but realistic goals for improvement that are likely to be attained within 6-8 instructional weeks. Select methods to monitor student progress during the intervention.

SAMPLE QUESTIONS:
- *Given the student's current functioning, what gains do you expect that the student will make in 6-8 weeks if the intervention that we design for him or her is successful?*
- *What is a realistic rate of progress for this student in oral reading fluency?*
- *Have we picked monitoring methods that are most efficient for monitoring the student's goal? Does the research support using these monitoring methods for tracking progress toward this particular goal?*
- *How frequently should data be collected using this progress-monitoring method?*
- *Is the monitoring method selected sufficiently sensitive to short-term student growth?*
- *Are there simple, already-existing sources of data to monitor progress toward this goal (e.g., using student homework grades to monitor completion and accuracy of homework assignments, collecting completed student work products as a means of tracking completion and accuracy of in-class assignments)?*

Exhibit 3-D, continued

In the Goal-Setting section, the recorder fills out a table with the key information about the goal that will be monitored and the assessment methods to be used in tracking student progress. Here are the specific questions asked in this section, with advice on how to respond:

1. *Describe in measurable, observable terms the behavior that is to be changed (taken from Step 4).*
   Refer to the definition that you used in Step 4 to define the target behavior. Also, check out the section, *Common Methods for Monitoring Student Progress Toward Behavioral and Academic Goals* that appears at the end of this *Companion Guide*. You may find the column 'Suggested Behavior Goals' in this section to be helpful!

2. *What is the target date to achieve this goal?*
   Generally, RTI Teams allow 6-8 instructional weeks for interventions to take effect. Your team can choose a shorter or longer time period however.

3. *Is the goal for the behavior listed in step 2 to be: ___ increased? or ___ decreased?*
   If your target behavior is a **problem** behavior (e.g., hitting), your team will want to decrease it. If the target behavior is **desired** (e.g., reading fluency), your team will want to increase it.

4. *What are the conditions under which the behavior typically appears (problem behaviors) or should be displayed (desired behaviors)?*
   Here are examples of 'condition' statements that give information about where, when, and under what circumstances the student's target behavior will be monitored: "When given a book at the fourth grade level', 'when given a directive by the teacher', 'when moving through the hallway', 'during math instruction'.

5. *What is the goal (level of proficiency) that the student is expected to achieve by the date listed above?*
   Levels of proficiency should be described in measurable, quantifiable terms. Examples of proficiency levels include 'on-task 80% or more', 'turning in homework at least 4 days per week', '85 correctly read words per minute'.

6. *What measure(s) will be used to monitor student progress?*
   Refer to Form 1, *Common Methods for Monitoring Student Progress Toward Behavioral and Academic Goals,* for widely used student monitoring methods (see last two pages of this Exhibit).

7. *How frequently will this student goal be monitored? (e.g., weekly?, daily?)*
   It is recommended that interventions be monitored at least weekly if possible, to provide sufficient information for the RTI Team to decide within 6-8 weeks whether the intervention plan is effective.

8. *Who is responsible for monitoring this student goal?*
   Often RTI Team members or other school staff assist the referring teacher to monitor student progress. Be sure to list the names of ALL personnel who take part in the monitoring effort.

Exhibit 3-D, continued

The RTI Team is ready to move on to the next meeting step when…
- The team has selected ambitious but realistic goals for improvement in the target academic or behavioral area.
- The referring teacher agrees that the outcome goals are appropriate for this student case.
- Each student goal is matched with at least two appropriate methods of progress-monitoring.

TIPS:
- Review the teacher's prioritized concerns to ensure that they are stated in specific, observable, measurable terms. It is much easier to set goals when concerns are clearly defined rather than vaguely worded.
- At the end of this Companion Guide is a section, *Common Methods for Monitoring Student Progress Toward Behavioral and Academic Goals.* This section lists suitable instruments or methods for assessing student academics and general behaviors. Refer to this document when writing student goal statements.
- Review additional information about assessment methods in Chapter 5 of this manual.
- Creative RTI Teams can often save time and effort by making full use of simple, already-existing sources of data to monitor progress toward student goals (e.g., using student homework grades to monitor completion and accuracy of homework assignments, collecting completed student work products as a means of tracking completion and accuracy of in-class assignments).

Step 6: Design an Intervention Plan   15-20 Minutes

GOALS:
- Select at least one intervention that addresses each of the selected referral concerns.
- Spell out the details of the intervention as a series of specific STEPS so that the teacher or other person(s) designated to implement it can do so correctly and efficiently.
- Note any important additional information about the intervention, including:
  — When and where the intervention will take place;
  — Whether specialized materials or training are required to implement the intervention;
  — Names of individuals responsible for carrying out the intervention.
- Review the intervention plan with the teacher to ensure that she or he finds the plan acceptable and feasible;
- Select a method to check up on how well the intervention is carried out ('intervention follow-through').

SAMPLE QUESTIONS:
- *Given the underlying reasons for this student's academic or behavioral problems, what research-based intervention ideas are most likely to address the student's needs?*

Exhibit 3-D, continued

- *What aspect of this particular intervention idea is likely to improve the student's academic or behavioral functioning in the area(s) specified?*
- *Are there specialized materials or training needed to implement this intervention successfully?*
- *How can our team assist you, the referring teacher, with the intervention?*
- *How can we work the student's strengths, talents, or interests into the intervention to make it more effective or motivating?*
- *What is a simple method that our team can use to track how successfully the intervention was put into practice (e.g., creation of a checklist of key steps to be implemented)?*

The RTI Team is ready to move on to the next meeting step when…
- The referring teacher and team members agree that the intervention:
  — Directly addresses the identified concern(s);
  — Is judged by the referring teacher to be acceptable, sensible, and achievable;
  — Is realistic, given the resources available;
  — Appears likely to achieve the desired goal for student improvement within the timeline selected.
- The team has selected a method for evaluating whether the intervention has been carried out as designed ('treatment integrity').

TIP:
Consider inviting staff members with expertise in a particular type of referral problem to attend your RTI Team meeting as 'intervention consultants' whenever you have students that present specialized concerns. For example, your team might invite a speech/language pathologist to a meeting for a student who appears to have difficulty acquiring language concepts.

Step 7: Plan to Contact Parents	Allotted Time: 5 Minutes

GOALS:
- If the parent(s) cannot attend the RTI Team meeting, the team selects an individual to contact the parent(s) after the meeting to review the main points of the student's intervention plan.

SAMPLE QUESTIONS:
- *Who will contact parents after this meeting to share the main points of our intervention plan?*
- *What specific details about the intervention plan would the parent(s) be most interested in hearing about?*

The RTI Team is ready to move on to the next meeting step when…
- At least one team member (often the referring teacher) has taken responsibility to contact the parent to share information about the student's intervention plan.

Exhibit 3-D, continued

TIP:
It is important for a representative from the RTI Team (usually the referring teacher) to contact parents prior to the initial RTI Team meeting to explain the purpose of the meeting and to extend an invitation to attend. This proactive outreach to parents establishes a tone of trust and open communication between school and home.

| Step 8: Review the Intervention & Monitoring Plans | Allotted Time: 5 Minutes |

GOALS:
- Review the main points of the intervention and monitoring plans with the referring teacher and other team members.
- (Case Manager) Schedule a time within a week of the initial meeting to meet with the referring teacher to:
  — review the intervention plan,
  — offer any needed assistance in carrying out the intervention,
  — ensure that the intervention plan is being put into practice as planned.
- Schedule a follow-up RTI Team meeting (usually within 6-8 weeks of the initial problem-solving meeting).
- As a team, take a moment to complete the *RTI Team Meeting Debriefing Form* (once the referring teacher has left the RTI Team meeting) at the end of the Minutes Form, Exhibit 3-A.

SAMPLE QUESTIONS:
- *Do the referring teacher and other members of our team all know what their responsibilities are in carrying out the intervention and monitoring plans for this student?*
- *(Meeting debriefing) Was our team able to support the referring teacher in identifying the most important referral concern(s)?*
- *(Meeting debriefing) Did our team help the teacher to put together a good intervention plan that is feasible and can be carried out with currently available resources?*

Adapted from the School-Based RTI Team Project Complete Forms & Related Resources, available at: http://www.interventioncentral.org/htmdocs/interventions/sbit.php. Used with permission.

Exhibit 3-D, Form 1

Common Methods for Monitoring Student Progress Toward Behavioral and Academic Goals

Directions: The selected measures listed below can be used to monitor student academic and behavioral goals. Select those measures that your RTI Team will use to monitor a particular student. Write the monitoring procedures you have chosen into Step 5 ('Goal-Setting') on the *RTI Team Meeting Minutes Form*.

ACADEMIC TARGETS

CBM: Curriculum-Based Measurement	
Description of Measure	**Suggested Behavior Goals**
☐ Oral Reading Fluency	Increase ___ Correct Read Words Per Minute to ___
☐ Maze Passages (Reading Comprehension)	Increase ___ Correct Maze Responses in 3 Minutes to ___
☐ Math Computation: Specify Computation Problem Type(s)	Increase ___ Correct Digits Per 2 Minutes to ___
☐ Writing: Total Words	Increase ___ Total Words in 3 Minutes to ___
☐ Writing: Correctly Spelled Words	Increase ___ Words Spelled Correctly in 3 Minutes to ___
☐ Writing: Correct Writing Sequences	Increase ___ Correct Writing Sequences in 3 Minutes to ___

Permanent Work Products (Classroom Assignments)	
Description of Measure	**Suggested Behavior Goals**
☐ Amount of Work Completed	Increase the Average Percentage of Class Assignments Completed to ___%
☐ Accuracy of Work Completed	Increase the Average Percentage of Work Done Correctly on Class Assignments to ___%
☐ Quality of Work Completed	• Increase the Average Grade in [Subject Area] to ___ • Increase Average Teacher Ratings on Class Assignments Using a [Subject Area] Rubric to ___

Homework Assignments	
Description of Measure	**Suggested Behavior Goals**
☐ Work Turned In	Increase the Average Number of Times per Week When Homework is Turned in to ___
☐ Amount of Work Completed	Increase the Average Amount of Homework Completed Correctly to ___
☐ Accuracy of Work Completed	Increase the Average Percentage of Homework Completely Correctly to ___
☐ Quality of Work Completed	Increase the Average Student Grade on Homework to ___ Increase Teacher Ratings of the Quality of Student Work Using an Evaluation Rubric to ___

Tests/Quizzes	
Description of Measure	**Suggested Behavior Goals**
☐ Global Measure of Student Performance	• Increase the Average Test/Quiz Grade in [Subject Area] to ___

Exhibit 3-D, Form 1, continued
BEHAVIORAL TARGETS

Daily Behavior Report Card (DBRCs). NOTE: Free DBRCs can be created conveniently online at: http://www.jimwrightonline.com/php/tbrc/tbrc.php	
Description of Measure	**Suggested Behavior Goal**
☐ [Each DBRC behavior-rating item is customized to match the student's presenting concern(s)]	• Increase the Average Teacher Ratings of 'Satisfactory' or Better on the DBRC Item *[Insert Item]* to ___ • Increase the Frequency of Teacher Ratings of 'Satisfactory' or Better on the DBRC Item *[Insert Item]* to ___ Times Per Week.

Verbal & Written Reports	
Description of Measure	**Suggested Behavior Goal**
☐ Teacher Written Reports	• [Depending on whether the goal is to INCREASE or to DECREASE specific student academic or general behaviors] • As reflected in teacher written reports, the student will INCREASE the behavior [*insert behavior*] to a level of ___ Times Per Hour/Class Period/Day/Week • As reflected in teacher written reports, the student will DECREASE the behavior [*insert behavior*] to a level of ___ Times Per Hour/Class Period/Day/Week
☐ Teacher Verbal Reports	• [Depending on whether the goal is to INCREASE or to DECREASE specific student academic or general behaviors] • As reflected in teacher verbal reports, the student will INCREASE the behavior [*insert behavior*] to a level of ___ Times Per Hour/Class Period/Day/Week • As reflected in teacher verbal reports, the student will DECREASE the behavior [*insert behavior*] to a level of ___ Times Per Hour/Class Period/Day/Week
☐ Student/Parent Journal	• [Depending on whether the goal is to INCREASE or to DECREASE specific student academic or general behaviors] • As reflected in student/parent journal entries, the student will INCREASE the behavior [*insert behavior*] to a level of ___ Times Per Hour/Class Period/Day/Week • As reflected in student/parent journal entries, the student will DECREASE the behavior [*insert behavior*] to a level of ___ Times Per Hour/Class Period/Day/Week
☐ Student/Parent Verbal Reports	• [Depending on whether the goal is to INCREASE or to DECREASE specific student academic or general behaviors] • As reflected in regular verbal reports that the student/parent will make to ___, the student will INCREASE the behavior [*insert behavior*] to a level of ___ Times Per Hour/Class Period/Day/Week • As reflected in regular verbal reports that the student/parent will make to ___, the student will DECREASE the behavior [*insert behavior*] to a level of

Exhibit 3-D, Form 1, continued

		___ Times Per Hour/Class Period/Day/Week

Compliance With the School Behavioral Code of Conduct		
	Description of Measure	**Suggested Behavior Goal**
☐	Office Disciplinary Referrals	• Reduce the Frequency of Office Disciplinary Referrals for [*insert behavioral concern*] to ___ Per Day/Week/Month

Attendance/Tardiness		
	Description of Measure	**Suggested Behavior Goal**
☐	Student Attendance	• Reduce the Percentage of Days Absent During the Next [*Insert Weeks*] Weeks to ____% • Reduce the Number of Days Absent During the Next [*Insert Weeks*] Weeks to No More Than ____
☐	Student Tardiness	• Reduce the Percentage of Days Tardy During the Next [*Insert Weeks*] Weeks to ____% • Reduce the Number of Days Tardy During the Next [*Insert Weeks*] Weeks to No More Than ____

Exhibit 3-E
RTI Team: Initial Meeting Minutes Form: Secondary Grades

| Step 1: Assess Teacher Concerns | Allotted Time: 5 Minutes |

Review concerns listed on the RTI Teacher Referral Form with the referring teacher and team. List primary concerns.

_____
_____
_____

| Step 2: Inventory Student Strengths & Talents | Allotted Time: 5 Minutes |

List student strengths, talents, and/or any preferred activities or incentives that motivate the student:

- _____
- _____
- _____

| Step 3: Review Background/Baseline Data | Allotted Time: 5 Minutes |

Review any background or baseline information collected on the student (e.g., attendance and office disciplinary referral records, student grades, Curriculum-Based Measurement data, Daily Behavior Report Card ratings, direct-observation data, etc.)

_____
_____
_____
_____
_____
_____
_____
_____

Adapted from the School-Based Intervention Team Project Complete Forms & Related Resources, available at: http://www.interventioncentral.org/htmdocs/interventions/sbit.php. Used with permission.

Exhibit 3-E, continued

| Step 4: Select Target Teacher Concerns | Allotted Time: 5-10 Minutes |

Define the top 1-2 concerns in specific, observable terms (top 1-2 difficulties that most interfere with the student's functioning in the classroom).

1. _____
   _____
   _____
   _____
   _____
   _____
   _____

   Likely Reason(s) for Student Concerns: Select up to 3 choices

   Behavioral
   ☐ Lacks necessary skills
   ☐ Has the necessary behavioral skills but is not motivated by the instructional task/setting to comply/behave appropriately
   ☐ Seeks att'n from adults
   ☐ Seeks att'n from peers
   ☐ Reacts to teasing/bullying
   ☐ Tries to escape from instructional demands or setting
   ☐ Attempts to hide academic deficits through noncompliance or other misbehavior
   ☐ _____

   Academic
   ☐ Is placed in work that is too difficult
   ☐ Lacks one or more crucial basic skills in the problem subject area(s)
   ☐ Needs drill & practice to strengthen and become more fluent in basic academic skills
   ☐ Has the necessary academic skills, fails to use them in the appropriate settings/situations
   ☐ Needs explicit guidance to connect current skills to new instructional demands
   ☐ Has the necessary academic skills but is not motivated by the instructional task/setting to actually do the work
   ☐ _____

2. _____
   _____
   _____
   _____
   _____
   _____
   _____

   Likely Reason(s) for Student Concerns: Select up to 3 choices

   Behavioral
   ☐ Lacks necessary skills
   ☐ Has the necessary behavioral skills but is not motivated by the instructional task/setting to comply/behave appropriately
   ☐ Seeks att'n from adults
   ☐ Seeks att'n from peers
   ☐ Reacts to teasing/bullying
   ☐ Tries to escape from instructional demands or setting
   ☐ Attempts to hide academic deficits through noncompliance or other misbehavior
   ☐ _____

   Academic
   ☐ Is placed in work that is too difficult
   ☐ Lacks one or more crucial basic skills in the problem subject area(s)
   ☐ Needs drill & practice to strengthen and become more fluent in basic academic skills
   ☐ Has the necessary academic skills, fails to use them in the appropriate settings/situations
   ☐ Needs explicit guidance to connect current skills to new instructional demands
   ☐ Has the necessary academic skills but is not motivated by the instructional task/setting to actually do the work
   ☐ _____

Exhibit 3-E, continued

Step 5: Set Academic and/or Behavioral Outcome Goals and Methods for Progress-Monitoring   **Allotted Time: 5 Minutes**

Fill out the details below for methods to monitor student progress for each target teacher concern.. Try to select at least TWO monitoring methods for each concern. NOTE: To view common methods of school data collection, refer to the guide *Common Methods for Monitoring Student Progress Toward Behavioral and Academic Goals* at the end of this form.

Target Teacher Concern 1 (From Step 4 of this Minutes Form): _____
_____

Progress-Monitoring Start Date: ____/____/____ End Date: ____/____/____

Total Number of Instructional Weeks for Progress-Monitoring: _____

Academic or Behavioral Measure	Expected Goal Reached at End of Monitoring	Person(s) Responsible for Data Collection

---

Target Teacher Concern 1 (From Step 4 of this Minutes Form): _____
_____

Progress-Monitoring Start Date: ____/____/____ End Date: ____/____/____

Total Number of Instructional Weeks for Progress-Monitoring: _____

Academic or Behavioral Measure	Expected Goal Reached at End of Monitoring	Person(s) Responsible for Data Collection

Exhibit 3-E, continued

Step 6: Design an Intervention Plan	Allotted Time: 15-20 Minutes

Intervention Script Builder   Date the intervention will begin: _____

Check the box that indicates the PRIMARY focus of intervention elements listed on this page:

☐ Academic Support   ☐ Behavioral Support   ☐ Social/Emotional Support

Intervention Check	Intervention Steps: Describe the elements of the intervention. Include enough detail so that the procedures are clear to all who must implement them. • If the intervention has multiple steps, describe each step separately. • If the intervention plan is made up of discrete, 'stand-alone' strategies, list each strategy separately.	Person(s) Responsible
This element was implemented Y___ N___	1. _____	
This element was implemented Y___ N___	2. _____	
This element was implemented Y___ N___	3. _____	
This element was implemented Y___ N___	4. _____	
This element was implemented Y___ N___	5. _____	
This element was implemented Y___ N___	6. _____	
This element was implemented Y___ N___	7. _____	
This element was implemented Y___ N___	8. _____	

Exhibit 3-E, continued

| Step 7: Plan to Contact Parents | Allotted Time: 5 Minutes |

Who will share a copy of the minutes from this meeting with the student's parent(s) and when?

_____

| Step 8: Review the Intervention & Monitoring Plans | Allotted Time: 5 Minutes |

At the close of the meeting:

- ☐ The recorder reviews the main points of the intervention & monitoring plans with the team.

- ☐ The team selects a date and time for the follow-up RTI Team meeting on this student. (NOTE: Generally, follow-up meetings are scheduled 6-8 instructional weeks from the start date of the intervention (Step 6).

    Next meeting date & time: _____

- ☐ The case manager reviews the agreed-upon time within the next school week to meet with the referring teacher(s):

    Date and time for case manager to meet with the referring teacher(s): _____

- ☐ The team completes the RTI Team Debriefing Form.

Exhibit 3-F
RTI Problem-Solving Team Effectiveness Self-Rating Scale

1-*Strongly Disagree* 2-*Disagree* 3-*Agree* 4-*Strongly Agree*

How Effective is Our Current RTI Team in…?

Coordinating Meetings ("How well do we coordinate & schedule?")
- Reviewing teacher referrals & checking in with teacher as needed 1 2 3 4
- Scheduling meetings 1 2 3 4
- Notifying referring teachers and RTI Team members about upcoming meetings 1 2 3 4
- Finding substitutes (if necessary) for team members, referring teachers 1 2 3 4
- Taking good meeting notes 1 2 3 4

Meeting Issues ("How well do we stick to a problem-solving framework and make referring teachers feel welcome & supported?")
- Having team members follow a 'problem-solving' format and avoid digressions 1 2 3 4
- Creating an atmosphere in which the referring teacher(s) feel welcome & supported 1 2 3 4

Interventions ("How well do we select, document, and monitor interventions?")
- Identifying school-wide resources available for use in team interventions 1 2 3 4
- Selecting interventions that are research-based 1 2 3 4
- Recording interventions thoroughly in clearly outlined steps 1 2 3 4
- Documenting intervention 'follow-through' by teachers 1 2 3 4

Communication and the RTI Team ("How well do we communicate our purpose and role to our audiences?")
- Publicizing the purpose and role of the RTI Team to faculty and other staff 1 2 3 4
- Publicizing the purpose and role of the RTI Team to parents 1 2 3 4
- Sharing information about meeting results, interventions with parents 1 2 3 4

RTI Team 'Process' Issues ("How well do we share our feelings and attitudes about the RTI Team?")
- Encouraging team members to share opinions about the RTI Team's direction, overall success 1 2 3 4
- Encouraging team members to identify positive, negative events occurring at meetings 1 2 3 4
- Reserving sufficient time for team 'debriefings' to communicate about 'process' issues 1 2 3 4

Additional Topics…
- Recruiting future RTI Team members 1 2 3 4
- Finding ways to save time in the RTI process 1 2 3 4
- Coordinating RTI Team and Special Education referrals 1 2 3 4
- Observing appropriate confidentiality with team, teacher, and student information 1 2 3 4
- Other: _____ 1 2 3 4
- Other: _____ 1 2 3 4

Exhibit 3-G
Creating a 'Multiple-Source' Process to Initiate Middle or High School Student Referrals to the RTI Problem-Solving Team

There should be multiple possible paths by which middle and high school students can be referred to the RTI Problem-Solving Team--to ensure that no student who needs intensive intervention help is overlooked. Schools should write down and share with school staff their own guidelines for how student referrals can be initiated to the RTI Team from different sources. Below are some recommendations for what an RTI Team referral process should look like in secondary schools.

RTI Team Referral Source	How to Initiate the RTI Team Referral	How to Evaluate the RTI Team Referral
Teacher	☐ The teacher completes a referral form for RTI assistance and sends it to the student's guidance counselor.	A 'gatekeeper' (e.g., administrator or guidance) reviews the referral to evaluate the severity of the concern and assess how to route the referral. Options include: • Scheduling an RTI Team meeting immediately • The administrator arranging a meeting with the teacher to discuss additional instructional or behavioral strategies that teacher can attempt prior to an RTI referral. • Scheduling a parent-teacher conference to discuss the concern • Getting additional information from other instructional staff who work with the student to better understand the concern
Non-Instructional Personnel	☐ The non-instructional staff member meets with guidance or administration to share instructional or behavioral concerns about the student.	Guidance and administration evaluate the severity of the concern and evaluate how to route the referral. Options include: • Scheduling an RTI Team meeting immediately and having teachers complete RTI referral forms on the student • Scheduling a parent-teacher conference to discuss the concern • Getting additional information from instructional staff to better understand the concern and decide how to proceed.
Administration & Guidance	☐ Guidance meets with administration to discuss any student that guidance or administration believes would benefit from an RTI referral.	As a result of the guidance/administration meeting, the referral is routed according to one of these options: • Scheduling an RTI Team meeting immediately and having teachers complete RTI referral forms on the student • Meeting with the student's teachers to help them to create appropriate Tier 1 (classroom) interventions • Getting more information from the student's teachers to better understand the concern before acting on it. • Scheduling a parent-teacher conference to discuss the concern • Monitoring the concern with no further action
Parent	☐ The parent calls or meets with guidance or administration to express concerns about the student, request general assistance, or request an RTI referral.	As a result of the parent phone call or meeting, the referral is routed according to one of these options: • Scheduling an RTI Team meeting immediately and having teachers complete RTI referral forms on the student • Scheduling a parent-teacher conference to discuss the concern.
School-Wide Academic Screening or 'Early Warning' Data Screening	☐ The school reviews data from grade-wide academic screenings completed 3 times yearly (e.g., CBM oral reading fluency; CBM writing sample) OR the school reviews archival data every 5 weeks on student grades, attendance, office referrals.	• The school sets 'cutpoint' scores for evaluating academic screening data or archival data (grades, attendance, office referrals). These cutpoint scores define students whose academic performance or behavior puts them 'at risk' or 'at high risk'. • When students fall within the 'at risk range' based on cutpoint scores, teachers may be alerted to attempt classroom (Tier 1) interventions. • When students fall within the 'high risk' range based on cutpoint scores, they are referred to the RTI Team.

Exhibit 3-H
The Case Manager-Teacher 'Pre-Meeting': Creating a More Efficient RTI Team Process

Prior to an initial RTI Problem-Solving Team meeting, it is recommended that a case manager from the RTI Team schedule a brief (15-20 minute) 'pre-meeting' with the referring teacher. The purpose of this pre-meeting is for the case manager to share with the teacher the purpose of the upcoming full RTI Team meeting, to clarify student referral concerns, and to decide what data should be collected and brought to the RTI Team meeting.

Here is a recommended agenda for the case manager-teacher pre-meeting:

1. *Explain the purpose of the upcoming RTI Problem-Solving Team meeting:* The case manager explains that the RTI Team meeting goals are to (a) fully understand the nature of the student's academic and/or behavioral problems; (b) develop an evidence-based intervention plan for the student; and (c) set a goal for student improvement and select means to monitor the student's response to the intervention plan.

2. *Define the student referral concern(s) in clear, specific terms.* The case manager reviews with the teacher the most important student referral concern(s), helping the teacher to define those concern(s) in clear, specific, observable terms. The teacher is also prompted to prioritize his or her top 1-2 student concerns. NOTE: Use the guides that appear on the next page for writing academic or behavioral problem-identification statements and for dividing global skills into component sub-skills.

Student Concern 1:_____

Student Concern 2:_____

3. *Decide what data should be brought to the RTI Team meeting.* The case manager and teacher decide what student data should be collected and brought to the RTI Team meeting to provide insight into the nature of the student's presenting concern(s). Use the table below to select data for RTI decision-making.

Data Source	Types of Data to Be Collected
Archival data: Select relevant information already in the cumulative folder or student database.	
Student work products. Collect examples of homework, tests, in-class assignments, work projects (with examples from typically performing students collected as well for purposes of comparison)	
Student interview. Meet with the student to get his or her perspective on the academic and/or behavioral problems.	
Specialized assessment. Decide whether more specialized, individual assessment is required (e.g., direct observations of the student's rate of on-task behavior; instructional assessment to map out in detail the student's skills in literacy, mathematics, etc.).	

Exhibit 3-H, continued

Identifying the Student Concern: Guides for Defining Academic and Behavioral Problems and for Breaking Global Skills into Component Sub-Skills

Academic Problems: Format for Writing Problem Definition Statement		
Environmental Conditions or Task Demands	**Problem Description**	**Typical/ Expected Level of Performance**
Example: For science homework…	…Tye turns in assignments an average of 50% of the time…	…while the classroom median rate of homework turned in is 90%.

Behavioral Problems: Format for Writing Problem Definition Statement		
Conditions. The condition(s) under which the problem is likely to occur	**Problem Description.** A specific description of the problem behavior	**Contextual Information.** Information about the frequency, intensity, duration, or other dimension(s) of the behavior
Example: When given a verbal teacher request…	…Jay fails to comply with that request within 3 minutes…	… an average of 50% of the time.

Discrete Categorization: Divide Global Skill into Essential Sub-Skills	
Global Skill:	**Example : Global Skill:** The student will improve classroom organization skills'
Sub-Skill 1:	**Example: Sub-Skills for 'Classroom Organization Skills'** ☐ Sub-Skill 1: Arrive to class on time
Sub-Skill 2:	☐ Sub-Skill 2: Bring work materials to class
Sub-Skill 3:	☐ Sub-Skill 3: Follow teacher directions in a timely manner
Sub-Skill 4:	☐ Sub-Skill 4: Know how to seek teacher assistance when needed
Sub-Skill 5:	☐ Sub-Skill 5: Maintain an uncluttered desk with only essential work materials

Exhibit 3-I
Engaging the Student as an Active RTI Partner in the Intervention Planning Process

Schools should strongly consider having middle and high school students attend and take part in their own RTI Problem-Solving Team meetings for two reasons. First, as students mature, their teachers expect that they will take responsibility in advocating for their own learning needs. Second, students are more likely to fully commit to RTI intervention plans if they attend the RTI Team meeting and have a voice in the creation of those plans.

Before the RTI Team Meeting. The student should be adequately prepared to attend the RTI Team meeting by first engaging in a 'pre-meeting' with a school staff member whom the student knows and trusts (e.g., school counselor, teacher, administrator). By connecting the student with a trusted mentor figure who can help that student to navigate the RTI process, the school improves the odds that the disengaged or unmotivated student will feel an increased sense of connection and commitment to their own school performance (Bridgeland, DiIulio, & Morison, 2006).

A student RTI 'pre-meeting' can be quite brief, lasting perhaps 15-20 minutes. Here is a simple agenda for the meeting:

- *Share information about the student problem(s).* Share with the student information about the problems with academic performance or behavior that led to an RTI Team referral. For example, the student may be shown RTI referral forms from teachers documenting their concerns or review recent grade reports.
- *Describe the purpose and steps of the RTI Problem-Solving Team meeting.* Be sure that the student understands that the goal of the upcoming RTI Team meeting is to develop an intervention plan designed to help the student to be successful.
- *Stress the student's importance in the intervention plan.* Emphasize the key role that the student can and should play in designing the intervention plan. Here the school is only acknowledging the obvious: a middle or high school student holds most of the power in deciding whether or not to commit to an intervention.
- *Have the student describe his or her learning needs.* Consider using the attached structured interview *Pre-RTI Team Meeting Student Interview: Sample Questions* to collect information about the student's learning needs.
- *Invite the student to attend the RTI Team meeting.* Reassure the student that he or she will not be singled out or 'attacked' at the problem-solving meeting. Assure the student that the meeting's purpose is simply to develop a plan to help that student to do better in school.

During the RTI Team Meeting. If the student agrees to attend the RTI Team meeting, he or she participates fully in the meeting. Teachers and other staff attending the meeting make an effort to keep the atmosphere positive and focused on finding solutions to the student's presenting concern(s). As each intervention idea is discussed, the team checks in with the student to determine that the student (a) fully understands how to access or participate in the intervention element being proposed and (b) is willing to take part in that intervention element. If the student appears hesitant or resistant, the team should work with the student either to win the student over to the proposed intervention idea or to find an alternative intervention that will accomplish the same goal.

Exhibit 3-I, continued

At the end of the RTI Team meeting, each of the intervention ideas that is dependent on student participation for success is copied into the *School Success Intervention Plan* (see below), which is then signed by the student, parent, and an adult school contact with whom the student has a positive connection. The student is directed to inform the assigned school contact if the student discovers that he or she is unable to carry out any element on the School Success Intervention Plan. The school contact person can then follow up to determine how to fix any problems encountered in the plan.

After the RTI Team Meeting. If the school discovers that the student is not carrying out his or her responsibilities as spelled out by the intervention plan, it is recommended that the staff member assigned as the RTI contact meet with the student and parent. At that meeting, the adult contact checks with the student to make sure that:

- the intervention plan continues to be relevant and appropriate for addressing the student's academic or behavioral needs
- the student understands and call access all intervention elements outlined on the *School Success Intervention Plan.*
- adults participating in the intervention plan (e.g., classroom teachers) are carrying out their parts of the plan.

If all evidence suggests that the student clearly has the capability to implement the intervention plan and that the student simply chooses not to do so, the adult contact should remind the student and parent that the intervention plan cannot work without the student's active cooperation. The student and parent are informed that the intervention plan will be discontinued if the student continues to refuse to comply but that the intervention plan can be reinstated immediately if the student decides once again to participate in the plan.

References

Bridgeland, J. M., DiIulio, J. J., & Morison, K. B. (2006). *The silent epidemic: Perspectives of high school dropouts.* Seattle, WA: Gates Foundation. Retrieved on May 4, 2008, from http://www.gatesfoundation.org/nr/downloads/ed/TheSilentEpidemic3-06FINAL.pdf

Exhibit 3-I, continued
Pre-RTI Team Meeting Student Interview: Sample Questions

Directions. Set aside time before the RTI Problem-Solving Team meeting to meet individually with the referred student. Ask the following questions to better determine the student's learning needs. Record student responses and bring the completed questionnaire to the RTI Team meeting.

1. Which of your courses are your favorite? Why?	
2. Which of your courses are the most challenging? Why?	
3. Describe how you study for quizzes and tests in your most challenging course(s).	
4. What strategies do you use to get help in your most challenging course(s)?	
5. Homework:	
a. Describe the physical setting in which you usually do your homework.	
b. How long do you typically work on homework each night?	
c. Do you have access to cell phones, TV, video games, or other entertainment while you do homework? If so, how frequently are you using them during homework time?	
d. How do you decide which homework assignment to do first?	
e. Do you spend time each night reviewing course notes or sections from your course textbooks? If so, about how much time do you usually spend doing this?	
f. What kinds of homework assignments do you like least or find most challenging?	
6. What would you want your teachers to know about your strengths and challenges as a student?	Strengths: _____ Challenges: _____
7. What are steps that you can take on your own to be more successful in school?	
8. What would you like to see as outcomes after the RTI Team meets to discuss your learning needs?	

Exhibit 3-I, Form 1

School Success Intervention Plan for: _____ Date: _____

The student agrees to carry out the strategies listed below to promote school success:	[Optional] If adults in school or at home will assist the student with a strategy, the ADULT responsibilities are listed below:	[Optional] Name of adult(s) assisting student with strategy
1. _____ _____	1. _____ _____	_____ _____
2. _____ _____	2. _____ _____	_____ _____
3. _____ _____	3. _____ _____	_____ _____
4. _____ _____	4. _____ _____	_____ _____

_____ _____ _____
Signature of Student Signature of Adult School Contact Signature of Parent

Chapter 4
Developing Student Intervention Plans

The ultimate mission of schools is to ensure that all students attain success and graduate. Too often, though, struggling students in secondary grades fall out of alignment with their learning environments into underperformance or even school failure. When a student experiences problems with schoolwork, those academic difficulties represent a mismatch between the student's characteristics as a learner and the demands of the instructional setting (e.g., Foorman & Torgesen, 2001). Behavior problems, too, are a sign of a disconnect between the student and the present learning environment. For example, it may be that a misbehaving student is not motivated to display more appropriate behaviors, does not know how to engage in those more acceptable behaviors, or is using disruptive behavior to escape academic demands (Witt, Daly & Noell, 2000).

The power of Response to Intervention is that it guides schools in identifying why particular students struggle with academic or behavioral issues and in matching those students to appropriate and effective intervention plans. This chapter addresses interventions, which lie at the vital center of RTI. It would be a mistake, however, to think of interventions as shrink-wrapped solutions that a school can randomly pull off a shelf and plug in to any student's RTI plan. Instead, the school must follow a multi-step process to ensure that the right intervention ideas are selected to address a student's unique problem(s) and that the resulting targeted intervention plan is correctly carried out.

A quick inventory of all the elements that a middle or high school must juggle as it assembles a student intervention illustrates why the topic of interventions deserves its own chapter. First, each school is expected to develop its own standards for determining whether a particular intervention idea can be considered evidence-based. Second, the school should make clear to teachers what kinds of support-interventions and accommodations for general education students are acceptable under RTI and what classroom practices are inappropriate (modification of core instruction resulting in a lowering of learning standards). Third, educators must have the ability to describe student academic and behavioral problems in clear and specific terms. After all, interventions are likely to work only if they closely match the student's needs and profile of skills. Fourth, before starting academic interventions, educators at all Tiers should be able to verify that 'critical components' of those interventions are in place. Fifth, the school should measure the integrity with which each RTI intervention is carried out—to assure that the quality of that intervention is high. And sixth, middle and high school educational leaders should adopt a building-wide plan to build the capacity of the entire school staff to provide student interventions as a routine part of their professional practice.

Develop Guidelines to Determine if Interventions are 'Evidence-Based'

The RTI model directs that educators use instructional and behavioral strategies that have been demonstrated through research to be effective. However, this directive is easier said than done. The field of public education lacks uniform guidelines to identify interventions that are 'evidence-based' (Odom et al., 2005). Furthermore, the number of interventions that are well-supported by research varies across academic and behavioral domains (Kratochwill, Clements, & Kalymon, 2007). In most school systems, even the day-to-day instruction and intervention techniques that teachers routinely use in classrooms rest on an uncertain research base (Fuchs, & Deshler, 2007).

Schools must therefore assume responsibility for coming up with their own guidelines for determining whether specific intervention practices or programs are in fact 'evidence-based' (Fuchs & Deshler, 2007). While there is difference of opinion about the level of evidence required to certify that an intervention practice or program is 'evidence-based', it is universally accepted that schools should at a minimum verify that any interventions that they use have been studied using high-quality research methodologies (e.g., Johnson, Mellard, Fuchs & McKnight, 2006). Steps that schools can adopt to enhance their capacity to discern whether interventions are adequately researched include writing their own definition of 'evidence-based', and compiling a list of research journals and professional organizations that can serve as sources of interventions because they have a reputation for producing impartial, high-quality research and scholarship. A more in-depth blueprint for defining the term 'evidence-based' is to be found in Exhibit 4-A, *Developing Shared Guidelines for Determining 'Evidence-Based': Recommendations for Schools.*

Adopt Shared Language to Describe Interventions and Related Terms

In order for teachers and other educational staff to serve as academic interventionists, they must have a shared definition of the key terms *intervention, accommodation,* and *modification*. Academic interventions strengthen a student's independent capacity to successfully meet academic expectations. *Interventions* comprise those practices or programs that "when taken, have demonstrated ability to change a fixed educational trajectory" (Methe & Riley-Tillman, 2008; p. 37). *Accommodations* do not directly strengthen academic skills but can help the student to fully access and participate in the general education curriculum. Importantly, accommodations do not water down the instructional content and do not reduce the student's rate of learning (Skinner, Pappas & Davis, 2005). *Modifications* are practices that actually lower the academic standards against which the student is to be evaluated. It should be noted that interventions and accommodatiions are appropriate for use on a general education student's RTI plan—but modifications are typically not included on an RTI plan. After all, it is impossible to imagine that modification strategies that lower learning expectations would help a struggling general education student to accelerate learning to close the academic gap with his or her peers. A more extensive set of definitions for intervention and related terms is to be found in Exhibit 4-B, *Intervention & Related RTI Terms: Definitions*. This Exhibit can be shared with faculty to ensure that strategies they employ with students meet acceptable RTI expectations as effective practices.

Define the Student Problem in Clear, Specific Terms

A student can be reliably matched to effective academic or behavioral interventions only if that student's presenting problem(s) are first clearly identified and understood (Bergan, 1995). Just as a physician cannot select an effective treatment for a patient without first diagnosing the illness, so too a school cannot choose an intervention with any confidence unless the student concern is first defined in specific terms. In fact, the task of clearly identifying the student problem is so fundamental that any intervention-development process that ignores this step should be considered 'fatally flawed' (Witt, VanDerHeyden & Gilbertson, 2004).

Both academic and behavioral problems should be described in sufficient detail so that, with the problem description in hand, any two independent observers could watch the same student and agree on instances when the student does or does not display the academic or behavioral concern. After the problem has been described, the school should then draw upon data from a variety of sources to develop a hypothesis, or 'best guess', about why the academic or behavioral concern is occurring (Christ, 2008). A student who talks with peers about non-instructional topics during independent seatwork, for example, may do so to attract the attention of peers or perhaps to avoid difficult academic work. The hypothesis that the school selects is the one that appears best to explain a student behavior and thus point the way toward appropriate intervention ideas—and may occasionally highlight certain intervention strategies that should be *avoided*. For example, if a teacher hypothesizes that a student is defiant because he wants to avoid in-class math work that is too difficult, this teacher would probably select an academic intervention designed to help the student to better understand the assigned math work. On the other hand, the problem would likely only be made worse if that teacher chose to regularly send the student to the principal's office for each episode of defiant behavior—as sending the student from the room would in fact reinforce the defiant behavior as a means of escaping classwork.

The following two exhibits can help schools to write clear, specific student problem-identification statements. Exhibit 4-C, *Defining Academic Problems: The First Step in Effective Intervention Planning,* provides a structure for defining academic problems that includes comparison to expected peer performance. A five-step process for defining behavior problems and linking them to effective interventions is to be found in Exhibit 4-D, *Defining Problem Student Behaviors and Matching to Appropriate Interventions: A 5-Step Process.*

Identify the 'Critical Components' of Academic Interventions

When working with struggling learners, teachers in the secondary grades feel tremendous pressure to help these students close the skill gap. Indeed, "each minute counts and schools cannot afford to support inefficient models of service delivery" (Batsche, Castillo, Dixon & Forde, 2008; p. 177). Schools can greatly increase the odds that an intervention will be successful by first developing quality indicators and then evaluating prospective intervention plans to ensure that they meet the following basic quality guidelines, to include:

- *Allocating sufficient contact time and assuring appropriate student-teacher ratio.* The cumulative time set aside for an intervention and the amount of direct teacher contact are two factors that help to determine that intervention's 'strength' (Yeaton & Sechrest, 1981).

- *Matching the intervention to the student problem.* Academic interventions are not selected at random. First, the student academic problem(s) is defined clearly and in detail. Then, the likely explanations for the academic problem(s) are identified to understand which intervention(s) are likely to help—and perhaps which should be avoided. The Instructional Hierarchy (Haring et al., 1978) is one useful tool for locating the best academic intervention for a student; it defines learners as being in the acquisition, fluency, generalization, or adaptation stage. Another important question to be answered when selecting an intervention is whether poor motivation plays a significant role in student underperformance.

- *Incorporating effective instructional elements.* The effective 'building blocks' of instruction are well-known and well-supported by the research. They include explicit instruction, appropriate level of challenge, active engagement, and timely performance feedback (Burns, VanDerHeyden & Boice, 2008; Skinner, Pappas & Davis, 2005). Schools should keep these effective instructional elements foremost in mind when selecting or creating any academic interventions.

- *Verifying teacher understanding and providing teacher support.* The teacher is an active agent in the intervention, with primary responsibility for putting it into practice in a busy classroom. It is important, then, that the teacher fully understands how to do the intervention, believes that he or she can do it, and knows whom to seek out if there are problems with the intervention.

- *Documenting the intervention and collecting data.* Interventions have meaning only if they are done within a larger data-based context. For example, interventions that lack baseline data, goal(s) for improvement, and a progress-monitoring plan are 'fatally flawed' (Witt, VanDerHeyden & Gilbertson, 2004).

A more detailed listing of 'critical components' for academic interventions can be found in Exhibit 4-E, *Academic Interventions 'Critical Components' Checklist*.

Develop the Capacity to Measure Intervention Integrity

If a student fails to respond to an RTI intervention, there are two possible explanations for this negative outcome. One possibility is that the intervention was implemented correctly but that the student simply failed to benefit. A second, more concerning possibility, however, is that the intervention was not carried out with integrity—that is, the manner in which the intervention was actually conducted fell short of its design. There are a number of explanations for why an intervention could be compromised: for example, students might have frequent absences that prevent them from accessing the intervention; a staff member might suddenly be assigned to different duties and thus no longer be available to serve as an interventionist; or a classroom teacher may not have received proper training before starting the intervention.

For a school to have confidence in its RTI interventions, then, it must make an effort to measure the quality with which these interventions are carried out. There are three general methods for measuring intervention integrity. Educators may want to use some combination of these approaches for any particular student case. First, an observer may prepare a checklist that details the essential steps of the intervention, visit the classroom to observe the intervention, and record the number of intervention steps correctly carried out. Second, the teacher or other interventionist might perform a self-check: periodically rating themselves or otherwise recording their own ability to carry out the intervention. Third, the intervention may yield work products or other physical evidence (e.g., dated student work from tutoring sessions) that provide indirect evidence that intervention sessions have taken place as scheduled and perhaps that intervention procedures have been followed correctly.

While the quality of any RTI intervention should be measured, schools should make a special effort to monitor the integrity of those interventions that require substantial resources to implement and are being used in student cases in which the stakes are high (e.g., there is the potential for school failure, referral to special education, or other negative outcomes). For a detailed review of options for tracking intervention integrity, review Exhibit 4-F, *Intervention Integrity: Methods to Track the Quality with Which Interventions Are Carried Out.* Forms 1, 2 and 3 of this exhibit are excellent guides to support this topic.

Schedule Tier 2 & Tier 3 Interventions

A basic expectation of RTI is that Tier 2 and 3 interventions should supplement, not replace, core instruction (Burns & Gibbons, 2008). Yet, finding the time in the schedules of struggling students to provide supplemental interventions can seem an insurmountable problem in middle and high schools. Indeed, in one recent survey, secondary-school principals flagged the issue of scheduling RTI interventions as one of the chief stumbling blocks to successful implementation of RTI (Sansosti, Noltemeyer & Goss, 2010). There are no simple solutions to the thorny problem of scheduling RTI in secondary schools. However, some scheduling strategies appear in Exhibit 4-G, *Scheduling RTI Supplemental Services in Middle and High Schools: Five Ideas.*

Create Schoolwide Procedures for Implementing Tier 1 (Classroom) Interventions

As schools gear up to provide interventions on a routine basis, the greatest number of interventions will almost surely be implemented in the general education classroom at Tier 1 because that is where struggling students spend most of their time. However, content-area teachers in the secondary grades may be reluctant to serve as interventionists, at least initially, because they do not view use of interventions as part of their job (Kamil et al., 2008), believe that only special education can help students with academic delays (Martens, 1993), or for other reasons. The objective of the middle or high school, then, is to expand 'teacher tolerance' of students with academic or behavioral needs (Gerber, 2003) by giving instructors specific guidance in how to select and use quality interventions. Teachers must know how to document interventions, for example, and have a menu of research-based academic and behavioral strategies at hand to choose from as they assemble Tier 1 intervention plans.

- An 8-step process to help schools attain the goal of creating uniform teacher intervention practices can be found in Exhibit 4-H of this chapter, *Tier 1 (Classroom) Interventions: Building Your School's Capacity.* At the end of this exhibit, there are three forms that can support the process.

- A standard form that general education teachers throughout a school building or district can use to document their Tier 1 intervention plans appears as Exhibit 4-I, *Documenting Tier 1 (Classroom) Interventions: A Sample Form.*

- Sample Tier 1 reading comprehension 'fix-up' strategies suitable for use by content-area teachers appear in Exhibit 4-J, *Reading Comprehension 'Fix-Up' Skills: A Toolkit.*

- A six-step approach to managing challenging classroom behaviors is featured as Exhibit 4-K, *'Defensive Behavior Management': Advance Planning, Connecting With the Student, and Defusing Crisis Situations.* Teachers may want to use this flexible framework as the starting point for Tier 1 behavior management plans.

- Strategies that content-area teachers can use to promote literacy skills with all students can be found as an Addendum, *Core Instructional Ideas to Promote Literacy Skills in Secondary Classrooms,* at the end of this book.

Middle and high schools face a challenging task as they strive to expand their capacity to deliver high-quality academic and behavioral interventions. And that task lacks an end point. Even when a school has established an initial continuum of evidence-based interventions that can be deployed as needed for struggling students, it will need to review those RTI intervention practices at least yearly to keep them in alignment with any significant changes occurring both within and outside of their school system. Internally, the school must continually monitor its student performance data and student demographics (e.g., number of students identified as English Language Learners) and adjust its array of intervention programs to address newly discovered student skill gaps or needs. Externally, the school will want to track and respond to changes in state and federal regulations that impact middle and high school RTI, particularly those regarding the selection, delivery, and documentation of interventions. Additionally, it is important that the school stay up to date on new developments in RTI intervention research (e.g., by reviewing peer-reviewed journals and other reputable publications and by visiting the *What Works Clearinghouse* website at http://ies.ed.gov/ncee/wwc/) to ensure that it has access to the best current intervention practices and programs.

References

Batsche, G. M., Castillo, J. M., Dixon, D. N., & Forde, S. (2008). Best practices in problem analysis. In A. Thomas & J. Grimes (Eds.), *Best practices in school psychology V* (pp. 177-193). Bethesda, MD: National Association of School Psychologists.

Bergan, J. R. (1995). Evolution of a problem-solving model of consultation. *Journal of Educational and Psychological Consultation,* 6(2), 111-123.

Burns, M. K., & Gibbons, K. A. (2008). *Implementing response-to-intervention in elementary and secondary schools.* Routledge: New York.

Burns, M. K., VanDerHeyden, A. M., & Boice, C. H. (2008). Best practices in intensive academic interventions. In A. Thomas & J. Grimes (Eds.), *Best practices in school psychology V* (pp.1151-1162). Bethesda, MD: National Association of School Psychologists.

Christ, T. (2008). Best practices in problem analysis. In A. Thomas & J. Grimes (Eds.), *Best practices in school psychology V* (pp. 159-176). Bethesda, MD: National Association of School Psychologists.

Foorman, B. R., & Torgesen, J. (2001). Critical elements of classroom and small-group instruction promote reading success in all children. *Learning Disabilities Research & Practice,* 16, 203-212.

Fuchs, D., & Deshler, D. D. (2007). What we need to know about responsiveness to intervention (and shouldn't be afraid to ask). *Learning Disabilities Research & Practice,* 22(2),129–136.

Gerber, M. M. (2003). *Teachers are still the test: Limitations of response to instruction strategies for identifying children with learning disabilities.* Paper presented at the National Research Center on Learning Disabilities Responsiveness-to-Intervention Symposium, Kansas City, MO.

Haring, N.G., Lovitt, T.C., Eaton, M.D., & Hansen, C.L. (1978). *The fourth R: Research in the classroom.* Columbus, OH: Charles E. Merrill Publishing Co.

Johnson, E., Mellard, D.F., Fuchs, D., & McKnight, M.A. (2006). *Responsiveness to Intervention (RTI): How to do it.*

Lawrence, KS: National Research Center on Learning Disabilities.

Kamil, M. L., Borman, G. D., Dole, J., Kral, C. C., Salinger, T., & Torgesen, J. (2008). *Improving adolescent literacy: Effective classroom and intervention practices: A practice guide* (NCEE #2008-4027). Washington, DC: National Center for Education Evaluation and Regional Assistance, Institute of Education Sciences, U.S. Department of Education. Retrieved from http://ies.ed.gov/ncee/wwc.

Kratochwill, T. R., Clements, M. A., & Kalymon, K. M. (2007). Response to intervention: Conceptual and methodological issues in implementation. In Jimerson, S. R., Burns, M. K., & VanDerHeyden, A. M. (Eds.), *Handbook of response to intervention: The science and practice of assessment and intervention.* New York: Springer.

Martens, B. K. (1993). A case against magical thinking in school-based intervention. *Journal of Educational and Psychological Consultation,* 4(2), 185-189.

Methe, S. A. & Riley-Tillman, T. C. (2008). An informed approach to selecting and designing early mathematics interventions. *School Psychology Forum,* 2(3), 29-41.

Sansosti, F. J., Noltemeyer, A., & Goss, S. (2010). Principals' perceptions of the importance and availability of response to intervention practices within high school settings. *School Psychology Review,* 39, 286-295.

Skinner, C. H., Pappas, D. N., & Davis, K. A. (2005). Enhancing academic engagement: Providing opportunities for responding and influencing students to choose to respond. *Psychology in the Schools,* 42, 389-403.

Witt, J. C., Daly, E. M., & Noell, G. (2000). *Functional assessments: A step-by-step guide to solving academic and behavior problems.* Longmont, CO: Sopris West.

Witt, J. C., VanDerHeyden, A. M., & Gilbertson, D. (2004). Troubleshooting behavioral interventions. A systematic process for finding and eliminating problems. *School Psychology Review,* 33, 363-383.

Yeaton, W. M. & Sechrest, L. (1981). Critical dimensions in the choice and maintenance of successful treatments: Strength, integrity, and effectiveness. *Journal of Consulting and Clinical Psychology,* 49, 156-167.

Frequently Asked Questions About…
…Middle & High School Interventions

1. **Why is it important that the school first clearly define the student academic or behavioral problem before selecting an intervention?** RTI interventions can best be described using a lock-and-key metaphor. The student who struggles in a particular academic or behavioral area can be thought of figuratively being 'locked'—effective school performance cannot take place until that problem is solved. To extend this metaphor, intervention strategies can be thought of as 'keys' that can open these locks—solving student problems and unlocking their learning potential. But there are many reasons why students struggle—they may lack an academic skill, for example, or be slow in performing a skill or lack motivation to engage in the skill. And, of course, interventions are equally varied and specific: some are designed to teach new skills, others to build fluency in existing skills, and still others to motivate a student to engage his or her best effort.

   If the wrong intervention is selected to address a student problem, it will probably not be effective, instead wasting precious time and instructional resources. In contrast, when an interventionist first takes the time to define the student problem in clear and specific terms and decide on the best explanation (hypothesis) for why the problem is occurring, that educator is much more likely to select the right intervention the first time and to help the student to achieve school success.

2. **Why do RTI interventions have to be 'evidence-based'?** Schools have limited resources, including time, to implement interventions, especially when attempting to address high-stakes cases of students with severe academic or behavioral deficits. It makes sense, then, that they attempt to increase the odds of student success by selecting as interventions only those strategies and programs that have been shown through reputable research to be effective. An additional advantage of evidence-based interventions—whether those drawn from journal article descriptions, accessed from web-

sites, or purchased as commercial programs—is that they are typically described in sufficient detail to provide clear direction to the teacher or other interventionist about how to implement them correctly. This specificity helps the interventionist to carry out the intervention with integrity.

3. **Aren't classroom RTI interventions just examples of 'good teaching'? If so, why do teachers have to document their Tier 1 (classroom) interventions?** If RTI interventions used in the classroom are evidence-based, they are certainly examples of 'good teaching' or 'good behavior management' practices. However, teachers should document their Tier 1 (classroom) intervention strategies for several reasons. First, if a student struggles to the point of requiring a classroom intervention plan, putting that plan into writing in advance allows the teacher to think through all of its elements. This pre-planning tends to increase the quality with which the actual intervention is carried out. Second, if a struggling student does not respond adequately to the Tier 1 (classroom) intervention, the teacher is able to use the plan documentation to communicate in detail with others in the school about what strategies were implemented and to make the case for seeking more RTI support for the student. Third, a written classroom RTI plan is a great starting point for a conference with the student and/or parent both to communicate the teacher's efforts to support the student and to identify roles that the student and parent might play in supporting the intervention plan.

4. **Who in the school is responsible for actually implementing academic or behavioral interventions?** Potentially, any educator or stakeholder in a middle or high school can serve as an interventionist, playing a part in implementing elements of an RTI intervention plan. The general education teacher is certainly a key interventionist for those day-to-day Tier 1 intervention strategies used in the classroom. Support staff such as reading teachers may provide supplemental interventions (Tier 2 or 3) for students who need that additional support. Mental health staff (e.g., counselors, school psychologists, social workers) and even school administrators may assist with RTI behavioral interventions. When appropriate, students can be given responsibility for

aspects of intervention plans—for example, being taught to use certain cognitive strategies independently or agreeing to seek help from an instructor when needed. Occasionally, even parents have volunteered to assist with elements of an RTI plan, such as serving as a homework coach for their child.

5. **Should a student's intervention plan be limited to only one strategy at a time?** No. If necessary, an intervention plan can have multiple strategies implemented by multiple people. Of course, if more than one intervention strategy is included on an RTI plan, each of the strategies should be evidence-based and each should logically address the area of identified student need. A plan with several intervention elements is sometimes referred to as an 'intervention package'.

    Educators sometimes express concern that, if more than one intervention strategy is implemented at a time on a successful RTI plan, it would be impossible to state with confidence precisely which element(s) of the plan actually contributed to the student's success. Although the need to isolate specific treatment variables is important in a formal research study, schools typically lack the time and resources for such painstaking methodologies. It is therefore acceptable in applied settings such as schools to assemble multi-element intervention packages and to simply evaluate the global impact of these plans on student academic performance or behavior.

6. **How can a content-area teacher find the time to implement student interventions in a busy classroom?** Teachers always feel the pressure of finding enough time to deliver strong instruction in complex material for students of a wide range of abilities. Yet good teaching also includes the expectation that the instructor attempts to differentiate instruction for students who need additional help to the degree that is feasible and reasonable in that classroom.

    Here are two ideas that a school can adopt to help teachers to efficiently deliver Tier 1 interventions when needed:

- *Create an intervention menu.* The school should compile a collection, or menu, of evidence-based intervention ideas to address common types of student concern (e.g., inattention in large-group settings; difficulty in locating the main-idea/gist sentence in a paragraph) and make those intervention ideas available to all faculty members. Having such a menu on hand is a great potential time-saver, as teachers then do not have to locate those strategies on their own.

- *Reteach student skills in core instruction.* If a large number of students show deficits in important academic skills (e.g., lack of reading comprehension 'fix-up' skills), the school should consider teaching or reteaching these skills as a core instructional module in a single core area class (e.g., English Language Arts, Social Studies, Science). Other instructors working with the same students would be knowledgeable of the strategies taught in this module and could then efficiently coach and support the use of the strategies in their classrooms as well.

7. **Is it ever an acceptable practice for schools to lower the instructional expectations for a general education student's as an RTI strategy?** In an attempt to engage unmotivated or struggling students, classroom teachers will sometimes lower academic expectations through such informal 'modification' practices as assigning these students fewer homework items or giving them less-demanding work assignments than peers. This approach of informally 'modifying' the struggling student's work is almost always a mistake. After all, in order for students with delays in school skills to close the academic gap with peers, they must accelerate their learning. And it is highly unlikely that *reducing* academic expectations of students will bring them up to grade level. On the contrary, such an approach will almost certainly have the opposite effect of leaving those students farther behind.

When teachers are tempted to modify general education students' instruction, they should instead attempt strategies that are beneficial to learning. Examples of pro-learning approaches include remediating skill deficits so that students have the tools to keep up with classroom instruction and using accommodations such as 'chunking' (breaking assignments into smaller 'chunks' to make them more manageable) that manipulate peripheral elements of the learning task but still hold students to the same general work expectations and performance standards as peers.

8. **How many interventions should be tried before a student is considered to be a 'non-responder'?** The school district must decide on uniform 'decision rules' that indicate when a student should be considered a 'non-responder' to intervention—and perhaps be referred to the special education eligibility team. A sufficient number of interventions should be attempted to allow a school with confidence to assert that a given student's academic problems are not simply due to controllable factors such as inadequate or mismatched instruction. For example, one district decided that—across Tiers 2 and 3—a student should go through at least 3 separate interventions of 6-8 instructional weeks each before the school could designate that student a 'non-responder' and refer him or her to special education. (NOTE: Some state education departments provide guidance to their schools on RTI decision rules regarding the appropriate number and duration of RTI interventions required to identify 'non-responding' students.)

9. **What is 'intervention integrity' and why are schools expected to measure it?** Students who present with serious academic or behavioral problems in middle and high schools can face high-stakes negative consequences (e.g., failing grades, failure on state tests required to graduate, long-term suspension from school for chronic misbehavior). If a student fails to respond to a specific academic or behavioral intervention, there are always at least two possible explanations. One possibility is that the student simply failed to respond to an intervention that was correctly carried out. Another more concerning possibility is that the student did not make progress because intervention was not implemented as designed and therefore was not effective. An intervention can be compromised for various reasons. For example, the student on intervention may be

absent for a significant length of time and thus not be available; the person providing the intervention (e.g., reading teacher) may be forced to interrupt intervention groups for several weeks to administer and score state assessments; a classroom teacher implementing an intervention may not have been trained properly and thus implements the intervention incorrectly.

The integrity of interventions can be measured directly by an observer watching the intervention take place and noting whether all steps have been correctly carried out. Intervention integrity can also be measured indirectly by having the teacher or other interventionist periodically self-evaluate his or her own ability to implement the intervention. Sometimes other information—such as intervention contact logs or work products created during an intervention session—can provide indirect evidence that interventions were carried out as designed.

Exhibit 4-A
Developing Shared Guidelines for Determining 'Evidence-Based': Recommendations for Schools

It is up to schools to evaluate their full range of instructional programs and interventions and to decide whether they are sufficiently supported by research to be used for RTI. There is no simple sequence of steps that will infallibly lead schools to the right, empirically supported intervention ideas. However, schools can take responsibility for evaluating whether instructional or intervention techniques have been adequately researched by:

- ☐ Defining in detail the academic or behavioral needs that require interventions;
- ☐ Developing consensus about what is meant by 'evidence-based';
- ☐ Using on-line rating sites when possible to evaluate commercial intervention products;
- ☐ Knowing the research-based components that are building blocks of effective interventions;
- ☐ Staying current with emerging intervention research through 'knowledge brokers'.

---

1. **Define in Detail the Academic or Behavioral Needs Requiring Intervention and Reference Them Using Standard Terminology.** Before attempting to track down evidence-based interventions to address particular academic or behavioral problems, the school should first carefully define and prioritize the specific student needs to be targeted—and use standard terminology to describe them.

   Effective interventions cannot be reliably identified and matched to student needs if those needs are only vaguely defined. For example, the high school that identifies as a common need that their students 'develop reading comprehension skills' will have difficulty finding effective interventions because the academic goal statement is overly broad. A more focused goal statement might be: *"When reading informational texts, our students will independently use reading comprehension fix-up skills as needed."* If schools put the effort into defining specifically those academic or behavioral problems common among their students, they are more likely to uncover effective intervention ideas to address those problems.

   Also, when possible, academic behaviors selected as intervention targets should be described using standard, widely accepted terminology to make it easier to locate evidence-based intervention ideas. For example, because student 'study skills' are sometimes referenced in the research literature under the more comprehensive term 'academic enabling skills' (DiPerna, 2006), schools should use both descriptors as search terms when looking for interventions in this area.

---

2. **Develop Consensus in Your School About What is Meant by 'Evidence-Based'.**
   At present, there is little agreement among intervention experts on a definition of 'evidence-based'. Therefore, schools must develop their own criteria to identify 'evidence-based' interventions. They can move forward in this process by:

Exhibit 4-A, continued

Drafting a definition of 'evidence-based.' Schools should write their own definition of what the term 'evidence-based' means. Useful guidelines for defining high-quality research come from the International Reading Association (2002), which states that a reading program or practice can be regarded as evidence-based if it is backed by research that shows its effectiveness. According to IRA, research studies that support research-based interventions in reading should also:

- Produce 'objective' data—so that different evaluators should be able to draw similar conclusions when reviewing the data from the studies;
- Have valid research results that can reasonably be applied to the kinds of real-world reading tasks that children must master in actual classrooms;
- Yield reliable and replicable findings that would not be expected to change significantly based on such arbitrary factors as the day or time that data on the interventions were collected or who collected them;
- Employ current best-practice methods in observation or experimentation to reduce the probability that other sources of potential bias crept into the studies and compromised the results;
- Be checked before publication by independent experts, who review the methods, data, and conclusions of the studies.

Compiling a list of trusted professional organizations and journals. To guide staff toward quality resources, schools may wish to compile a list of professional organizations and educational research journals that they find generally provide useful and trustworthy as sources of information about evidence-based interventions. For example, the National Association of School Psychologists (http://www.nasponline.org), National Association of Secondary School Principals (http://www.principals.org), and the International Reading Association (http://www.reading.org) are examples of reputable organizations that schools might turn to for intervention information; the School Psychology Review, the Journal of Special Education, and Reading Research Quarterly are examples of reputable peer-reviewed educational journals. The school can continue to add to its list of trusted organizations and journals over time.

Adopting a 'research continuum'. Schools may sometimes find that no interventions in a particular academic or behavioral area meet the stringent criteria to be regarded as 'evidence-based'. In such instances, schools must be prepared to sift through existing research to locate the best available intervention ideas, even if the research base that supports them falls short of the ideal. It can be useful in this sifting process for schools to use a 'research continuum' that establishes categories for interventions in descending levels of research quality. The continuum would be used as an aid to judge whether specific instructional practices or interventions are supported by research of sufficient quantity and quality for use in their schools.

To cite one example, the US Department of Education (2003) provides guidelines for judging the strength of research evidence supporting an intervention.

Exhibit 4-A, continued

- **Strong evidence.** Programs with 'strong' evidence of effectiveness are supported by studies with well-designed, well-implemented randomized controlled trials that were conducted in at least two different 'typical' school settings. Furthermore, at least one of the studies included a school whose characteristics are similar to the school or classroom that is considering adopting the program.

- **Possible evidence.** Programs with 'possible' evidence of effectiveness are supported by studies that may have used non-random comparison groups instead of randomized controlled trials but took pains to closely match the groups in academic achievement and other important student characteristics.

- **No evidence.** Programs that are 'not supported by meaningful evidence of effectiveness' include those whose studies used a simple pre-post design, failed to match treatment and comparison groups carefully, used meta-analytic techniques to analyze studies of lesser quality, or contained other significant flaws in design or implementation.

View the full US Department of Education (2003) research-continuum guide at http://www2.ed.gov/rschstat/research/pubs/rigorousevid/rigorousevid.pdf

---

3. **Use Impartial On-Line Rating Sites to Evaluate Commercial Intervention Products.** Websites now exist that provide ratings and reviews of commercial instructional and intervention products. The best of these sites apply evidence-based criteria to identify the most effective programs for schools to consider. Schools should use such sites as one resource when determining whether specific educational products are evidence-based.

An example of an impartial intervention-rating site is the What Works Clearinghouse (http://ies.ed.gov/ncee/wwc)--probably the most influential website for rating commercial products for general instruction and intervention. This site is sponsored by the U.S. Department of Education's Institute of Education Sciences and bills itself as 'a central and trusted source of scientific evidence for what works in education.' The WWC reviews existing research on commercial products to determine if they show evidence of being effective for instruction or supplemental intervention with school-age populations. Just as important, the WWC screens out those research studies about a product that fail to meet its rigorous research standards. The WWC compiles 'intervention reports' that summarize its findings of whether a particular program or product meets criteria of being 'evidence-based'. The WWC has rated programs in a number of academic and behavioral domains.

When evaluating intervention-clearinghouse websites, here are two cautionary points to consider:

- *Reliance on Existing Research.* Intervention-rating sites typically lack the ability to independently research commercial products. Instead, they depend on existing research studies for their analyses. Therefore, if a commercial product is relatively new

Exhibit 4-A, continued

and has not yet been researched or if the only available studies of that product are of lesser quality, that product may be screened out or overlooked by these rating sites.

- *Potential Delays in Program Ratings.* The resources of intervention-rating sites are limited, so there can be a considerable delay between the advent of a new commercial product and the time when the rating site issues a report about the product's effectiveness. Limited resources also mean that, for the foreseeable future, no single site is likely to have adequate staff and funds to rate commercial instructional and intervention products in all academic and behavioral areas and across all grade levels.

4. **Know the Research-Based Components That Are Building Blocks of Effective Interventions.** Research indicates (Burns, VanDerHeyden, & Boice, 2008) that, to be maximally effective, any academic intervention should:
   - be matched to the student's academic needs;
   - be delivered using explicit instruction;
   - provide the student with adequate success in the instructional task;
   - give the student a high opportunity to respond;
   - provide timely performance feedback.

   Schools that know these basic components that make academic interventions effective have more options as they design intensive intervention plans for struggling students. For example, a school may decide not to use an evidence-based commercial intervention program—either because one does not exist, is too expensive, or is otherwise not readily available. But if the school designs an intervention of its own to include the effective components described here, that school is likely to create an intervention that is effective (Burns, VanDerHeyden, & Boice, 2008). Or in another scenario, the school may locate a commercial intervention product that looks promising but that does not yet have a sufficient body of research to support it. If the school can verify that the commercial program contains the five effective intervention components, it can have increased confidence that the program will work.

5. **Keep Up With Emerging Intervention Research Through 'Knowledge Brokers'.** Districts must stay current on a large volume of intervention research in their quest to build and maintain a knowledge base of the most effective instructional and behavior management programs and strategies. One idea to manage the ongoing load of intervention research is to divide it up by appointing 'knowledge brokers' (Ervin & Schaughency, 2008). Districts first define key intervention topic areas that match common needs of students in their schools, such as 'reading comprehension fix-up skills' or 'organizational skills'. Then district or school staff members are selected to serve as 'knowledge brokers' based on their training, experience, and/or interest. Knowledge brokers regularly keep up with emerging research in their intervention topic area by reading educational research journals and other publications from reputable organizations or government agencies, attending training conferences, etc. They periodically funnel this new information about effective programs and practices to

Exhibit 4-A, continued

teachers, support staff, and administrators to ensure that the schools are using the best available intervention ideas.

References

Burns, M. K., VanDerHeyden, A. M., & Boice, C. H. (2008). Best practices in intensive academic interventions. In A. Thomas & J. Grimes (Eds.), *Best practices in school psychology V* (pp.1151-1162). Bethesda, MD: National Association of School Psychologists.

DiPerna, J. C. (2006). Academic enablers and student achievement: Implications for assessment and intervention services in the schools. *Psychology in the Schools, 43*, 7-17.

Ervin, R. A., & Schaughency, E. (2008). Best practices in accessing the systems change literature. In A. Thomas & J. Grimes (Eds.), *Best practices in school psychology V* (pp. 853-873).

International Reading Association. (May, 2002). *What is evidence-based reading instruction?: A position statement of the International Reading Association.* Retrieved December 14, 2010, from http://www.reading.org/General/AboutIRA/Position Statements/EvidencedBasedPosition.aspx

Kratochwill, T. R., Clements, M. A., & Kalymon, K. M. (2007). Response to intervention: Conceptual and methodological issues in implementation. In Jimerson, S. R., Burns, M. K., & VanDerHeyden, A. M. (Eds.), *Handbook of response to intervention: The science and practice of assessment and intervention.* New York: Springer.

Odom, S. L., Brantlinger, E., Gersten, R., Horner, R. H., Thompson, B., & Harris, K. R. (2005). Research in special education: Scientific methods and evidence-based practices. *Exceptional Children, 71*(2), 137-148.

US Department of Education. (2003). *Identifying and implementing educational practices supported by rigorous evidence: A user friendly guide.* [Brochure]. Washington, DC: Author. Retrieved on September 23, 2010, from http://www2.ed.gov/rschstat/research/pubs/rigorousevid/rigorousevid.pdf

Exhibit 4-B
Intervention & Related RTI Terms: Definitions

Educators who serve as interventionists should be able to define and distinguish among the terms *core instruction, intervention, accommodation,* and *modification.* (In particular, interventionists should avoid using modifications as part of an RTI plan for a general education student, as they can be predicted to undermine the student's academic performance.) Here are definitions for these key terms.

- [ ] **Core Instruction.** Those instructional strategies that are used routinely with all students in a general education setting are considered 'core instruction'. High-quality instruction is essential and forms the foundation of RTI academic support. NOTE: While it is important to verify that a struggling student receives good core instructional practices, those routine practices do not 'count' as individual student interventions.

- [ ] **Intervention.** An academic intervention is a strategy used to teach a new skill, build fluency in a skill, or encourage a child to apply an existing skill to new situations or settings. An intervention can be thought of as "a set of actions that, when taken, have demonstrated ability to change a fixed educational trajectory" (Methe & Riley-Tillman, 2008; p. 37). As an example of an academic intervention, the teacher may select question generation (Davey & McBride,1986.; Rosenshine, Meister & Chapman, 1996), a strategy in which the student is taught to locate or generate main idea sentences for each paragraph in a passage and record those 'gist' sentences for later review.

- [ ] **Accommodation.** An accommodation is intended to help the student to fully access and participate in the general education curriculum without changing the instructional content and without reducing the student's rate of learning (Skinner, Pappas & Davis, 2005). An accommodation is intended to remove barriers to learning while still expecting that students will master the same instructional content as their typical peers. An accommodation for students who are slow readers, for example, may include having them supplement their silent reading of a novel by listening to the book on tape. An accommodation for unmotivated students may include breaking larger assignments into smaller 'chunks' and providing students with performance feedback and praise for each completed 'chunk' of assigned work (Skinner, Pappas & Davis, 2005).

- [ ] **Modification.** A modification changes the expectations of what a student is expected to know or do—typically by lowering the academic standards against which the student is to be evaluated. Examples of modifications are giving a student five math computation problems for practice instead of the 20 problems assigned to the rest of the class or letting the student consult course notes during a test when peers are not permitted to do so. Instructional modifications are essential elements on the Individualized Education Plans (IEPs) or Section 504 Plans of many students with special needs. Modifications are generally not included on a general education student's RTI intervention plan, however, because the assumption is that the student can be successful in the curriculum with appropriate interventions and accommodations alone. In fact, modifying the work of struggling general education students is likely to have a negative effect that works *against* the goals of RTI. Reducing academic expectations will result in these students falling further behind rather than closing the performance gap with peers.

References

Davey, B., & McBride, S. (1986). Effects of question-generation training on reading comprehension. *Journal of Educational Psychology,* 78, 256-262.

Methe, S. A., & Riley-Tillman, T. C. (2008). An informed approach to selecting and designing early mathematics interventions. *School Psychology Forum: Research into Practice,* 2, 29-41.

Rosenshine, B., Meister, C., & Chapman, S. (1996). Teaching students to generate questions: A review of the intervention studies. *Review of Educational Research,* 66, 181-221.

Skinner, C. H., Pappas, D. N., & Davis, K. A. (2005). Enhancing academic engagement: Providing opportunities for responding and influencing students to choose to respond. *Psychology in the Schools,* 42, 389-403.

Exhibit 4-C
Defining Academic Problems:
The First Step in Effective Intervention Planning

Students who struggle with academic deficits do not do so in isolation. Their difficulties are played out in the larger context of the school environment and curriculum—and represent a 'mismatch' between the characteristics of the student and the instructional demands of the classroom (Foorman & Torgesen, 2001). It may surprise educators to learn that the problem-identification step is the most critical for matching the student to an effective intervention (Bergan, 1995). Problem identification statements should be defined in clear and specific terms sufficient to pass 'the stranger test' (Howell, Hosp, & Kurns, 2008). That is, the student problem can be judged as adequately defined if a person with no background knowledge of the case and equipped only with the problem-identification statement can observe the student in the academic setting and know with confidence when the problem behavior is displayed and when it is not.

Here are recommendations for increasing teacher capacity to frame student skills in relation to curriculum requirements, describe student academic problems in specific terms, and generate a hypothesis about why the problem is occurring.

1. **Be knowledgeable of the school academic curriculum and key student academic skills that are taught.** Academic abilities can best be described in terms of the specific curriculum skills or knowledge that students are required to demonstrate. Therefore, the general-education teacher should have a good survey-level knowledge of the general academic skills that students at a given grade level are expected to have mastered as well as key curriculum goals for that course. If the curriculum alone is not adequate for describing a student's academic deficit, the instructor can make use of research-based definitions to further define the academic problem area. Here are guidelines for consulting curriculum and research-based definitions of academic skills:

    - *Curriculum.* The teacher can review the school's curriculum and related documents (e.g., score-and-sequence charts; curriculum maps) to formulate specific academic skill or performance goals. Of course, if the student is performing well below grade-level (e.g., in math skills), the teacher may want to go 'off-level' by reviewing curriculum goals from earlier grades. First, determine the approximate grade or level in the curriculum that matches the student's skills. Then, review the curriculum at that alternate grade level to find appropriate descriptions of the student's relevant academic deficit(s).

    - *Research-Based Skill Definitions.* Even when a school's curriculum identifies key skills, schools may find it useful to corroborate or elaborate on those skill definitions by reviewing alternative definitions published in research reports, journals or other trusted sources.

Exhibit 4-C, continued

For example, an algebra teacher had a student with delays in solving quadratic equations. The instructor found that the school's math curriculum did not provide a detailed description of the various skills required to successfully complete quadratic equations. So the teacher reviewed the report issued by the National Mathematics Advisory Panel (Fennell et al., 2008) The teacher discovered in that document a detailed description of the component skills for solving quadratic equations, including "factors and factoring of quadratic polynomials with integer coefficients", "completing the square in quadratic expressions" and "quadratic formula and factoring of general quadratic polynomials". By combining the skill definitions from the school curriculum with the more detailed descriptions taken from the research-based document, the teacher was better able to pinpoint the student's area of academic deficit in specific terms.

---

2. **Describe the academic problem in specific, skill-based terms with a meaningful instructional context** (Batsche et al., 2008; Upah, 2008). Write a clear, brief description of the academic skill or performance deficit that focuses on a specific skill or performance area. Include information about the conditions under which the academic problem is observed and typical or expected level of performance.

- *Environmental Conditions or Task Demands.* Describe the environmental conditions or task demands in place when the academic problem is observed.

- *Problem Description.* Describe the actual observable academic behavior in which the student is engaged. Include rate, accuracy, or other quantitative information of student performance.

- *Typical or Expected Level of Performance.* Provide a typical or expected performance criterion for this skill or behavior. Typical or expected academic performance can be calculated using a variety of sources,

Academic Problems: Sample Definitions		
Environmental Conditions or Task Demands	**Problem Description**	**Typical or Expected Level of Performance**
When completing a beginning-level algebra word problem…	…Ann is unable to translate that word problem into an equation with variables…	…while most peers in her class have mastered this skill.
During social studies large-group instruction…	…Franklin attends to instruction an average of 45% of the time…	… while peers in the same room attend to instruction an average of 85% of the time.
For science homework…	… Tye turns in assignments an average of 50% of the time…	… while the classroom median rate of homework turned in is 90%.
On weekly 30-minute in-class writing assignments…	… Angela produces compositions that average 145 words…	…while a sampling of peer compositions shows that the typical student writes an average of 254 words.

Exhibit 4-C, continued

3. Develop a hypothesis statement to explain the academic skill or performance problem. The hypothesis states the assumed reason(s) or cause(s) for the student's academic problems. Once it has been developed, the hypothesis statement acts as a compass needle, pointing toward interventions that most logically address the student academic problems. Listed below are common reasons for academic problems. Note that more than one hypothesis may apply to a particular student (e.g., a student may have both a skill deficit and a motivation deficit).

Academic Problems: Possible Hypotheses & Recommendations	
Hypothesis	**Recommendation**
☐ *Skill Deficit.* The student has not yet acquired the skill.	Provide direct, explicit instruction to acquire the skill. Reinforce the student for effort and accuracy.
☐ *Fluency Deficit.* The student has acquired the basic skill but is not yet proficient.	Provide opportunities for the student to practice the skill and give timely performance feedback. Reinforce the student for fluency as well as accuracy.
☐ *Generalization Deficit.* The student possesses the basic skill but fails to use it across appropriate situations or settings.	Train the student to identify the relevant characteristics of situations or settings when the skill should be used. Provide incentives for the student to use the skill in the appropriate settings.
☐ *Motivation (Performance) Deficit.* The student is capable of performing the skill and can identify when use of the skill is appropriate—but nonetheless fails to use the skill.	Use various strategies to engage the student in the skill (e.g., select high-interest learning activities; offer incentives to the student for successful use of the skill, etc.).
☐ *Escape or Avoidance.* The student may or may not be able to perform the academic task. However, the student's behavior is intended to stop the academic activity (escape) or to prevent participation in the activity (avoidance).	Check for appropriate instructional match to ensure that the student experiences sufficient success in the activity. Use motivation strategies (see above) to promote student interest and engagement. Offer the student opportunities for choice in the academic activity.

References

Batsche, G. M., Castillo, J. M., Dixon, D. N., & Forde, S. (2008). Best practices in designing, implementing, and evaluating quality interventions. In A. Thomas & J. Grimes (Eds.), *Best practices in school psychology V* (pp. 177-193). Bethesda, MD: National Association of School Psychologists.

Bergan, J. R. (1995). Evolution of a problem-solving model of consultation. *Journal of Educational and Psychological Consultation, 6*(2), 111-123.

Fennell, F., Faulkner, L. R., Ma, L., Schmid, W., Stotsky, S., Wu, H., & Flawn, T. (2008). *Foundations for success: The final report of the National Mathematics Advisory Panel: Chapter 3: Report of the task group on conceptual knowledge and skills.* U.S., Department of Education: Washington, D.C. Retrieved from http://www.ed.gov/about/bdscomm/list/mathpanel/reports.html

Exhibit 4-C, continued

Foorman, B. R., & Torgesen, J. (2001). Critical elements of classroom and small-group instruction promote reading success in all children. *Learning Disabilities Research & Practice,* 16, 203-212.

Howell, K. W., Hosp, J. L., & Kurns, S. (2008). Best practices in curriculum-based evaluation. In A. Thomas & J. Grimes (Eds.), Best practices in school psychology V (pp. 349-362). Bethesda, MD: National Association of School Psychologists.

Upah, K. R. F. (2008). Best practices in designing, implementing, and evaluating quality interventions. In A. Thomas & J. Grimes (Eds.), *Best practices in school psychology V* (pp. 209-223). Bethesda, MD: National Association of School Psychologists.

Exhibit 4-D
Defining Problem Student Behaviors and Matching to Appropriate Interventions: A 5-Step Process

Teachers can select effective interventions for student behavior problems only if they first clearly define the problem behavior(s) and the reason(s) that a behavior is occurring. By following the five steps below, the teacher is more likely to describe a student's problem behavior(s) with clarity and to identify effective interventions to address them. Use the worksheet at the end of this exhibit to implement this process.

1. Define the problem behavior in clear, observable, measurable terms (Batsche et al., 2008; Upah, 2008). Write a clear description of the problem behavior. Avoid vague problem identification statements such as "The student is disruptive."

    A good method to judge whether the problem has been adequately defined is to apply the "stranger test": Can a stranger read the problem definition statement, then observe the student, and be able to judge reliably when the behavior occurs and when it does not? A useful self-prompt to come up with a more detailed description of the problem is to ask, "What does <problem behavior> look like in the classroom?"

    A well-written problem definition should include three parts:
    - Conditions. The condition(s) under which the problem is likely to occur
    - Problem Description. A specific description of the problem behavior
    - Contextual information. Information about the frequency, intensity, duration, or other dimension(s) of the behavior that provide a context for estimating the degree to which the behavior presents a problem in the setting(s) in which it occurs.

Sample Problem Behavior Definitions		
Conditions. The condition(s) under which the problem is likely to occur	Problem Description. A specific description of the problem behavior	Contextual Information. Information about the frequency, intensity, duration, or other dimension(s) of the behavior
During 20-minute independent seatwork literacy tasks…	…John talks with peers about non-instructional topics…	…an average of three times.
In school settings such as the playground or gymnasium, when unsupervised by adults…	…Angela is reported by peers to use physically threatening language…	…at least once per week.
When given a verbal teacher request…	…Jay fails to comply with that request within 3 minutes…	… an average of 50% of the time.

Exhibit 4-D, continued

2. Develop examples and non-examples of the problem behavior (Upah, 2008). Writing both examples and non-examples of the problem behavior helps to resolve uncertainty about when the student's conduct should be classified as a problem behavior. Examples should include the most frequent or typical instances of the student problem behavior. Non-examples should include any behaviors that are acceptable conduct but might possibly be confused with the problem behavior.

Examples and Non-Examples of Problem Behavior		
Problem Behavior	**Examples**	**Non-Examples**
During 20-minute independent seatwork literacy tasks, John talks with peers about non-instructional topics	• John chats with another student that he encounters at the pencil sharpener. • John whispers to a neighboring student about a comic book in his desk.	• At the direction of the teacher, John pairs up with another student to complete an assignment. • John verbally interacts with students in an appropriate manner while handing out work materials as requested by the teacher.
When given a verbal teacher request, Jay fails to comply with that request within 3 minutes.	• Jay does not comply when directed by the teacher to open his math book and begin work. • Jay is verbally defiant and uncooperative when requested by an adult to stop running in the hall.	• Jay does not comply with a teacher request because he does not hear that request. • Jay asks the teacher to explain directions that he does not understand.

3. Write a behavior hypothesis statement (Batsche et al., 2008; Upah, 2008). The next step in problem-solving is to develop a hypothesis about why the student is engaging in an undesirable behavior or not engaging in a desired behavior. Teachers can gain information to develop a hypothesis through direct observation, student interview, review of student work products, and other sources. The behavior hypothesis statement is important because (a) it can be tested, and (b) it provides guidance on the type(s) of interventions that might benefit the student.

Behavior Hypothesis Statements		
Problem Behavior	**<Because>**	**Hypothesis**
During 20-minute independent seatwork literacy tasks, John talks with peers about non-instructional topics…	…because…	…he is avoiding academic work.
When given a verbal teacher request, Jay fails to comply with that request…	…because…	…he is reinforced by the negative adult attention that results from his noncompliance.

Exhibit 4-D, continued

4. Select a replacement behavior (Batsche et al., 2008). Behavioral interventions should be focused on increasing student skills and capacities, not simply on suppressing problem behaviors. By selecting a positive behavioral goal that is an appropriate replacement for the student's original problem behavior, the teacher reframes the student concern in a manner that allows for more effective intervention planning.

Selection of Replacement Behavior	
Problem Behavior	**Replacement Behavior**
During 20-minute independent seatwork literacy tasks, John talks with peers about non-instructional topics.	During 20-minute independent seatwork literacy tasks, John is engaged in active accurate academic responding.
When given a verbal teacher request, Jay fails to comply with that request.	When given a verbal teacher request, Jay carries out the request without argument or complaint within 3 minutes.

5. Write a prediction statement (Batsche et al., 2008; Upah, 2008). The prediction statement proposes a strategy (intervention) that is predicted to improve the problem behavior. The importance of the prediction statement is that it spells out specifically the expected outcome if the strategy is successful. The formula for writing a prediction statement is to state that if the proposed strategy ('Specific Action') is adopted, then the rate of problem behavior is expected to decrease or increase in the desired direction.

Prediction Statement		
Specific Action	**Problem Behavior**	**Rate of Behavior**
If prior to independent seatwork, John meets with a tutor to review key vocabulary terms and rehearse the assigned reading,..	...the amount of time that John spends talking with peers about non-instructional topics during independent work...	...will decrease.
If adults avoid engaging Jay in long exchanges when he fails to comply with their requests and instead impose appropriate pre-selected consequences...	...the frequency of Jay's timely compliance with adult requests...	...will increase.

References

Batsche, G. M., Castillo, J. M., Dixon, D. N., & Forde, S. (2008). Best practices in designing, implementing, and evaluating quality interventions. In A. Thomas & J. Grimes (Eds.), *Best practices in school psychology V* (pp. 177-193). Bethesda, MD: National Association of School Psychologists.

Upah, K. R. F. (2008). Best practices in designing, implementing, and evaluating quality interventions. In A. Thomas & J. Grimes (Eds.), *Best practices in school psychology V* (pp. 209-223). Bethesda, MD: National Association of School Psychologists.

Exhibit 4-D, Form 1
Finding the Right Behavioral Intervention:
Five Steps to Defining Student Problem Behaviors: Worksheet

Teachers can select effective interventions for student behavior problems only if they first clearly define the problem behavior(s) and the reason(s) that a behavior is occurring.

The process of defining student problem behaviors goes more smoothly if the teacher has first collected relevant information about the student's problem behavior (e.g., examples of seatwork, anecdotal notes of student behavior, frequency counts of behavior, student interview, etc.).

By following the five steps below, the teacher is more likely to describe a student's problem behavior(s) with clarity and to identify effective interventions to address them.

1. Define the problem behavior in clear, observable, measurable terms.

Sample Problem Behavior Definitions		
Conditions. The condition(s) under which the problem is likely to occur	*Problem Description.* A specific description of the problem behavior	*Contextual Information.* Information about the frequency, intensity, duration, or other dimension(s) of the behavior

2. Develop examples and non-examples of the problem behavior.

Examples and Non-Examples of Problem Behavior	
Examples	Non-Examples

Exhibit 4-D, Form 1, continued

3. Write a behavior hypothesis statement.

Behavior Hypothesis Statements		
Problem Behavior	**<Because>**	**Hypothesis**
	...because...	

4. Select a replacement behavior.

Selection of Replacement Behavior	
Replacement Behavior	

5. Create a prediction statement.

Prediction Statement		
Specific Action	**Problem Behavior**	**Rate of Behavior**

Exhibit 4-E
Academic Interventions 'Critical Components' Checklist

This checklist summarizes the essential components of academic interventions. When preparing a student's Tier 1, 2, or 3 academic intervention plan, use this document as a 'pre-flight checklist' to ensure that the academic intervention is of high quality, is sufficiently strong to address the identified student problem, is fully understood and supported by the teacher, and can be implemented with integrity. NOTE: While the checklist refers to the 'teacher' as the interventionist, it can also be used as a guide to ensure the quality of interventions implemented by non-instructional personnel, adult volunteers, parents, and peer (student) tutors.

Directions: When creating an academic intervention plan, review that plan by comparing it to each of the items below.
- If a particular intervention element is missing or needs to be reviewed, check the 'Critical Item?' column for that element.
- Write any important notes or questions in the 'Notes' column.

Allocating Sufficient Contact Time & Assuring Appropriate Student-Teacher Ratio		
The cumulative time set aside for an intervention and the amount of direct teacher contact are two factors that help to determine that intervention's 'strength' (Yeaton & Sechrest, 1981).		
Critical Item?	Intervention Element	Notes
☐	**Time Allocated.** The time set aside for the intervention is appropriate for the type and level of student problem (Burns & Gibbons, 2008; Kratochwill, Clements & Kalymon, 2007). When evaluating whether the amount of time allocated is adequate, consider: • Length of each intervention session. • Frequency of sessions (e.g.., daily, 3 times per week) • Duration of intervention period (e.g., 6 instructional weeks)	
☐	**Student-Teacher Ratio.** The student receives sufficient contact from the teacher or other person delivering the intervention to make that intervention effective. NOTE: Generally, supplemental intervention groups should be limited to 6-7 students (Burns & Gibbons, 2008).	

Exhibit 4-E, continued

Matching the Intervention to the Student Problem

Academic interventions are not selected at random. First, the student academic problem(s) is defined clearly and in detail. Then, the likely explanations for the academic problem(s) are identified to understand which intervention(s) are likely to help—and which should be avoided.

Critical Item?	Intervention Element	Notes
☐	**Problem Definition.** The student academic problem(s) to be addressed in the intervention are defined in clear, specific, measureable terms (Bergan, 1995; Witt, VanDerHeyden & Gilbertson, 2004). The full problem definition describes: • *Conditions.* Describe the environmental conditions or task demands in place when the academic problem is observed. • *Problem Description.* Describe the actual observable academic behavior in which the student is engaged. Include rate, accuracy, or other quantitative information of student performance. • *Typical or Expected Level of Performance.* Provide a typical or expected performance criterion for this skill or behavior. Typical or expected academic performance can be calculated using a variety of sources,	
☐	**Appropriate Target.** Selected intervention(s) are appropriate for the identified student problem(s) (Burns, VanDerHeyden & Boice, 2008). TIP: Use the Instructional Hierarchy (Haring et al., 1978) to select academic interventions according to the four stages of learning: • *Acquisition.* The student has begun to learn how to complete the target skill correctly but is not yet accurate in the skill. Interventions should improve accuracy. • *Fluency.* The student is able to complete the target skill accurately but works slowly. Interventions should increase the student's speed of responding (fluency) as well as to maintain accuracy. • *Generalization.* The student may have acquired the target skill but does not typically use it in the full range of appropriate situations or settings. Or the student may confuse the target skill with 'similar' skills. Interventions should get the student to use the skill in the widest possible range of settings and situations, or to accurately discriminate between the target skill and 'similar' skills. • *Adaptation.* The student is not yet able to modify or adapt an existing skill to fit novel task-demands or situations. Interventions should help the student to identify key concepts or elements from previously learned skills that can be adapted to the new demands or situations.	
☐	**'Can't Do/Won't Do' Check.** The teacher has determined whether the student problem is primarily a skill or knowledge deficit ('can't do') or whether student motivation plays a main or supporting role in academic underperformance ('wont do'). If motivation appears to be a significant factor contributing to the problem, the intervention plan includes strategies to engage the student (e.g., high interest learning activities; rewards/incentives; increased student choice in academic assignments, etc.) (Skinner, Pappas & Davis, 2005; Witt, VanDerHeyden & Gilbertson, 2004).	

Exhibit 4-E, continued

	Incorporating Effective Instructional Elements	
	These effective 'building blocks' of instruction are well-known and well-supported by the research. They should be considered when selecting or creating any academic intervention.	
Critical Item?	Intervention Element	Notes
☐	**Explicit Instruction.** Student skills have been broken down "into manageable and deliberately sequenced steps" and the teacher provided" overt strategies for students to learn and practice new skills" (Burns, VanDerHeyden & Boice, 2008, p.1153).	
☐	**Appropriate Level of Challenge.** The student experienced sufficient success in the academic task(s) to shape learning in the desired direction as well as to maintain student motivation (Burns, VanDerHeyden & Boice, 2008).	
☐	**Active Engagement.** The intervention ensures that the student is engaged in 'active accurate responding' (Skinner, Pappas & Davis, 2005).at a rate frequent enough to capture student attention and to optimize effective learning.	
☐	**Performance Feedback.** The student receives prompt performance feedback about the work completed (Burns, VanDerHeyden & Boice, 2008).	
☐	**Maintenance of Academic Standards.** If the intervention includes any accommodations to better support the struggling learner (e.g., preferential seating, breaking a longer assignment into smaller chunks), those accommodations do not substantially lower the academic standards against which the student is to be evaluated and are not likely to reduce the student's rate of learning (Skinner, Pappas & Davis, 2005).	

Exhibit 4-E continues on next page

Exhibit 4-E, continued

Verifying Teacher Understanding & Providing Teacher Support		
The teacher is an active agent in the intervention, with primary responsibility for putting it into practice in a busy classroom. It is important, then, that the teacher fully understands how to do the intervention, believes that he or she can do it, and knows whom to seek out if there are problems with the intervention.		
Critical Item?	Intervention Element	Notes
☐	**Teacher Responsibility.** The teacher understands his or her responsibility to implement the academic intervention(s) with integrity.	
☐	**Teacher Acceptability.** The teacher states that he or she finds the academic intervention feasible and acceptable for the identified student problem.	
☐	**Step-by-Step Intervention Script.** The essential steps of the intervention are written as an 'intervention script'--a series of clearly described steps—to ensure teacher understanding and make implementation easier (Hawkins, Morrison, Musti-Rao & Hawkins, 2008).	
☐	**Intervention Training.** If the teacher requires training to carry out the intervention, that training has been arranged.	
☐	**Intervention Elements: Negotiable vs. Non-Negotiable.** The teacher knows all of the steps of the intervention. Additionally, the teacher knows which of the intervention steps are 'non-negotiable' (they must be completed exactly as designed) and which are 'negotiable' (the teacher has some latitude in how to carry out those steps) (Hawkins, Morrison, Musti-Rao & Hawkins, 2008).	
☐	**Assistance With the Intervention.** If the intervention cannot be implemented as designed for any reason (e.g., student absence, lack of materials, etc.), the teacher knows how to get assistance quickly to either fix the problem(s) to the current intervention or to change the intervention.	

Exhibit 4-E, continued

Documenting the Intervention & Collecting Data		
Interventions only have meaning if they are done within a larger data-based context. For example, interventions that lack baseline data, goal(s) for improvement, and a progress-monitoring plan are 'fatally flawed' (Witt, VanDerHeyden & Gilbertson, 2004).		
Critical Item?	Intervention Element	Notes
☐	**Intervention Documentation.** The teacher understands and can manage all documentation required for this intervention (e.g., maintaining a log of intervention sessions, etc.).	
☐	**Checkup Date.** Before the intervention begins, a future checkup date is selected to review the intervention to determine if it is successful. Time elapsing between the start of the intervention and the checkup date should be short enough to allow a timely review of the intervention but long enough to give the school sufficient time to judge with confidence whether the intervention worked.	
☐	**Baseline.** Before the intervention begins, the teacher has collected information about the student's baseline level of performance in the identified area(s) of academic concern (Witt, VanDerHeyden & Gilbertson, 2004).	
☐	**Goal.** Before the intervention begins, the teacher has set a specific goal for predicted student improvement to use as a minimum standard for success (Witt, VanDerHeyden & Gilbertson, 2004). The goal is the expected student outcome by the checkup date if the intervention is successful.	
☐	**Progress-Monitoring.** During the intervention, the teacher collects progress-monitoring data of sufficient quality and at a sufficient frequency to determine at the checkup date whether that intervention is successful (Witt, VanDerHeyden & Gilbertson, 2004).	

References

Bergan, J. R. (1995). Evolution of a problem-solving model of consultation. *Journal of Educational and Psychological Consultation,* 6(2), 111-123.

Burns, M. K., & Gibbons, K. A. (2008). *Implementing response-to-intervention in elementary and secondary schools.* Routledge: New York.

Burns, M. K., VanDerHeyden, A. M., & Boice, C. H. (2008). Best practices in intensive academic interventions. In A. Thomas & J. Grimes (Eds.), *Best practices in school psychology V* (pp.1151-1162). Bethesda, MD: National Association of School Psychologists.

Haring, N.G., Lovitt, T.C., Eaton, M.D., & Hansen, C.L. (1978). *The fourth R: Research in the classroom.* Columbus, OH: Charles E. Merrill Publishing Co.

Hawkins, R. O., Morrison, J. Q., Musti-Rao, S., & Hawkins, J. A. (2008). Treatment integrity for academic interventions in real- world settings. *School Psychology Forum,* 2(3), 1-15.

Exhibit 4-E, continued

Kratochwill, T. R., Clements, M. A., & Kalymon, K. M. (2007). Response to intervention: Conceptual and methodological issues in implementation. In Jimerson, S. R., Burns, M. K., & VanDerHeyden, A. M. (Eds.), *Handbook of response to intervention: The science and practice of assessment and intervention.* New York: Springer.

Skinner, C. H., Pappas, D. N., & Davis, K. A. (2005). Enhancing academic engagement: Providing opportunities for responding and influencing students to choose to respond. *Psychology in the Schools,* 42, 389-403.

Witt, J. C., VanDerHeyden, A. M., & Gilbertson, D. (2004). Troubleshooting behavioral interventions. A systematic process for finding and eliminating problems. *School Psychology Review,* 33, 363-383.

Yeaton, W. M. & Sechrest, L. (1981). Critical dimensions in the choice and maintenance of successful treatments: Strength, integrity, and effectiveness. *Journal of Consulting and Clinical Psychology,* 49, 156-167.

Exhibit 4-F
Intervention Integrity:
Methods to Track the Quality with Which Interventions Are Carried Out

As schools implement academic and behavioral interventions, they strive to implement those interventions with consistency and quality in classrooms that are fluid and fast-evolving instructional environments. On the one hand, teachers must be prepared to improvise moment by moment to meet classroom needs that suddenly arise: for example, reordering their lesson plans on the fly to maintain student engagement, spending unanticipated extra time answering student questions, or responding to sudden behavior problems. On the other hand, it is a basic expectation that specific RTI interventions will be carefully planned and carried out as designed.

So how can a school ensure that interventions are implemented with consistency even in the midst of busy and rapidly shifting instructional settings? The answer is for the school to find efficient ways to track 'intervention integrity'. After all, if the school lacks basic information about whether an intervention was done right, it cannot have confidence in the outcome of that intervention. And uncertainty about the quality with which the intervention was conducted will prevent the school from distinguishing truly 'non-responding' students from cases in which the intervention did not work simply because it was done incorrectly or inconsistently.

There are three general sources of data that can provide direct or indirect information about intervention integrity: (1) work products and records generated during the intervention, (2) teacher self-reports and self-ratings, and (3) direct structured observation of the intervention as it is being carried out. Each of these approaches has potential strengths and drawbacks.

☐ *Work products and records generated during the intervention.* Often student work samples and other records generated naturally as part of the intervention can be collected to give some indication of intervention integrity (Gansle & Noell, 2007). If student work samples are generated during an intervention, for example, the teacher can collect these work samples and write onto them the date, start time, and end time of the intervention session. Additionally, the teacher can keep a simple intervention contact log to document basic information for each intervention session, including the names of students attending the session (if a group intervention); date; and start time and end time of the intervention session.

An advantage of using work products and other records generated as a natural part of the intervention is that they are easy to collect. However, such work products and records typically yield only limited information on intervention integrity, such as whether interventions occurred with the expected frequency or whether each intervention session met for the appropriate length of time. (*The Intervention Contact Log,* Form 1 of this exhibit, is an example of a documentation tool that would track frequency, length of

Exhibit 4-F, continued

session, and group size for group interventions—although the form can also be adapted as well for individual students.)

☐ *Teacher self-reports and self-ratings.* As another source of data, the teacher or other educators responsible for the intervention can periodically complete formal or informal self-ratings to provide information about whether the intervention is being carried out with integrity. Teacher self-ratings can be done a variety of ways. For example, the instructor may be asked at the end of each intervention session to complete a brief rating scale (e.g., 0 = intervention did not occur; 4 = intervention was carried out completely and correctly). Or the teacher may periodically (e.g., weekly) be emailed an intervention integrity self-rating to complete.

One advantage of teacher self-ratings is that they are easy to complete, a definite advantage in classrooms where time is a very limited resources. A second advantage of self-ratings, as with any form of self-monitoring of behaviors, is that they may prompt teachers to higher levels of intervention compliance (e.g., Kazdin, 1989). A limitation of teacher self-reports and self-ratings, though, is that they tend to be biased in a positive direction (Gansle & Noell, 2007), possibly resulting in an overly optimistic estimate of intervention integrity. Form 1, *Intervention Contact Log,* includes a teacher self-rating component to be completed after each intervention session.

☐ *Direct observation of the intervention steps.* The most direct way to measure the integrity of any intervention is through observation. First, the intervention is divided into a series of discrete steps to create an observation checklist. An observer would then visit the classroom with checklist in hand to watch the intervention being implemented and to note whether each step of the intervention is completed correctly (Roach & Elliott, 2008).

The direct observation of intervention integrity yields a single figure: 'percentage of intervention steps correctly completed'. To compute this figure, the observer (1) adds up the number of intervention steps correctly carried out during the observation, (2) divides that sum by the total number of steps in the intervention, and (3) multiplies the quotient by 100 to calculate the percentage of steps in the intervention that were done in an acceptable manner. For example, a teacher conducts a 5-step reading fluency intervention with a student. The observer notes that 4 of the 5 steps were done correctly and that one was omitted. The observer divides the number of correctly completed steps (4) by the total number of possible steps (5) to get a quotient of .80. The observer then multiples the quotient by 100 (.80 X 100), resulting in an intervention integrity figure of 80 percent.

The advantage of directly observing the steps of an intervention is that it gives objective, first-hand information about the degree to which that intervention was carried out with integrity. However, this approach does have several drawbacks. The first possible hurdle is one of trust: Teachers and other intervention staff may believe that the observer who documents the quality of interventions will use the information to evaluate global job per-

Exhibit 4-F, continued

formance rather than simply to give feedback about the quality of a single intervention (Wright, 2007).

A second drawback of direct observations tied to an intervention checklist is that this assessment approach typically assigns equal weight to all intervention steps—when in actual fact some steps may be relatively unimportant while others may be critical to the success of the intervention (Gansle & Noell, 2007). Schools can construct interventions more precisely at the design stage to improve the ability of intervention-integrity checklists to distinguish the relative importance of various intervention elements. When first developing a step-by-step intervention script, schools should review the research base to determine which of the steps comprising a particular intervention are essential and which could be considered optional or open to interpretation by the interventionist. The teacher would then clearly understand which intervention steps are 'negotiable' or 'non-negotiable' (Hawkins, Morrison, Musti-Rao, & Hawkins, 2008). Of course, the intervention integrity checklist would also distinguish between the critical and non-critical intervention elements. (Form 2, *Intervention Script Builder,* at the end of this exhibit, guides schools to break an intervention down into its constituent steps and to identify specific steps as 'negotiable' or 'non-negotiable.' The form also has an 'Intervention Check' column that an independent observer can use to observe an intervention and verify that each step is correctly carried out.)

As schools develop procedures to measure the quality with which interventions are implemented, the majority will probably come to rely on an efficient mix of different data sources to verify intervention integrity—including products generated during interventions, teacher self-ratings, and direct observations. (Schools can use Form 3, *Selecting Methods to Track Intervention Integrity,* to brainstorm various ways to collect intervention integrity data on a particular student.)

Let's consider an intervention integrity example: The integrity of a small-group time-drill math computation intervention (Rhymer et al., 2002) could be measured concurrently in several ways. The teacher might maintain an intervention contact log (record generated during the intervention) that documents group size as well as the frequency and length of intervention sessions. As a part of each contact log entry, the teacher may be asked to rate the degree to which she was able to implement the intervention that day (teacher self-rating). The teacher could also collect examples of student worksheets (work products): saving at least one computation-drill worksheet per student from each intervention session and recording on each worksheet the date, start time, and end time for the computation time drill. These work products would supply at least indirect evidence that the intervention was being administered according to research recommendations (Rhymer et al., 2002) for math time drills. And finally, an observer might drop into the class at least once per week (*direct observation*) to observe the math time drill intervention using a step-by-step integrity checklist customized for that intervention. Collectively, these various direct and indirect measures would assure the school that the intervention plan is being implemented with sufficient integrity to inspire confidence in the outcome.

Exhibit 4-F, continued

References

Gansle, K. A., & Noell, G. H. (2007). The fundamental role of intervention implementation in sssessing response to intervention. In S. R. Jimerson, M. K. Burns, & A. M. VanDerHeyden (Eds.), *Response to intervention: The science and practice of assessment and intervention* (pp. 244-251). New York: Springer Publishing.

Hawkins, R. O., Morrison, J. Q., Musti-Rao, S., & Hawkins, J. A. (2008). Treatment integrity for academic interventions in real- world settings. *School Psychology Forum,* 2(3), 1-15.

Kazdin, A. E. (1989). *Behavior modification in applied settings (4th ed.).* Pacific Gove, CA: Brooks/Cole.

Rhymer, K. N., Skinner, C. H., Jackson, S., McNeill, S., Smith, T., & Jackson, B. (2002). The 1-minute explicit timing intervention: The influence of mathematics problem difficulty. *Journal of Instructional Psychology,* 29(4), 305-311.

Roach, A. T., & Elliott, S. N. (2008). Best practices in facilitating and evaluating intervention integrity. In A. Thomas & J. Grimes (Eds.), *Best practices in school psychology V* (pp.195-208).

Wright, J. (2007). *The RTI toolkit: A practical guide for schools.* Port Chester, NY: National Professional Resources, Inc.

Exhibit 4-F, Form 1

Intervention Contact Log

Staff Member(s) Implementing Intervention: _____

Classroom/Location: _____ Intervention Description: _____

Students in Group: (Note: Supplemental intervention groups generally should be capped at 6-7 students.)

A. _____ D. _____ G. _____
B. _____ E. _____ H. _____
C. _____ F. _____ I. _____

Date: _____ Time Start: ___:___ AM Time End: ___:___ AM | Students Absent: _____
To what degree were you able to carry out the intervention
as designed? **1 2 3 | 4 5 6 | 7 8 9** | Comments: _____
            Not at all Somewhat   Fully

Date: _____ Time Start: ___:___ AM Time End: ___:___ AM | Students Absent: _____
To what degree were you able to carry out the intervention
as designed? **1 2 3 | 4 5 6 | 7 8 9** | Comments: _____
            Not at all Somewhat   Fully

Date: _____ Time Start: ___:___ AM Time End: ___:___ AM | Students Absent: _____
To what degree were you able to carry out the intervention
as designed? **1 2 3 | 4 5 6 | 7 8 9** | Comments: _____
            Not at all Somewhat   Fully

Date: _____ Time Start: ___:___ AM Time End: ___:___ AM | Students Absent: _____
To what degree were you able to carry out the intervention
as designed? **1 2 3 | 4 5 6 | 7 8 9** | Comments: _____
            Not at all Somewhat   Fully

Date: _____ Time Start: ___:___ AM Time End: ___:___ AM | Students Absent: _____
To what degree were you able to carry out the intervention
as designed? **1 2 3 | 4 5 6 | 7 8 9** | Comments: _____
            Not at all Somewhat   Fully

Date: _____ Time Start: ___:___ AM Time End: ___:___ AM | Students Absent: _____
To what degree were you able to carry out the intervention
as designed? **1 2 3 | 4 5 6 | 7 8 9** | Comments: _____
            Not at all Somewhat   Fully

Date: _____ Time Start: ___:___ AM Time End: ___:___ AM | Students Absent: _____
To what degree were you able to carry out the intervention
as designed? **1 2 3 | 4 5 6 | 7 8 9** | Comments: _____
            Not at all Somewhat   Fully

Exhibit 4-F, Form 2

Intervention Script Builder

Student Name: _____ Grade: _____

Teacher/Team: _____ Intervention Start Date: ___ /___ /___

Description of the Target Academic or Behavior Concern: _____

Intervention Check	Intervention Preparation Steps: Describe any preparation (creation or purchase of materials, staff training, etc.) required for this intervention.	Negotiable? (Hawkins et al., 2008)
This step took place Y___ N___	1. _____	☐ Negotiable Step ☐ Non-Negotiable Step
This step took place Y___ N___	2. _____	☐ Negotiable Step ☐ Non-Negotiable Step
This step took place Y___ N___	3. _____	☐ Negotiable Step ☐ Non-Negotiable Step
Intervention Check	Intervention Steps: Describe the steps of the intervention. Include enough detail so that the procedures are clear to all who must implement them.	Negotiable? (Hawkins et al., 2008)
This step took place Y___ N___	1. _____	☐ Negotiable Step ☐ Non-Negotiable Step
This step took place Y___ N___	2. _____	☐ Negotiable Step ☐ Non-Negotiable Step
This step took place Y___ N___	3. _____	☐ Negotiable Step ☐ Non-Negotiable Step
This step took place Y___ N___	4. _____	☐ Negotiable Step ☐ Non-Negotiable Step
This step took place Y___ N___	5. _____	☐ Negotiable Step ☐ Non-Negotiable Step
This step took place Y___ N___	6. _____	☐ Negotiable Step ☐ Non-Negotiable Step

Exhibit 4-F, Form 2, continued

Research Citation(s) / References: List the published source(s) that make this a 'scientifically based' intervention. _____
_____

Intervention Quality Check: How will data be collected to verify that this intervention is put into practice as it was designed? (Select at least one option.)

❑ Classroom Observation: Number of observations planned? _____

   Person responsible for observations?: _____

❑ Teacher Intervention Rating Log: How frequently will the teacher rate intervention follow-through?

   Daily _____ Weekly _____

❑ Teacher Verbal Report: Who will check in with the teacher for a verbal report of how

   the intervention is progressing? _____

   Approximately when during the intervention period will this verbal 'check in' occur?

   _____

❑ Intervention Checklist: Select either the classroom teacher/team or an outside observer to rate the quality of the intervention and check the appropriate set of directions below.
   ____ *Teacher Directions*: Make copies of this intervention script. Once per week, review the steps in the intervention script and note (Y/N) whether each step was *typically* followed. Then write any additional notes about the intervention in the blank below

   ____ *Independent Observer Directions*: Make copies of this intervention script. At several points during the intervention, make an appointment to observe the intervention in action. While observing the intervention, go through the steps in the intervention script and note (Y/N) whether each step was typically followed. Then write any additional notes about the intervention in the space below

Intervention Observation Notes: _____
_____
_____

Reference

Hawkins, R. O., Morrison, J. Q., Musti-Rao, S., & Hawkins, J. A. (2008). Treatment integrity for academic interventions in real-world settings. *School Psychology Forum,* 2(3), 1-15.

Exhibit 4-F, Form 3
Selecting Methods to Track Intervention Integrity

Student Name: _____ Date: _____

Directions: Schools can use three general sources of data to obtain direct or indirect information about intervention integrity: (1) work products and records generated during the intervention, (2) teacher self-reports and self-ratings, and (3) direct classroom observation of the intervention as it is being carried out. Use this form to select an efficient combination of methods to measure the overall integrity with which an intervention is being implemented.

Work products and records generated during the intervention. Student work samples and other records such as intervention contact logs generated naturally as part of the intervention can be collected to give some indication of intervention integrity (Gansle & Noell, 2007). What work products or other intervention records can be collected to help to track the integrity of the intervention?

Type of Work Product/Other Intervention Documentation	Person(s) Responsible	Frequency of Data Collection
_____	_____	_____
_____	_____	_____
_____	_____	_____

Teacher self-reports and self-ratings. The teacher or other educators responsible for the intervention can periodically complete formal or informal self-ratings to provide information whether the intervention is being carried out with integrity (Gansle & Noell, 2007).. Teacher self-ratings can be done a variety of ways. At the end of each intervention session, for example, the instructor may complete a brief rating scale (e.g., 0 = intervention did not occur; 4 = intervention was carried out completely and correctly). Or the teacher may periodically be emailed a short, open-ended intervention integrity questionnaire. What method(s) of teacher self-reports/self-ratings will be used to track the integrity of this intervention?

Type of Teacher Self-Report or Self-Rating	Person(s) Responsible	Frequency of Data Collection
_____	_____	_____
_____	_____	_____
_____	_____	_____

Direct observation of the intervention steps. The intervention is divided into a series of discrete steps to create an observation checklist. An observer then visits the classroom with checklist in hand to watch the intervention being implemented and to note whether each step of the intervention is completed correctly (Roach & Elliott, 2008). The direct observation of intervention integrity yields a single figure: 'percentage of intervention steps correctly completed'. To compute this figure, the observer (1) adds up the number of intervention steps correctly carried out during the observation, (2) divides that sum by the total number of steps in the intervention, and (3) multiplies the quotient by 100 to calculate the percentage of steps in the intervention that were done in an acceptable manner.

Exhibit 4-F, Form 3, continued

Who will be responsible for creating an intervention-integrity checklist containing the essential steps of the intervention?	Who will use the intervention-integrity checklist to conduct observations of the intervention?	How often or on what dates will classroom observations of the intervention be conducted?
_____	_____	_____
_____	_____	_____
_____	_____	_____

References

Gansle, K. A., & Noell, G. H. (2007). The fundamental role of intervention implementation in assessing response to intervention. In S. R. Jimerson, M. K. Burns, & A. M. VanDerHeyden (Eds.), *Response to intervention: The science and practice of assessment and intervention* (pp. 244-251). New York: Springer Publishing.

Roach, A. T., & Elliott, S. N. (2008). Best practices in facilitating and evaluating intervention integrity. In A. Thomas & J. Grimes (Eds.), *Best practices in school psychology V* (pp.195-208).

Exhibit 4-G
Scheduling RTI Supplemental Services in Middle and High Schools: Five Ideas

A basic expectation of RTI is that Tier 2 and 3 interventions should supplement, not replace, core instruction (Burns & Gibbons, 2008). Yet, finding the time in the schedules of struggling students to provide supplemental interventions can seem an insurmountable problem in middle and high schools. Indeed, in one recent survey, secondary-school principals flagged the issue of scheduling RTI interventions as one of the chief stumbling blocks to successful implementation of RTI (Sansosti, Noltemeyer & Goss, 2010).

There are no simple solutions to the thorny problem of scheduling RTI in secondary schools. Five possible scheduling strategies appear below—but they do have limitations. (For example, two ideas require course work outside of the school day, and depend upon active parent and student support and participation.) However, schools might find these suggestions to be a useful starting point as they brainstorm their own strategies to find the necessary time to deliver supplemental RTI services.

RTI Scheduling Strategy	Considerations
1. RTI Period. The school sets aside one period per day (e.g., 35-45 minutes) during which all students have the opportunity to receive appropriate academic support. Tier 2/3 students are provided with interventions during this period. Non-RTI students may use this time as a study hall or for other academically relevant activities.	Schools are often inventive in finding the time to schedule a schoolwide RTI period: (1) One idea is to trim a brief amount of time (e.g., five minutes) from each class period in the daily schedule to free up sufficient time for a stand-alone period. (2) In schools in which staff by contract must report before students or remain for a period after student dismissal each day, the school might lengthen the student day to overlap with the morning or afternoon additional staff time, potentially freeing up at least some of the minutes needed to cobble together an RTI period.
2. Zero Period. The school creates an optional period before the official start of the school day. During that 'zero period', students can elect to take core or elective courses. Those students needing RTI support can take an essential class during zero period, freeing up a time-slot during the school day to receive their RTI assistance.	This option requires that staff teaching zero-period classes receive extra compensation or adjustment of their school-day teaching schedule. Also, parents and students must make a firm commitment to attend zero-period classes, as this option entails additional work and potential inconvenience—including an earlier wake-up time and home responsibility for transportation.
3. Credit Recovery. A school that has access to online 'credit recovery' courses offers a struggling student the option to take a core course online (via credit recovery) on his or her own time. This option frees up a time-slot during the school day for that student to get RTI assistance.	The credit-recovery option requires that a student be self-motivated and willing to take on extra work in order to access RTI help. While this option may be a good fit for some students, many may lack the motivation and skill-set necessary for success in an online course taken outside of the school day.

Exhibit 4-G, continued

4. Core Course with Extended Time. The school creates two-period sections of selected core-area classes (e.g., English, Introductory Algebra). General-education students are recruited for these extended-time sections because they were found through academic screening and/or archival records to need additional time to master course concepts and/or complete assigned work. The two-period course affords sufficient time for the teacher to provide core instruction and (at least potentially) to provide supplemental interventions in such areas as literacy.	Students placed in an extended-time core course that occupies two class periods may have to give up or postpone the opportunity to take another course. The extended-time course can be made more effective if the school can assign additional staff (e.g., co-teacher; trained paraprofessional) to push into the setting for at least part of the class to provide additional, more individualized support to struggling students.
5. Study Hall Schedule Coordinated with RTI Services. Using academic screening and/or archival records, the school identifies students who require RTI support. These students are scheduled as a bloc in a common study hall. The school then schedules RTI services at the same time as the study hall. Reading teachers, other trained interventionists, and/or tutors run short-term (5-10 week) Tier 2/3 group or individual sessions. Students are recruited from the study hall and matched to the appropriate RTI service based on shared need. They are discharged from the RTI service and rejoin the study hall if they show sufficient improvement. (NOTE: If the study hall meets daily, students in RTI groups who are in less-intensive interventions may be scheduled for alternate days between study hall and RTI groups.) This model is fluid: After each 5-10 week period, new RTI groups or tutoring assignments can be created, with students again being matched to these services based on need.	A school that puts students with a shared intervention need into the same study hall should take care that these students do not feel stigmatized or singled out because of their academic delays. To expand the pool of RTI interventionists available during the common study hall, the school may wish to recruit paraprofessionals, community volunteers, or other non-instructional personnel to serve as tutors. Of course, these personnel will require training in research-based intervention practices, as well as ongoing supervision by school personnel.

References

Burns, M. K., & Gibbons, K. A. (2008). *Implementing response-to-intervention in elementary and secondary schools.* Routledge: New York.

Sansosti, F. J., Noltemeyer, A., & Goss, S. (2010). Principals' perceptions of the importance and availability of response to intervention practices within high school settings. *School Psychology Review, 39,* 286-295.

Exhibit 4-H
Tier 1 (Classroom) Interventions: Building Your School's Capacity

Directions: Schools must plan carefully to build their capacity to carry out evidence-based Tier 1 interventions in the classroom. Below is an 8-point checklist that schools can follow to expand their capacity to provide appropriate teacher-led classroom interventions available to all students who might need them.

1. **Train Teachers to Write Specific, Measureable, Observable 'Problem Identification Statements.**
2. **Inventory Tier 1 Interventions Already in Use.**
3. **Create a Standard Menu of Evidence-Based Tier 1 Intervention Ideas for Teachers.**
4. **Set Up a System to Locate Additional Evidence-Based Tier 1 Intervention Ideas.**
5. **Establish Tier 1 Coaching and Support Resources.**
6. **Provide Classroom (Tier 1) Problem-Solving Support to Teachers.**
7. **Create Formal Guidelines for Teachers to Document Tier 1 Strategies.**
8. **Develop Decision Rules for Referring Students from Tier 1 to Higher Levels of Intervention.**

☐ **1. Train Teachers to Write Specific, Measureable, Observable 'Problem Identification Statements'.** Teachers are able to describe common student academic and behavioral problems accurately in specific, observable, measurable terms.

If training in this skill is required, how will teachers receive this training?_____

_____

_____

If training is required, who will provide the training?_____

Tip: Review past student cases referred to your school's RTI Team (Problem-Solving Team). For each case, list the primary reason(s) that the student was referred. Review this cumulative list of referral concerns to determine (a) the kinds of student referral concerns that teachers are most likely to encounter and (b) whether referring teachers are able to articulate clearly and specifically their concerns about students.

Exhibit 4-H, continued

☐ **2. Inventory Tier 1 Interventions Already in Use.** The school surveys teachers' current classroom intervention practices to discover those effective strategies that they are already using. This information can assist the school in understanding the staff's present capacity to deliver classroom interventions, as well as gaps in intervention knowledge and use.

1. Generate a list of 4-6 TOP teacher RTI referral concerns for your school (e.g., 'lack of study/organizational skills', 'limited content-area vocabulary').
2. Create a survey form for teachers that lists each top RTI referral concern and asks that teachers write down those whole-group or individual student strategies that they routinely use in the classroom to address that concern. Teachers are encouraged to write enough detail so that the strategy is clear to others. (Note: As a sample survey, review Form 1, *Teacher Survey: What Classroom (Tier 1) Instruction/Intervention Strategies Do You Currently Use?* of this exhibit.)
3. Review the surveys. Compile a list of the best teacher strategies—organized by referral concern. Include only those classroom intervention ideas that are supported by research.
4. Analyze the results on the classroom intervention survey to determine current teacher intervention practices; variability of intervention use among classrooms, grade levels, teams, or departments; intervention areas in which teachers require additional training, etc.

Tips:
- Your school can identify potential 'intervention coaches' among your staff by reviewing teacher responses to the intervention surveys. Contact those teachers who list innovative and effective intervention ideas and ask whether they might be willing to serve as informal 'intervention coaches', being available to demonstrate those strategies to other teachers and coach those teachers in their use.
- Once your school has created a list of the 'best' classroom intervention ideas organized by referral concern, give a copy of that list to teachers. Point out that staff already routinely provides Tier 1 interventions to students—and that over time the RTI model will simply build on this existing capacity.
- Scan the teacher Tier 1 intervention survey results. Select the strongest entries to add to the schoolwide Tier 1 intervention menu (see next section).

Exhibit 4-H, continued

☐ **3. Create a Standard Menu of Evidence-Based Tier 1 Intervention Ideas for Teachers.** When given a menu of evidence-based classroom interventions, teachers can independently access and use them to address common student academic and behavioral concerns.

1. Generate a list of the academic and behavioral concerns for which your teachers appear most in need of classroom intervention strategies (e.g., 'reading fluency', 'inattention in class'). (Note: To record these areas of student concern, you can use Form 2, *Grade- or Building-Wide Student Academic/Behavioral Concerns for Which Tier 1 Intervention Menus Will Be Developed,* of this exhibit.)
2. For each common student concern, locate evidence-based intervention ideas from research journals and other print publications, websites, etc.
3. Write each intervention idea in a teacher-friendly format, including sufficient detail for the instructor to implement the strategy in the classroom. Organize all of the collected ideas into a Tier 1 intervention menu. Group each intervention under the appropriate category of teacher concern (e.g., 'reading fluency', 'inattention in class'). Share these intervention menus with teachers.

Tip: The What Works Clearinghouse has an expanding series of 'practice guides' with empirically supported classroom ideas for instruction and behavior management. These guides are one good source for Tier 1 intervention ideas. You can review these practice guides at: http://ies.ed.gov/ncee/wwc/publications/practiceguides/

☐ **4. Set Up a System to Locate Additional Evidence-Based Tier 1 Intervention Ideas.** As research identifies additional effective classroom strategies, the school is able routinely to learn of those strategies and add them to its Tier 1 intervention menu.

1. Appoint staff members to serve as 'knowledge brokers' who monitor different intervention topic areas (e.g., inattention in class, study skills, reading fluency, etc.).
2. These knowledge brokers read research journals, attend workshops and otherwise stay current on emerging research into school intervention in their topic area(s).
3. Knowledge brokers periodically make recommendations to the school on innovative intervention ideas that should be added to the Tier 1 intervention menu.

Tip: Consider appointing at least two school staff members to serve as knowledge brokers for each intervention topic area. Sharing responsibilities for staying current on intervention research allows knowledge brokers to collaborate and pool their knowledge—thus making the task more manageable.

Exhibit 4-H, continued

☐ **5. Establish Tier 1 Coaching and Support Resources.** Teachers are encouraged to access colleagues as needed who can demonstrate how to use effective Tier 1 interventions—and can also provide coaching and feedback in those intervention skills.
1. Identify personnel in your school (and perhaps district-wide) who can be available to meet with teachers as intervention coaches. 2. Train these personnel to be effective Tier 1 coaches by ensuring that they follow a structured sequence in their coaching: a. meet with the teacher to select one or more ideas from the school's Tier 1 intervention menu, b. show the teacher how to use each selected strategy, c. go into the teacher's class if needed to demonstrate the strategy, d. observe the teacher use the strategy and give performance feedback. 3. Compile a list of people in the school who can serve as intervention coaches. Share that list with teachers. Include information about how teachers can contact coaches and how to schedule coaching sessions.
Tip: Find creative ways to make Tier 1 intervention coaching time-efficient. If your school has grade-level / teaching team / department meetings, for example, consider bringing coaches to those meetings occasionally to show all teachers how to use interventions for shared concerns.

Exhibit 4-H continues on next page

Exhibit 4-H, continued

☐ **6. Provide Classroom (Tier 1) Problem-Solving Support to Teachers.** Teachers can reach out to colleagues for additional Tier 1 classroom intervention ideas that they can try before referring a student to higher levels of intervention.

OPTION A: Time is regularly reserved at grade-level / teaching team / department meetings for teachers to bring students up for discussion. The team and teacher generate a list of evidence-based interventions that the teacher can implement.

How frequently will this team meet to discuss students struggling at Tier 1? _____

How will those intervention ideas be documented? _____

_____

OPTION B: The school generates a list of building-level (and perhaps district-level) personnel who can serve as Tier 1 intervention consultants, meeting individually with teachers to brainstorm classroom intervention ideas.

How will this consultant list be developed and shared with teachers? _____

_____

How will those intervention ideas be documented? _____

_____

Who are candidates to serve as Tier 1 consultants? (Use Form 3 of this exhibit, *Tier 1 (Classroom) Intervention Consultant List*).

Tips:
- Invite personnel with specialized training (e.g., reading teachers) to attend grade-level/teaching team/department Tier 1 intervention planning meetings when appropriate to generate additional intervention ideas.
- When selecting candidates for a consultant list, prepare a simple anonymous teacher survey. On that survey, list the most common academic and behavioral concerns that lead to RTI student referrals in your school. Next to each concern, ask teachers to write in the names of building (and perhaps district) personnel whom they would seek out for intervention ideas. Recruit those people for your consultant list whose names appear most frequently on completed teacher surveys.

Exhibit 4-H, continued

☐ **7. Create Formal Guidelines for Teachers to Document Tier 1 Strategies.** Teachers have a single format for documenting their Tier 1 strategies for students who may be referred for higher levels of intervention.
Create one form that all teachers use to document their classroom interventions in a uniform manner. (See Exhibit 4-I, Form 1, *Tier 1 Intervention Planning Sheet* as a sample documentation format.)
Tip: Be sure that teachers use the standard classroom intervention documentation form at the point when they seek out additional Tier 1 intervention ideas from their fellow teachers or school consultants. Intervention documentation is much easier to do at the point that an intervention is first planned than after that intervention has already been implemented.

☐ **8. Develop Decision Rules for Referring Students from Tier 1 to Higher Levels of Intervention.** Teachers know when they have attempted a sufficient number of classroom strategies for a still-struggling student and should refer the student for more intervention support.
Establish general decision rules to guide teachers in determining whether they have put sufficient effort into classroom interventions before seeking additional intervention support. These rules should include: • The minimum number of evidence-based classroom interventions that the teacher should implement and document. • The minimum period of time that classroom interventions should typically be implemented before teachers should consider a higher level of RTI intervention. • The expected documentation that teachers should complete describing their Tier 1 classroom intervention efforts.
Tip: Include teachers in the development of decision rules for Tier 1 interventions. When presenting those decision rules to school faculty, be sure to emphasize that the decision rules are simply a formal structured version of good instruction and behavior management.

Exhibit 4-H, Form 1

Teacher Survey: What Classroom (Tier 1) Instruction/Intervention Strategies Do You Currently Use?

Name: _____ Date: _____

Directions. For the academic or behavioral concern below, write down those whole-group or individual student strategies that you routinely use in the classroom to address that concern. Please write enough detail so that your strategy is clear to those reviewing this survey.

If we share any of your intervention ideas with staff, may we cite you as the source?
　　　　　　　　　　　　　　　　　　　　　　　　　　　　　　____Y ____N

Academic or Behavioral Concern: _____

	Teacher Strategy
1.	
2.	
3.	
4.	
5.	
6.	
7.	
8.	
9.	
10.	

Exhibit 4-H, Form 2

Grade- or Building-Wide Student Academic/Behavioral Concerns for Which Tier 1 Intervention Menus Will Be Developed

School: _____

Academic Concerns	Behavioral Concerns

Exhibit 4-H, Form 3

Tier 1 (Classroom) Intervention Consultant List	
Consultant	**Area(s) of Expertise**

Exhibit 4-I
Documenting Tier 1 (Classroom) Interventions: A Sample Form

When general education students begin to struggle with academic or behavioral issues, the classroom teacher will typically select and implement one or more evidence-based intervention strategies to assist those students. But a strong intervention plan needs more than just well-chosen interventions. It also requires 4 additional components (Witt, VanDerHeyden, & Gilbertson, 2004): (1) student concerns should be clearly and specifically defined; (2) one or more methods of formative assessment should be used to track the effectiveness of the intervention; (3) baseline student data should be collected prior to the intervention; and (4) a goal for student improvement should be calculated before the start of the intervention to judge whether that intervention is ultimately successful. If a single one of these essential 4 components is missing, the intervention is to be judged as fatally flawed (Witt, VanDerHeyden, & Gilbertson, 2004) and as not meeting minimum RTI standards.

Teachers need a standard format to use in documenting their 'Tier 1' (classroom) intervention plans. The Form 1, *Tier 1/Classroom Intervention Planning Sheet,* is designed to include all of the essential RTI elements of an effective intervention plan. The form includes space to document:

- *Definition of up to two student academic or behavioral problems.* The most significant step in selecting an effective classroom intervention is to correctly identify the target student concern(s) in clear, specific, measureable terms (Bergan, 1995). The teacher selects no more than two student concerns to address on the intervention plan.
- *Intervention description.* The teacher describes the evidence-based intervention(s) that will be used to address the identified student concern(s).
- *Intervention delivery.* The teacher writes down details necessary for implementing the intervention in the classroom (e.g., where and when the intervention will be used; the adult-to-student ratio; how frequently the intervention will take place; the length of time each session of the intervention will last; materials needed for the intervention, etc.
- *Checkup date.* The teacher notes the date at which the intervention will be reviewed to determine whether it has been sufficiently effective. NOTE: For academic interventions, it is advisable to allow at least 4 instructional weeks before deciding whether the intervention has been effective.
- *Assessment data.* For each intervention, the teacher selects the type(s) of classroom data that will be collected formatively throughout the intervention period to judge its effectiveness. For each data source, in turn, the teacher collects baseline data on student performance—and calculates an outcome goal that the student is expected to attain if the intervention is successful. During the period in which the intervention is in effect, the teacher collects ongoing data to judge student performance and attaches that data to Form 1.

Exhibit 4-I, continued

While a Tier 1/classroom intervention documentation form is a helpful planning tool, schools should remember that teachers will need other resources and types of assistance as well to be successful in selecting and using Tier 1 interventions. For example, teachers should have access to an 'intervention menu' that contains evidence-based strategies to address the most common academic and behavioral concerns and should be able to get coaching support as they learn how to implement new classroom intervention ideas.

References

Bergan, J. R. (1995). Evolution of a problem-solving model of consultation. *Journal of Educational and Psychological Consultation,* 6(2), 111-123.

Witt, J. C., VanDerHeyden, A. M., & Gilbertson, D. (2004). Troubleshooting behavioral interventions. A systematic process for finding and eliminating problems. *School Psychology Review,* 33, 363-383.

Exhibit 4-I, Form 1

Tier 1/Classroom Intervention Planning Sheet

Teacher/Team: _____ Date: _____ Student: _____

Student Problem Definition #1: _____

Student Problem Definition #2: _____

[Optional] Person(s) assisting with intervention planning process: _____

Interventions: Essential Elements (Witt et al., 2004)
- Clear problem-definition(s)
- Baseline data
- Goal for improvement
- Progress-monitoring plan

Intervention Description	Intervention Delivery	Check-Up Date	Assessment Data
Describe each intervention that you plan to use to address the student's concern(s).	List key details about delivery of the intervention, such as: (1) where & when the intervention will be used; (2) the adult-to-student ratio; (3) how frequently the intervention will take place; (4) the length of time each session of the intervention will last.	Select a date when the data will be reviewed to evaluate the intervention.	Note what classroom data will be used to establish baseline, set a goal for improvement, and track the student's progress during this intervention.
			Type(s) of Data to Be Used: Baseline | Goal by Check-Up
			Type(s) of Data to Be Used: Baseline | Goal by Check-Up
			Type(s) of Data to Be Used: Baseline | Goal by Check-Up

Witt, J. C., VanDerHeyden, A. M., & Gilbertson, D. (2004). Troubleshooting behavioral interventions. A systematic process for finding and eliminating problems. *School Psychology Review, 33*, 363-383.

Exhibit 4-J
Reading Comprehension 'Fix-Up' Skills: A Toolkit

Good readers continuously monitor their understanding of informational text. When necessary, they also take steps to improve their understanding of text through use of reading comprehension 'fix-up' skills. Presented here are a series of fix-up skill strategies that can help struggling students to better understand difficult reading assignments.

☐ [Core Instruction] **Providing Main Idea Practice through 'Partner Retell'** (Carnine & Carnine, 2004). Students in a group or class are assigned a text selection to read silently. Students are then paired off, with one student assigned the role of 'reteller' and the other appointed as 'listener'. The reteller recounts the main idea to the listener, who can comment or ask questions. The teacher then states the main idea to the class. Next, the reteller locates two key details from the reading that support the main idea and shares these with the listener. At the end of the activity, the teacher does a spot check by randomly calling on one or more students in the listener role and asking them to recap what information was shared by the reteller.

☐ [Accommodation] **Developing a Bank of Multiple Passages to Present Challenging Concepts** (Hedin & Conderman, 2010; Kamil et al., 2008; Texas Reading Initiative, 2002). The teacher notes which course concepts, cognitive strategies, or other information will likely present the greatest challenge to students. For these 'challenge' topics, the teacher selects alternative readings that present the same general information and review the same key vocabulary as the course text but that are more accessible to struggling readers (e.g., with selections written at an easier reading level or that use graphics to visually illustrate concepts). These alternative selections are organized into a bank. Students are encouraged to engage in wide reading by choosing selections from the bank as a means to better understand difficult material.

☐ [Student Strategy] **Promoting Understanding & Building Endurance through Reading-Reflection Pauses** (Hedin & Conderman, 2010). The student decides on a reading interval (e.g., every four sentences; every 3 minutes; at the end of each paragraph). At the end of each interval, the student pauses briefly to recall the main points of the reading. If the student has questions or is uncertain about the content, the student rereads part or all of the section just read. This strategy is useful both for students who need to monitor their understanding as well as those who benefit from brief breaks when engaging in intensive reading as a means to build up endurance as attentive readers.

☐ [Student Strategy] **Identifying or Constructing Main Idea Sentences** (Davey & McBride, 1986; Rosenshine, Meister & Chapman, 1996). For each paragraph in an assigned reading, the student either (a) highlights the main idea sentence or (b) highlights key details and uses them to write a 'gist' sentence. The student then writes the main idea of that paragraph on an index card. On the other side of the card, the

Exhibit 4-J, continued

student writes a question whose answer is that paragraph's main idea sentence. This stack of 'main idea' cards becomes a useful tool to review assigned readings.

☐ **[Student Strategy] Restructuring Paragraphs with Main Idea First to Strengthen 'Rereads'** (Hedin & Conderman, 2010). The student highlights or creates a main idea sentence for each paragraph in the assigned reading. When rereading each paragraph of the selection, the student (1) reads the main idea sentence or student-generated 'gist' sentence first (irrespective of where that sentence actually falls in the paragraph); (2) reads the remainder of the paragraph, and (3) reflects on how the main idea relates to the paragraph content.

☐ **[Student Strategy] Summarizing Readings** (Boardman et al., 2008). The student is taught to summarize readings into main ideas and essential details--stripped of superfluous content. The act of summarizing longer readings can promote understanding and retention of content while the summarized text itself can be a useful study tool.

☐ **[Student Strategy] Linking Pronouns to Referents** (Hedin & Conderman, 2010). Some readers lose the connection between pronouns and the nouns that they refer to (known as 'referents')—especially when reading challenging text. The student is encouraged to circle pronouns in the reading, to explicitly identify each pronoun's referent, and (optionally) to write next to the pronoun the name of its referent. For example, the student may add the referent to a pronoun in this sentence from a biology text: "The Cambrian Period is the first geological age that has large numbers of multi-celled organisms associated with it Cambrian Period."

☐ **[Student Strategy] Apply Vocabulary 'Fix-Up' Skills for Unknown Words** (Klingner & Vaughn, 1999). When confronting an unknown word in a reading selection, the student applies the following vocabulary 'fix-up' skills:

1. Read the sentence again.
2. Read the sentences before/after the problem sentence for clues to the word's meaning.
3. See if there are prefixes or suffixes in the word that can give clues to meaning.
4. Break the word up by syllables and look for 'smaller words' within.

☐ **[Student Strategy] Compiling a Vocabulary Journal from Course Readings** (Hedin & Conderman, 2010). The student highlights new or unfamiliar vocabulary from course readings. The student writes each term into a vocabulary journal, using a standard 'sentence-stem' format: e.g., "Mitosis means…" or "A chloroplast is…". If the student is unable to generate a definition for a vocabulary term based on the course reading, he or she writes the term into the vocabulary journal without definition and then applies other strategies to define the term: e.g., look up the term in a dictionary; use Google to locate two examples of the term being used correctly in context; ask the instructor, etc.).

Exhibit 4-J, continued

☐ **[Student Strategy] Encouraging Student Use of Text Enhancements** (Hedin & Conderman, 2010). Text enhancements can be used to tag important vocabulary terms, key ideas, or other reading content. If working with photocopied material, the student can use a highlighter--but should limit highlighting to important text elements such as main idea and key vocabulary terms. Another enhancement strategy is the 'lasso and rope' technique—using a pen or pencil to circle a vocabulary term and then drawing a line that connects that term to its underlined definition. If working from a textbook, the student can cut sticky notes into strips. These strips can be inserted in the book as pointers to text of interest. They can also be used as temporary labels—e.g., for writing a vocabulary term and its definition.

☐ **[Student Strategy] Reading Actively Through Text Annotation** (Harris, 1990; Sarkisian et al., 2003). Students are likely to increase their retention of information when they interact actively with their reading by jotting comments in the margin of the text. Using photocopies, the student is taught to engage in an ongoing 'conversation' with the writer by recording a running series of brief comments in the margins of the text. The student may write annotations to record opinions about points raised by the writer, questions triggered by the reading, or unknown vocabulary words.

References

Boardman, A. G., Roberts, G., Vaughn, S., Wexler, J., Murray, C. S., & Kosanovich, M. 2008). *Effective instruction for adolescent struggling readers: A practice brief.* Portsmouth, NH: RMC Research Corporation, Center on Instruction.

Carnine, L., & Carnine, D. (2004). The interaction of reading skills and science content knowledge when teaching struggling secondary students. *Reading & Writing Quarterly,* 20, 203-218.

Davey, B., & McBride, S. (1986). Effects of question-generation training on reading comprehension. *Journal of Educational Psychology,* 78, 256-262.

Harris, J. (1990). Text *annotation and underlining as metacognitive strategies to improve comprehension and retention of expository text.* Paper presented at the Annual Meeting of the National Reading Conference (Miami).

Hedin, L. R., & Conderman, G. (2010). Teaching students to comprehend informational text through rereading. *The Reading Teacher,* 63(7), 556–565.

Kamil, M. L., Borman, G. D., Dole, J., Kral, C. C., Salinger, T., & Torgesen, J. (2008). *Improving adolescent literacy: Effective classroom and intervention practices: A practice guide* (NCEE #2008-4027). Washington, DC: National Center for Education Evaluation and Regional Assistance, Institute of Education Sciences, U.S. Department of Education. Retrieved from http://ies.ed.gov/ncee/wwc.

Klingner, J. K., & Vaughn, S. (1999). Promoting reading comprehension, content learning, and English acquisition through collaborative strategic reading (CSR). *The Reading Teacher,* 52(7), 738-747.

Exhibit 4-J, continued

Rosenshine, B., Meister, C., & Chapman, S. (1996). Teaching students to generate questions: A review of the intervention studies. *Review of Educational Research,* 66, 181-221.

Sarkisian V., Toscano, M., Tomkins-Tinch, K., & Casey, K. (2003). *Reading strategies and critical thinking.* Retrieved October 15, 2006, from http://www.academic.marist.edu/alcuin/ssk/stratthink.html

Texas Reading Initiative. (2002). *Promoting vocabulary development: Components of effective vocabulary instruction.* Austin, TX: Author. Retrieved November 15, 2010, from http://www.tea.state.tx.us/reading/practices/redbk5.pdf

Exhibit 4-K
'Defensive Behavior Management': Advance Planning, Connecting With the Student, and Defusing Crisis Situations

Description: 'Defensive behavior management' (Fields, 2004) is a teacher-friendly six-step approach to avert student-teacher power struggles that emphasizes providing proactive instructional support to the student, elimination of behavioral triggers in the classroom setting, relationship-building, strategic application of defusing techniques when needed, and use of a 'reconnection' conference after behavioral incidents to promote student reflection and positive behavior change.

Purpose: When students show non-compliant, defiant, and disruptive behaviors in the classroom, the situation can quickly spin out of control. In attempting to maintain authority, the teacher may instead fall into a power struggle with the student, often culminating in the student being removed from the classroom. The numerous negative consequences of chronic student misbehavior include classwide lost instructional time, the acting-out student's frequent exclusion from instruction, and significant teacher stress (Fields, 2004). Defensive management can prevent these negative outcomes.

Materials: No specialized materials are needed.

Preparation: Preparation steps are included in the intervention itself (see below).

Intervention Steps: Defensive behavior management is implemented through these steps:

1. **Understanding the Problem and Using Proactive Strategies to Prevent It.** The teacher collects information—through direct observation and perhaps other means—about specific instances of student problem behavior and the instructional components and other factors surrounding them. The teacher analyzes this information to discover specific 'trigger' events that seem to set off the problem behavior(s). Examples of potential triggers include lack of skills; failure to understand directions; fatigue because of work volume; reluctance to demonstrate limited academic skills in the presence of peers or adults; etc.).

   As the teacher identifies elements in the classroom environment that appear to trigger student non-compliance or defiance, the instructor adjusts instruction to provide appropriate student support to prevent behavioral episodes (e.g., providing the student with additional instruction in a skill; repeating directions and writing them on the board; 'chunking' larger work assignments into smaller segments; restructuring academic tasks to reduce the likelihood of student embarrassment in front of peers).

2. **Promoting Positive Teacher-Student Interactions.** Early in each class session, the teacher makes a point to engage in at least one positive verbal interaction with the student. Throughout the class period, the teacher continues to interact in positive ways

Exhibit 4-K, continued

with the student (e.g., brief conversation, smile, thumbs up, praise comment after a student remark in large-group discussion, etc.). In each interaction, the teacher adopts a genuinely accepting, polite, respectful tone.

3. **Scanning for Warning Indicators.** During the class session, the teacher monitors the target student's behavior for any behavioral indicators suggesting that the student is becoming frustrated or angry. Examples of behaviors that precede non-compliance or open defiance may include stopping work; muttering or complaining; becoming argumentative; interrupting others; leaving his or her seat; throwing objects, etc.).

4. **Exercising Emotional Restraint.** Whenever the student begins to display problematic behaviors, the teacher makes an active effort to remain calm. To actively monitor his or her emotional state, the teacher tracks physiological cues such as increased muscle tension and heart rate, as well as fear, annoyance, anger, or other negative emotions. The teacher also adopts calming or relaxation strategies that work for him or her in the face of provocative student behavior--such as taking a deep breath or counting to 10 before responding.

5. **Using Defusing Tactics.** If the student begins to escalate to non-compliant, defiant, or confrontational behavior (e.g., arguing, threatening, other intentional verbal interruptions), the teacher draws from a range of possible deescalating strategies to defuse the situation. Such strategies can include private conversation with the student while maintaining a calm voice, open-ended questions, paraphrasing the student's concerns, acknowledging the student's emotions, etc.

6. **Reconnecting with the Student.** Soon after any in-class incident of student non-compliance, defiance, or confrontation, the teacher makes a point to meet with the student individually to discuss the behavioral incident, identify the triggers in the classroom environment that may have led to the problem, and brainstorm with the student to create a written plan to prevent the reoccurrence of such an incident. Throughout this conference, the teacher maintains a supportive, positive, polite, and respectful tone.

Adjusting/Troubleshooting: Here are recommendations for using defensive management as an intervention strategy and addressing issues that might arise:

Consider adopting defensive behavior management across classrooms. Particularly in middle and high schools, students who are chronically non-compliant or defiant often display those maladaptive behaviors across instructional settings. If all teachers who work with a challenging student use the defensive management approach, there is a greater likelihood that the student will find classrooms more predictable and supportive—and that teachers will experience greater success with that student.

Exhibit 4-K, continued

Do not use defensive management to respond to physically aggressive behaviors or other serious safety concerns. While the defensive-management process can work quite effectively to prevent or minimize verbal outbursts and non-compliance, the teacher should not attempt on his or her own to manage serious physical aggression using this classroom-based approach. Instead, teachers should respond to any episodes of student physical aggression by immediately notifying building administration.

Reference

Fields, B. (2004). Breaking the cycle of office referrals and suspensions: Defensive management. *Educational Psychology in Practice,* 20, 103-115.

Chapter 5
Using Data to Guide RTI: Screening, Instructional Assessment, and Progress-Monitoring

At the middle and high school level, RTI attempts to lower the risk of underperformance or school dropout by finding struggling students at the earliest possible moment and then matching those learners to the right intervention strategies. However, schools can proactively identify and provide support to marginal and disengaged students through RTI, only when guided by data.

This chapter reviews three major roles that data collection and interpretation play in the RTI model (Hosp, Hosp & Howell, 2007). First, schools use existing student data (e.g., records of grades, attendance, and behavior) and academic assessments as universal screeners for the entire school population to identify those students who are at significant risk of academic failure and underperformance. Second, schools conduct more detailed 'instructional assessments' for those students with serious academic delays whose skill deficits are not yet fully understood. Third, the school develops the capacity to regularly monitor the academic or behavioral progress of students on intervention at Tiers 1, 2, and 3 to determine as quickly as possible whether those interventions are successful. These three data requirements are explained in greater detail below:

Universal Screening:
Assessing the Entire Student Population at Tier 1

Group academic screening measures are an efficient means to estimate the typical skill level of a grade level and also to proactively locate those students in the group who have substantial academic deficits and need supplemental interventions. The school first identifies a standard set of academic measures to use in the screening. These should be quick to administer and provide predictive information about student academic success. Universal screenings at each grade level are then conducted at least three times per year, typically in the fall, winter, and spring.

In addition to flagging students who may require additional academic-intervention support, universal academic screening data has other important uses. The school can share screening results with general-education teachers to help them to adjust their instruction—if needed—to meet the needs of the full range of learners in their classrooms. Additionally, schools can use universal screening information to better allocate instructional and intervention resources to the grade levels or pockets of struggling students where needs are greatest (Stewart & Silberglit, 2008).

There is broad agreement that universal screenings of some type should be a central part of RTI implementation (Glover & DiPerna, 2007). However, the routine use of academic screeners in the secondary grades is not yet a settled question. The foremost objection is simply that middle and high schools can already locate most struggling learners who require supplemental interventions by using teacher nominations, state test results, grades, or other information that already exists or is easy to collect (Fuchs, Fuchs, & Compton, 2010). So it is possible that the additional cost of screening students 3 times per year using predictive academic measures will not yield additional benefits that would justify the time and expense required.

At the present time, then, middle and high schools may want to adopt an exploratory approach as they consider whether—and if so how—they might adopt academic screening tools to assess the risk status of their universal student population. To start with, a school should allow itself adequate time—three to five years—to fully investigate and implement a building-wide screening program (Stewart & Silberglit, 2008). And when considering specific screening measures, the school might first want to pilot them at a single grade level or even within selected classrooms to gauge whether those assessments add real value as 'early warning' indicators of problem academic performance before deciding to adopt such screeners schoolwide.

In the meantime, the school can investigate sources of information already collected and stored in the building or district database that might be analyzed and used to flag students who have emerging problems with academic performance or school conduct. Such existing school data as grades or attendance records can be used as 'screeners' to identify students at-risk (Stewart & Silberglit, 2008). One recent study, for example, found that as early as sixth grade, attendance, grades, and disciplinary data were significant predictors of student drop-out status (Balfanz, Herzog, MacIver, 2007).

Schools that would like a structured planning form to assist them in setting up a universal screening program are encouraged to check out Exhibit 5-A, *Finding Students At-Risk: How to Create a Comprehensive Middle or High School-Wide Screening Plan*. The accompanying forms prompt the user to consider archival data, curriculum-based measures, and a sample computerized curriculum-skills assessment program as screening tools and provide information about where to locate screening resources on the Internet.

Instructional/Diagnostic Decision-Making: Understanding the Individual Student

The role of a middle or high school content-area teacher is to build academic skills and knowledge so that students can master increasingly challenging curriculum goals. Teachers are guided in their instruction each day by streams of formal and informal classroom data that indicate whether students are mastering the instructional content—e.g., frequent observations of students working on in-class assignments, work samples completed in-class or as homework, grades, school-wide literacy screening results, student performance on state tests, and so on. Just as a compass allows a sailor to judge whether the boat is moving on the correct course, the right data allow teachers to pinpoint student academic needs and to adjust instruction flexibly to address those needs.

With data from gradewide screenings in hand, schools will probably find that they have sufficient information to decide what supplemental instructional support is needed for most students who have mild academic delays or deficits. However, screening results may also reveal a small number of students in the classroom who have large apparent skill gaps—and for these students the screening data alone are not likely to provide enough information to fully understand the reason(s) for their academic problems. Therefore, when faced with a student with a significant learning delay, the teacher (or other school-based interventionist) may need to collect more detailed instructional information about the student in order to analyze that student's learning needs and match those needs to an individualized intervention plan. This flexible, open-ended problem-solving approach has two main steps: (1) Analyzing existing data from various sources so that the teacher can choose possible reason(s), or hypotheses, that best explain the student's learning problems; (2) Collecting additional data as needed to verify or rule out various hypotheses until a single explanation has been identified that is the best candidate as the primary reason for the student problem.

The most frequent reasons, or hypotheses, for poor student academic performance are:

- *The student cannot perform the academic skill or cannot do the academic work.* The problem is a skill deficit. The student has failed to acquire the necessary academic skills to complete course requirements (Haring, Lovitt, Eaton, & Hansen, 1978).

- *The student can perform the academic skill or do the academic work but is not yet fluent.* The problem is fluency. The student has the basic skill but is slow and inefficient in using it (Haring et al., 1978).

- *The student has the academic skill but does not realize times or situations when it should be used.* The problem lies in reliably accessing a skill. The student lacks the metacognitive capacity to analyze a learning task, inventory his or her current skills, and to realize the need to match an existing skill to complete the task (Hosp, 2008).

- *The student has the necessary academic skills but chooses not to put effort into completing the task.* (Witt, VanDerHeyden, & Gilbertson, 2004). The problem is one of motivation. The student has the essential skills but is not sufficiently invested in the learning task to put forth his or her best effort.

- *The student has the necessary academic skills but lacks important 'academic enabling' skills.* Poor academic performance may stem from the student's lack of key academic support or 'enabling' skills (DiPerna, 2006) such as strategies to study efficiently, to complete homework, or to create a work plan to carry out a multi-step assignment.

In the early stages of problem-solving, a teacher may come up with several possible hypotheses or explanations for why a student may be performing poorly in the class. The next step is to collect and analyze classroom data to uncover likely patterns that explain why a specific student has academic delays. Because no two students are alike, this step is an exploratory process. However, teachers can streamline the process and work most efficiently to locate the most valuable classroom information if they use a structured framework (Hosp, 2008). In particular, teachers should collect information on the student from a variety of sources, including:

- review of existing records
- interviews with school staff, parent, and student
- observation of the student during work situations

As teachers assemble information on a particular student, they should check to ensure that the data answers questions about:

- instructional practices that do and do not benefit the student;

- key academic skills the student possesses or lacks that are essential for success in the classroom curriculum;

- non-instructional factors in learning environments that can hinder or help the student (e.g., being seated in the classroom next to supportive peers; lack of a structured setting at home for the student to complete homework);

- any traits that the student presents across settings (e.g., a strong work ethic; high levels of inattention across settings) that can contribute to or interfere with learning.

A more formal description of the open-ended investigative framework presented here appears as Exhibit 5-B, *The RIOT/ICEL Matrix: Organizing Data to Answer Questions About Student Academic Performance & Behavior.* A sample tool for measuring global student abilities such as study and organizational skills can be found as Exhibit 5-C, *'Academic Enabler' Observational Checklists: Measuring Students' Ability to Manage Their Own Learning.*

Progress-Monitoring Decision-Making: Using Data to Evaluate the Effectiveness of Interventions

One simple but useful definition of RTI is "a change in performance or behavior due to intervention" (Duhon, Mesmer, Atkins, Greguson & Olinger, 2009; p. 102). This definition implies that, without data, the teacher or other interventionist is operating blindly, unsure whether an intervention is in fact resulting in a positive outcome. So whenever a student is being administered an RTI intervention at any of the Tiers, it is essential that progress-monitoring data be collected regularly to judge whether that intervention is effective. To ensure that the monitoring of any student on intervention yields trustworthy information, schools should follow these quality guidelines: (1) use sources of data that provide quantitative summaries of academic performance or behavior; (2) calculate baseline prior to beginning the intervention and set a student outcome goal as a standard for judging success; and (3) monitor the student often enough to judge quickly whether the intervention is actually effective.

- *Use quantitative progress-monitoring data.* Any measure used to track a student's ongoing progress on intervention must provide objective, quantitative data to allow the interventionist to directly compare the student's performance across successive observation dates and (if desired) plot the results on a time-series graph. Progress-monitoring measures at any Tier should be efficient to administer, be repeatable (e.g., with multiple alternate forms), provide prompt feedback on student performance, and be a reliable predictor of student success on the targeted skill(s) (Hosp, 2008). With a modest investment of effort, teachers can package information already available or readily collectible in the classroom into a quantitative format. Examples of classroom data that can be used to monitor Tier 1 interventions include grades, behavioral frequency count, rating scales, and global skill checklists. Exhibit 5-D, *Teacher-Friendly Methods to Monitor Tier 1 (Classroom) Interventions,* provides a more detailed listing of Tier 1/classroom progress-monitoring methods. Because the stakes are higher for students on interventions at Tiers 2 and 3, schools should take care to use progress-monitoring measures at these levels that have strong 'technical adequacy', including published research on their reliability and validity. Schools can visit the National Center on RTI at http://www.rti4success.org to review a Progress-Monitoring Tools Chart that evaluates various commercially available intervention-monitoring measures.

- *Calculate student baseline and establish an outcome goal.* Progress-monitoring data being collected for a student on an RTI intervention can be accurately interpreted only if it is placed in a meaningful context that includes baseline and outcome goal. Baseline is a pre-assessment of the student's targeted academic skill(s) or behavior prior to the beginning of the intervention. Baseline information is an estimate of the student's academic or behavioral starting point and serves as a point of comparison against which to evaluate student progress (Barnett, Daly, Jones & Lentz, 2004). The outcome goal is an estimate of the progress that a student is expected to make if the intervention is successful (Burns & Gibbons, 2008). Indeed, baseline and outcome goals are considered so crucial to judging the impact of an intervention that the absence of either can be considered a 'fatal flaw' that would render that intervention of little worth in RTI decision-making (Witt, VanDerHeyden & Gilbertson, 2004). A useful form that any educator can use to organize progress-monitoring data collection can be found in Exhibit 5-E, *RTI Classroom Progress-Monitoring Worksheet.* This form guides the interventionist through collection of baseline and goal-setting.

- *Monitor student progress at the appropriate frequency.* During the intervention, ongoing data should be collected to measure student progress at a frequency that will indicate within a reasonable time period whether the intervention is in fact working (Witt, VanDerHeyden & Gilbertson, 2004). At Tier 1, classroom interventions should be monitored at least weekly, to allow the teacher to judge the outcome of the intervention within a brief timespan (e.g., 5-6 weeks). As mentioned earlier in this chapter, however, Tier 1 methods of progress-monitoring can often make use of information that is either already available or readily collectible within the classroom setting. At Tier 2, interventions should be monitored at least 1-2 times per month (Burns & Gibbons, 2008), while Tier 3 interventions should be monitored at least weekly (Howell, Hosp & Kurns, 2008).

The RTI process is truly data-based, with different types of measurement information being used to answer different questions. School-wide screenings compiled from existing data or gathered through academic screening tools can answer the question: Which struggling learners in the general-education population might need supplemental intervention? When conducting more detailed instructional assessments with students who have greater academic deficits, teachers collect detailed information from a variety of sources to answer the question: What is the pattern of specific academic needs for these students? The academic or behavioral progress of students on intervention at Tiers 1 through 3 is measured on any ongoing basis; that stream of data is compared to baseline levels and students' outcome goals to answer the question: Are these interventions effective?

But in concluding this chapter on RTI and data collection, it is worth remembering that student data of any kind, however rigorously collected and technically adequate, is of value only if educators use it to make sound and reliable decisions about student instruction and intervention.

References

Balfanz, R., Herzog, L., MacIver, D. J. (2007). Preventing student disengagement and keeping students on the graduation path in urban middle grades schools: Early identification and effective interventions. *Educational Psychologist,* 42, 223–235.

Barnett, D. W., Daly, E. J., Jones, K. M., & Lentz, F.E. (2004). Response to intervention: Empirically based special service decisions from single-case designs of increasing and decreasing intensity. *Journal of Special Education,* 38, 66-79.

Burns, M. K., & Gibbons, K. A. (2008). *Implementing response-to-intervention in elementary and secondary schools.* Routledge: New York.

DiPerna, J. C. (2006). Academic enablers and student achievement: Implications for assessment and intervention services in the schools. *Psychology in the Schools,* 43, 7-17.

Duhon, G. J., Mesmer, E. M., Atkins, M. E., Greguson, L. A., & Olinger, E. S. (2009). Quantifying intervention intensity: A systematic approach to evaluating student response to increasing intervention frequency. *Journal of Behavioral Education,* 18, 101-118.

Fuchs L. S., Fuchs, D., and Compton, D. L. (2010). Rethinking response to intervention at middle and high school. *School Psychology Review,* 39, 22-28.

Glover, T. A., & DiPerna, J. C. (2007). Service delivery for response to intervention: Core components and directions for future research. *School Psychology Review,* 36, 526-540.

Haring, N.G., Lovitt, T.C., Eaton, M.D., & Hansen, C.L. (1978). *The fourth R: Research in the classroom.* Columbus, OH: Charles E. Merrill Publishing Co.

Hosp, J. L. (2008). Best practices in aligning academic assessment with instruction. In A. Thomas & J. Grimes (Eds.), *Best practices in school psychology V* (pp.363-376). Bethesda, MD: National Association of School Psychologists.

Hosp, M. K., Hosp, J. L., & Howell, K. W. (2007). *The ABCs of CBM.* New York: Guilford Press.

Howell, K. W., Hosp, J. L., & Kurns, S. (2008). Best practices in curriculum-based evaluation. In A. Thomas & J. Grimes (Eds.), *Best practices in school psychology V* (pp.349-362). Bethesda, MD: National Association of School Psychologists.

Stewart, L. H. & Silberglit, B. (2008). Best practices in developing academic local norms. In A. Thomas & J. Grimes (Eds.), *Best practices in school psychology V* (pp. 225-242). Bethesda, MD: National Association of School Psychologists.

Witt, J. C., VanDerHeyden, A. M., & Gilbertson, D. (2004). Troubleshooting behavioral interventions. A systematic process for finding and eliminating problems. *School Psychology Review,* 33, 363-383.

Frequently Asked Questions About...
...Middle & High School Assessment & Progress-Monitoring

Tier 1: Universal Screening of All Students

1. **What are schoolwide academic screenings?** Middle and high schools may choose to administer schoolwide screening measures as a proactive means to locate students at risk for academic or behavioral failure. For academic screenings, the school selects a standard set of measures to use in the screening that are quick to administer and provide predictive information about student academic success. Academic screenings are conducted at least three times per year—typically in fall, winter, and spring. The school shares that screening data with classroom teachers to help them to adjust their instructional practices. Additionally, the school uses academic screening data to determine which students are performing below academic expectations and require supplemental intervention.

    Universal academic screening data has several important uses. It can help the school to estimate efficiently the typical academic skill level of any grade, as well as to proactively identify those struggling students who need supplemental intervention support. Additionally, schools can use universal screening information to better allocate instructional and intervention resources to the appropriate grade levels or pockets of struggling students.

2. **What academic screening tools can be used in middle and high schools to proactively identify students at risk?** There is broad agreement that universal screenings should be a central part of RTI implementation. However, one size does not fill all: The types of academic screeners that a given middle and high school adopts should be matched to the typical levels of student performance at that school. Schools whose students often perform below expectations on basic skills such as reading fluency or comprehension may find curriculum-based measures such as CBM Oral Reading Fluency to be helpful in flagging students at

risk. In contrast, buildings whose students have typically mastered basic academic skills might adopt assessments that track higher-level problem-solving abilities and advanced curriculum goals. A listing of academic screening tools with good measurement characteristics can be found on the National Center for RTI website at http://www.rti4success.org.

3. **Can existing data be used as a source of screening information for at-risk students?** Yes. Schools can use archival information about student grades, attendance records, and office disciplinary referrals as one source of screening information. At key points during the school year (e.g., every five weeks), the school could review this existing information to identify students who appear to be having problems with their academic performance, school attendance, or classroom behavior. Identified students might then be provided with appropriate interventions.

Tier 1: Collecting Background and Diagnostic Information

4. **What kind of background information can a teacher collect to better understand why a student is experiencing an academic or behavioral problem?** When a student is having academic or behavioral difficulties in the classroom, the teacher can use a systematic approach to collecting information that will increase the chance of finding a solution to the student's problem. First, the teacher should pose and answer questions that are most likely to result in better student outcomes. The acronym **ICEL** can remind the teacher to ask what role if any each of the following factors may play in the student's presenting problems: **Instruction** ("What instructional techniques used in the current classroom appear to help or hinder the student?"); **Curriculum** ("What are the student's current academic skills as they map to the school's curriculum expectations?"); **Environment** ("What non-instructional factors in the student's academic environment—such as interactions with peers—exist that may impact learning?"); **Learner** ("What traits might the student possess such as chronic inattention or lack of self-confidence in math skills that could impact learning?").

Second, the teacher should take care to collect information across a range of sources to reduce the possibility that any one source will bias the findings. The acronym **RIOT** can help the teacher to remember to sample the several possible sources of student information: **Review** of records; **Interview** of other teachers, parents, or the student; **Observation** of the student engaged in academic tasks; and more structured in-class **Testing** of the student if needed.

5. **How can the classroom teacher survey a student's academic skills when needed to diagnose specific skill deficits?** For students who present with large apparent skill gaps, schoolwide screening data alone will probably not give enough information to fully understand the reason(s) for their academic problems. For selected students with significant academic delays, then, teachers or schools may wish to conduct an in-depth instructional assessment (sometime also referred to as an *analytic* or *diagnostic* assessment) to identify specific areas of academic deficit or delay. Schools can purchase commercial academic products to conduct diagnostic assessments. While it may be convenient to have a ready-made assessment package to survey student skills, however, such products can be expensive and do not necessarily assess all of the relevant skills in a particular middle or high school curriculum.

   Another option is for teachers to create their own customized instructional assessments, to include items that match the real-life academic demands of the classroom. When creating instructional assessments, the teacher first decides what academic skills to assess by reviewing the district curriculum to identify academic skills from the student's current and earlier grades that are essential for success in the course. Once the teacher has selected the important curriculum or course academic skills to be assessed, the next step is to convert those skills to actual assessment items. For each academic skill being tested, the teacher should construct several test items—to provide enough information to allow the teacher to make accurate judgments about whether the student has mastered a given skill. Just how many test items should be created to assess a skill will depend on how specific the skill definition is. If an academic skill is narrowly defined, 3 to 5 teacher-constructed items should be sufficient to assess that skill. However, if a skill is defined in broad terms, more than five items may be required to fully assess it.

Tiers 1, 2 and 3: Monitoring Student Progress

6. **Once an intervention has begun, what is the interventionist's responsibility in monitoring students' progress?** When a student receiving an RTI intervention at the Tier 1, 2, or 3 level, the educator implementing that intervention (the interventionist) is expected to monitor the student's progress regularly to judge whether the intervention is effective. It is recommended that the classroom teacher monitor Tier 1 interventions at least once per week. Tier 2 interventions should be monitored 1-2 times per month. Intensive Tier 3 interventions should be monitored at least weekly. The interventionist should measure the student's baseline level in the academic or behavioral target skill before the intervention begins and should also calculate a performance goal that the student will attain by the end of the intervention period if that intervention is successful.

7. **What role does a clear problem identification statement play in student progress-monitoring?** The success of any RTI intervention hinges on a problem-identification statement that describes in crystal-clear terms the student academic or behavioral problem that is to be the focus of the intervention. A clear problem-identification statement can greatly simplify the task of selecting a method of progress-monitoring. For example, a teacher is initially unable to think of a way to measure the Tier 1 progress of a student whose behavioral problem is vaguely defined as "Frank is off-task in class." However, the teacher then restates the student problem as "On 20-minute in-class writing assignments, Frank talks with peers about non-instructional topics and requires an average each session of 3 redirections back to task by the teacher." This teacher discovers in the process of redefining the student problem that she can use the method of tallying the number of times that she has to redirect the student to task to calculate the baseline level of the student problem (an average of 3 teacher redirections

required), to set a student goal for improvement, and even to monitor the student's progress.

8. **Why is it important to determine baseline performance and to set a goal before monitoring the progress of a student on intervention?** Baseline and goal are the two 'bookend' measurements that are essential to allow the classroom teacher or other interventionist to make sense of progress-monitoring data. Before starting the intervention, the interventionist first needs to collect baseline information to calculate the student's starting point on the academic skill or behavior that is the intervention target. With baseline in hand, the interventionist can next set a goal for improvement that the student is expected to reach by the end of the intervention period if that intervention is actually effective. When the intervention concludes, the interventionist can compare the student's actual performance to the goal to determine if the intervention was indeed a success. If an interventionist monitors student progress on intervention but has not both calculated baseline and set an outcome goal, the monitoring data lacks a meaningful context and will be of little use.

9. **How can the student be involved in collecting and interpreting progress-monitoring data?** Giving the student responsibilities in monitoring their progress on intervention can both motivate and teach the student to take greater responsibility for his or her own learning and behavior. One idea is to have students collect their own progress-monitoring data. For example, a student on an intervention to increase homework completion might maintain a homework log, noting each assignment and the date it was turned in. A second idea is to have students set or review the intervention goal and then regularly monitor their progress toward the goal. For example, a teacher who assigns homework every day may meet with a student and set the goal that the student turn in completed homework on time on at least 80 percent of the days (4 days out of five)—a considerable improvement from the student's current 40 percent completion rate. Then every Friday during the intervention period, teacher and student meet briefly to review the student's actual homework completion rate for the week.

RTI Decision Rules

10. **How does a school set data decision rules to judge whether a student is an RTI 'non-responder'?** Districts that have adopted an RTI model must develop their own decision rules for determining whether a general-education student who has received interventions across the Tiers is an RTI 'non-responder'. Those decision rules should include answers to the following questions:

    - What is the minimum length of time that interventions at Tiers 1, 2, & 3 should last? (Recommendation: Interventions at Tier 1 should last at least 4-8 instructional weeks, while those at Tiers 2 and 3 should last at least 6-8 instructional weeks.)

    - What is the minimum number of intervention trials that should be attempted? (Recommendation: Across Tiers 2 and 3, a total of at least 3 separate intervention trials should be attempted before deciding that a student is a non-responder to intervention.)

    Of course, data collected during each intervention trial should be of high quality, with baseline, goal, and regular progress-monitoring.

Exhibit 5-A
Finding Students At-Risk: How to Create a Comprehensive Middle or High School-Wide Screening Plan

Schools can use screening data efficiently to identify those students who are experiencing problems with academic performance, behavior, and attendance. Providing intervention in the beginning stages of middle or high school student's academic or behavioral problems is more likely to be effective and is typically less costly than attempting to intervene when a student's problems have spiraled into full-blown crisis. The purpose of school-wide screening, therefore, is to allow buildings to proactively flag struggling students at an early point and match them to appropriate interventions.

Schools should remember that whole-group screening results are often not sufficient to map out completely what a specific student's skill deficits might be—nor are they designed to do so. Rather, screenings help schools to single out quickly and with the minimum required investment of resources those students who need more intervention assistance. Some students picked up in a screening will require additional, detailed follow-up "instructional assessment" (Hosp, 2008) in order to better understand their learning needs and select appropriate interventions.

There are three general steps to implementing a school-wide screening program in a middle or high school:
1. First, the school must decide on the range of measures or sources of data that will be used to screen their student population.
2. Next, the school must line up the required resources to conduct the screening. This step includes scheduling time for screening measures to be administered and finding personnel to administer, score, and interpret the results of those measures.
3. Finally, the school must build a process for communicating the screening results to classroom teachers and other interventionists, and for using the screening data to identify students who need supplemental (Tier 2 or 3) interventions.

Selecting the Assessment Tools or Sources of Data to Be Used for School-Wide Screening

Schools can make use of several possible types of screening data: existing data on grades, behavior, and attendance; Curriculum-Based Measurement to track basic academic skills; and computerized adaptive measures that help to determine appropriate instructional placement. Those types of screening data are described in greater detail below:

- *Existing data* (Form 1). Schools collect data on student academic performance (grades), behavior (office disciplinary referrals), and attendance (daily attendance report). Measures of grades, behavior, and attendance have been found to predict student drop-out status as early as grade 6 (Balfanz, Herzog, & MacIver, 2007). Existing data (sometimes called 'archival' or 'extant' data) requires limited effort to access (Chafouleas, Riley-Tillman & Sugai, 2007)—because it has already

Exhibit 5-A, continued

been collected—and can be used proactively to find those students who are experiencing problems in school (Steward & Silberglit, 2008). Use of existing data would be appropriate across all middle and high school grades. See Form 1 of this exhibit, *Existing Data: Creating a Screening Plan for Your Middle or High School,* that is structured to help schools to incorporate existing data into their screening plan.

Existing data screening example. A high school monitors its teacher grade reports every five weeks. Students failing at least one course are discussed at weekly instructional team meetings to brainstorm additional Tier 1 (classroom intervention) ideas. Those students are also considered for possible supplemental reading or writing lab (Tier 2) support. Students failing two or more courses are flagged and referred to the building RTI Problem-Solving Team for a comprehensive Tier 3 intervention plan.

- *Curriculum-Based Measurement (CBM).* A series of brief, timed academic tools known as Curriculum-Based Measurement (CBM) have been developed that can assess student mastery of academic skills (Hosp, Hosp, & Howell, 2007). The most widely used types of CBM in middle and high schools are Oral Reading Fluency, Maze (Reading Comprehension), Writing, Math Computation, and Math Concepts & Applications. Schools should give some thought to matching CBMs as screening tools to the demographics of their student populations (Stewart & Silberglit, 2008). A middle school with large numbers of high-performing students, for example, may decide not to screen its 7th grade for the basic academic skill of reading fluency. However, a high school with many students whose reading skills are below grade level may choose to screen its 9th grade for reading fluency. Review Form 2 of this exhibit, *CBM: 'RTI-Ready' Curriculum-Based Measures for Middle and High Schools,* to browse different CBM options suitable to secondary schools, with Internet sources for obtaining these assessment materials.

CBM screening example. A middle school (grades 5-8) decided to use DIBELS Oral Reading Fluency (ORF) CBM probes to screen its 5th and 6th grades three times per year—both to evaluate the quality of its core literacy program and to identify students who need supplemental (Tier 2) reading fluency intervention. After using the ORF probes for one year, the school decided not to extend their use to screen grades 7 and 8, because by the spring screening date in grade 6 the great majority of students were found to be at low risk for reading fluency problems.

- *Computerized Adaptive Measures.* In many middle and high schools, the majority of students have attained fluency in basic academic skills and now face the challenges of a more demanding, advanced instructional curriculum. One solution for schools is to administer adaptive computer assessments that evaluate student curriculum knowledge. Such measures can fill an information gap as students move beyond acquisition of basic academic skills and move into higher level vocabulary,

Exhibit 5-A, continued

concepts, text interpretation, applied problem-solving and specialized knowledge. Look at Form 3 of this exhibit, *Adaptive Computerized Assessments for Middle and High Schools: Example,* to learn more about one type of computerized academic screening tool, the Measures of Academic Progress (MAP).

Computerized adaptive measures screening example. A district housed its combined middle (grades 6-8) and high schools in one building. In addition to other sources of screening information, the school selected a computerized adaptive measure to assess general student academic-curriculum skills in reading and mathematics through the end of grade 10. This information was used to verify the effectiveness of the school's English Language Arts and Mathematics instruction, as well as to flag the handful of students needing additional supplemental (Tier 2 or 3) intervention support.

Expert Guidance in Evaluating Screening/Progress-Monitoring Tools

The National Center on Response to Intervention rates the 'technical adequacy' of commercially available academic screening and progress-monitoring tools. To review their findings, go to: http://www.rti4success.org/chart/progressMonitoring/progressmonitoringtoolschart.htm

References

Balfanz, R., Herzog, L., MacIver, D. J. (2007). Preventing student disengagement and keeping students on the graduation path in urban middle grades schools: Early identification and effective interventions. *Educational Psychologist,* 42, 223–235. .

Chafouleas, S., Riley-Tillman, T.C., & Sugai, G. (2007). *School-based behavioral assessment: Informing intervention and instruction.* New York: Guilford Press.

Hosp, J. L. (2008). Best practices in aligning academic assessment with instruction. In A. Thomas & J. Grimes (Eds.), *Best practices in school psychology V* (pp.363-376). Bethesda, MD: National Association of School Psychologists.

Hosp, M. K., Hosp, J. L., & Howell, K. W. (2007). *The ABCs of CBM.* New York: Guilford Press.

Stewart, L. H. & Silberglit, B. (2008). Best practices in developing academic local norms. In A. Thomas & J. Grimes (Eds.), *Best practices in school psychology V* (pp. 225-242). Bethesda, MD: National Association of School Psychologists.

Exhibit 5-A, Form 1. Existing Data: Creating a Screening Plan for Your Middle or High School

Directions. Existing school information on grades, attendance, and behavior can be used as one source of student screening data (Stewart & Silberglit, 2008). Use this form to select sources of existing data and to decide how that information will be organized for use in screening students.

☐ **Grades.** Teachers focus closely on student grades as indicators of academic success and curriculum mastery.

Grades: What Grade Levels? At what grade level(s) will this information be collected?

Grades Screening Schedule. On what schedule will grades be monitored building-wide? (e.g., at 5-week intervals):

Grade Risk Threshold. What is the threshold at which a grade report will identify a student as being at-risk? (e.g., failing two or more subjects)?

Grades—Person(s) Responsible. Who is responsible for periodically reviewing grades to flag students who fall within the at risk range?

Grades—RTI Actions. What action(s) will be taken for any students identified as at risk because of grades?

- _____
- _____
- _____

☐ **Attendance.** Problems with school attendance are strongly predictive of academic problems and drop-out.

Attendance: What Grade Levels? At what grade level(s) will this information be collected?

Attendance Screening Schedule. On what schedule will attendance be monitored building-wide? (e.g., at 5-week intervals):

Attendance Risk Threshold. What is the threshold at which an attendance report will identify a student as being at-risk? (e.g., missing an average of three or more school days per month with unexcused absence)?

Attendance—Person(s) Responsible. Who is responsible for periodically reviewing attendance data to flag students who fall within the at risk range?

Attendance—RTI Actions. What action(s) will be taken for any students identified as at risk because of attendance?

- _____
- _____
- _____

☐ **Behavior.** Office disciplinary referrals provide relevant information about problem school behaviors.

Behavior: What Grade Levels? At what grade level(s) will this information be collected?

Behavior Screening Schedule. On what schedule will office disciplinary referrals be monitored building-wide? (e.g., at 5-week intervals):

Behavior Risk Threshold. What is the threshold at which frequency or type of disciplinary referrals will identify a student as being at-risk? (e.g., 2 or more disciplinary referrals of any kind per month)?

Behavior—Person(s) Responsible. Who is responsible for periodically reviewing disciplinary data to flag students who fall within the at risk range?

Behavior RTI Actions. What action(s) will be taken for any students identified as at risk because of discipline?

- _____
- _____
- _____

Stewart, L. H. & Silberglit, B. (2008). Best practices in developing academic local norms. In A. Thomas & J. Grimes (Eds.), *Best practices in school psychology V* (pp. 225–242). Bethesda, MD: National Association of School Psychologists.

Exhibit 5-A, Form 2. CBM: 'RTI-Ready' Curriculum-Based Measures for Middle and High Schools

Directions: Select those CBM measures below to be used in your school-wide screening. Select also the grades and screening points during the school year when each selected measure will be administered. ('F'= Fall, 'W' = Winter, 'S' = Spring).

☐ **CBM Oral Reading Fluency**

GR	5	6	7	8	9	10	11	12
	F|W|S	F|W|S	F|W|S	F|W|S	F|W|S	F|W|S	F|W|S	F|W|S

Time: 1 minute
Administration: 1:1
Description: The student reads aloud from a passage and is scored for fluency and accuracy. Passages are controlled for level of reading difficulty.

Online Sources for This Measure

- AimsWeb (http://www.aimsweb.com/). [Pay]. Site has both English and Spanish reading probes.
- DIBELS (https://dibels.org/next/index.php).[Free].
- Easy CBM (http://www.easycbm.com/).[Free for individual teachers; subscription pricing available to school districts].
- EdCheckup (http://www.edcheckup.com/). [Pay].
- iSteep (http://www.isteep.com/). [Pay].
- Intervention Central (http://www.rti2.org/rti2/oralReadings). [Free]. Application that creates an oral reading fluency probe based on text supplied by the user.

☐ **CBM Maze (Reading Comprehension)**

GR	5	6	7	8	9	10	11	12
	F|W|S	F|W|S	F|W|S	F|W|S	F|W|S	F|W|S	F|W|S	F|W|S

Time: 1-3 minutes
Administration: Group
Description: The student is given a passage in which every 7th word has been removed. The student reads the passage silently. Each time the student comes to a removed word, the student chooses from among 3 replacement words: the correct word and two distractors. The student circles the replacement word that he or she believes best restores the meaning of the text.

Online Sources for This Measure

- AimsWeb (http://www.aimsweb.com/). [Pay].
- EdCheckup (http://www.edcheckup.com/). [Pay].
- iSteep (http://www.isteep.com/). [Pay].
- Intervention Central (http://www.rti2.org/rti2/mazes).[Free]. Application that creates a maze passage probe based on text typed in by the user.
- Yearly ProgressPro (http://www.ctb.com/yearlyprogresspro). [Pay]. Computer-delivered Maze passages.

Exhibit 5-A, Form 2, continued

☐ CBM Writing
Time: 4 minutes
Administration: Group

GR	5	6	7	8	9	10	11	12
	F W S	F W S	F W S	F W S	F W S	F W S	F W S	F W S

Description: The student is given a story starter as a writing prompt. The student spends one minute thinking about the story starter topic, then has 3 minutes to write the story. The CBM writing probe offers three scoring options: Total Number of Words Written, Correctly Spelled Words, and Correct Writing Sequences (a scoring approach that takes into account the mechanics and conventions of writing such as punctuation, spelling, capitalization, and correct semantic and syntactic usage).

Online Sources for This Measure
- AimsWeb (http://www.aimsweb.com/). [Pay].
- EdCheckup (http://www.edcheckup.com/). [Pay].
- Intervention Central (http://www.rti2.org/rti2/writtenExpressions). [Free]. Application that creates a writing probe using pre-entered story starters or text typed in by the user.

☐ CBM Math Computation
Time: 2 minutes
Administration: Group

GR	5	6	7	8	9	10	11	12
	F W S	F W S	F W S	F W S	F W S	F W S	F W S	F W S

Description: The student is given a worksheet with math computation problems. The worksheet may be a single-skill probe (all problems of a single type) or a mixed-skill probe (several different problem types). The completed worksheet is scored for the number of Correct Digits (digits in student answers that are of the correct value and appear in the correct place-value location).

Online Sources for This Measure
- AimsWeb (http://www.aimsweb.com/). [Pay].
- EdCheckup (http://www.edcheckup.com/). [Pay].
- iSteep (http://www.isteep.com/). [Pay].
- Intervention Central (http://www.rti2.org/rti2/writtenExpressions). [Free]. Application that creates a writing probe using pre-entered story starters or text typed in by the user.
- Yearly ProgressPro (http://www.ctb.com/yearlyprogresspro). [Pay].

Exhibit 5-A, Form 2, continued

☐ **CBM Math Concepts & Applications**

GR	5			6			7			8			9			10			11			12		
	F	W	S	F	W	S	F	W	S	F	W	S	F	W	S	F	W	S	F	W	S	F	W	S

Time: 8–10 minutes
Administration: Group
Description: The student is given a worksheet (or completes an online assessment) that contains a mix of applied math problems that are tied to larger concepts (e.g., to the Math Focal Points from the National Council of Teachers of Mathematics.

Online Sources for This Measure
- AimsWeb (http://www.aimsweb.com/). [Pay].
- Easy CBM (http://www.easycbm.com/). [Free for individual teachers; subscription pricing available to school districts]. Student probes can be completed online.
- iSteep (http://www.isteep.com/). [Pay].
- Yearly ProgressPro (http://www.ctb.com/yearlyprogresspro). [Pay]. Computer-delivered assessments.

Chapter 5 • Using Data to Guide RTI: Screening, Instructional Assessment, and Progress-Monitoring 179

Exhibit 5-A, Form 3 Adaptive Computerized Assessments for Middle and High Schools: Example

A screening approach that is becoming increasingly popular for middle and high schools is to assess students' academic skills relative to curriculum expectations. Such measures can fill an information gap as students move beyond acquisition of basic academic skills and move into higher level vocabulary, concepts, text interpretation, applied problem-solving and specialized knowledge. An example of a computerized, adaptive curriculum-skills assessment is the Measures of Academic Progress (MAP) system (http://www.nwea.org), described below.

Directions: Select when a measure like the MAP would be used in your school-wide screening. Select also the grades and screening points during the school year when each selected measure will be administered. ('F' = Fall, 'W' = Winter, 'S' = Spring).

☐ CBM Measures of Academic Progress (MAP)	GR	5	6	7	8	9	10	11	12
		F W S	F W S	F W S	F W S	F W S	F W S	F W S	F W S

Time: Untimed
Administration: Computer-administered
Description (taken from MAP basics overview, 2009): The student can complete any one of four computer assessment modules: Reading, Language Usage, Mathematics, or Science. The assessments are untimed. The MAP program is adaptive: students are dynamically presented with new assessment items based on their previous responses. The purpose of MAP is to find students' optimal 'instructional level' rather than to demonstrate content mastery. MAP assessments can be administered 3-4 times per year. The MAP system also provides expected growth rates for students and can predict student performance on state tests based on MAP scores.

Online Sources for This Measure
- Northwest Evaluation Association (http://www.nwea.org)

Reference

Measures of Academic Progress™ (MAP) basics overview (2009). Lake Oswego, OR: Northwest Evaluation Association. Retrieved from http://www.nwea.org/sites/www.nwea.org/files/resources/MAP%20Basics_Overview.pdf

Exhibit 5-B
The RIOT/ICEL Matrix: Organizing Data to Answer Questions About Student Academic Performance & Behavior

When a student displays serious academic or behavioral deficits, the Response to Intervention model adopts an inductive approach that begins with educators collecting a range of information to better analyze and understand the student's intervention needs (Fuchs, Fuchs & Compton, 2010).

However, this investigative RTI problem-solving approach can be compromised at the outset in several ways (Hosp, 2008). For example, educators may draw from too few sources when pulling together information about the presenting problem(s)—e.g., relying primarily on interviews with one classroom teacher—which can bias the findings. Also, educators may not consider the full range of possible explanations for the student's academic or behavioral problems—such as instructional factors or skill-deficits—and thus fail to collect information that would confirm or rule out those competing hypotheses. And finally, educators may simply not realize when they have reached the 'saturation point' in data collection (Hosp, 2008) when stockpiling still more data will not significantly improve the understanding of the student problem.

One tool that can assist schools in their quest to sample information from a broad range of sources and to investigate all likely explanations for student academic or behavioral problems is the RIOT/ICEL matrix. This matrix helps schools to work efficiently and quickly to decide what relevant information to collect on student academic performance and behavior—and also how to organize that information to identify probable reasons why the student is not experiencing academic or behavioral success.

The RIOT/ICEL Matrix, Form 1, is not itself a data collection instrument. Instead, it is an organizing framework, or heuristic, that increases schools' confidence both in the quality of the data that they collect and the findings that emerge from the data (Hosp, 2006, May). The top horizontal row of the RIOT/ICEL table includes four potential sources of student information: **R**eview, **I**nterview, **O**bservation, and **T**est (RIOT). Schools should attempt to collect information from a range of sources to control for potential bias from any one source.

The leftmost vertical column of the RIOT/ICEL table includes four key domains of learning to be assessed: **I**nstruction, **C**urriculum, **E**nvironment, and **L**earner (ICEL). A common mistake that schools often make is to assume that student learning problems exist primarily in the learner and to underestimate the degree to which teacher instructional strategies, curriculum demands, and environmental influences impact the learner's academic performance. The ICEL elements ensure that a full range of relevant explanations for student problems are examined.

Select Multiple Sources of Information: RIOT. The elements that make up the top horizontal row of the RIOT/ICEL table (**R**eview, **I**nterview, **O**bservation, and **T**est) are defined as follows:

Exhibit 5-B, continued

- **Review.** This category consists of past or present records collected on the student. Obvious examples include report cards, office disciplinary referral data, state test results, and attendance records. Less obvious examples include student work samples, physical products of teacher interventions (e.g., a sticker chart used to reward positive student behaviors), and emails sent by a teacher to a parent detailing concerns about a student's study and organizational skills.

- **Interview.** Interviews can be conducted face-to-face, via telephone, or even through email correspondence. Interviews can also be structured (that is, using a pre-determined series of questions) or follow an open-ended format, with questions guided by information supplied by the respondent. Interview targets can include those teachers, paraprofessionals, administrators, and support staff in the school setting who have worked with or had interactions with the student in the present or past. Prospective interview candidates can also consist of parents and other relatives of the student as well as the student himself or herself.

- **Observation.** Direct observation of the student's academic skills, study and organizational strategies, degree of attentional focus, and general conduct can be a useful channel of information. Observations can be more structured (e.g., tallying the frequency of call-outs or calculating the percentage of on-task intervals during a class period) or less structured (e.g., observing a student and writing a running narrative of the observed events). Obvious examples of observation include a teacher keeping a frequency count of the times that she redirects an inattentive student to task during a class period and a school psychologist observing the number of times that a student talks with peers during independent seatwork Less obvious examples of observation include having a student periodically rate her own academic engagement on a 3-point scale (self-evaluation) and encouraging a parent to send to school narrative observations of her son's typical routine for completing homework.

- **Test.** Testing can be thought of as a structured and standardized observation of the student that is intended to test certain hypotheses about why the student might be struggling and what school supports would logically benefit the student (Christ, 2008). Obvious examples of testing include a curriculum-based measurement Oral Reading Fluency probe administered to determine a student's accuracy and fluency when reading grade-level texts and a state English Language Arts test that evaluates students' mastery of state literacy standards. A less obvious example of testing might be a teacher who teases out information about the student's skills and motivation on an academic task by having that student complete two equivalent timed worksheets under identical conditions—except that the student is offered an incentive for improved performance on the second worksheet but not on the first ('Can't Do/Won't Do Assessment'). Another less obvious example of testing might be a student who has developed the capacity to take chapter pre-tests in her math book, to self-grade the test, and to write down questions and areas of confusion revealed by that test for later review with the math instructor.

Exhibit 5-B, continued

Investigate Multiple Factors Affecting Student Learning: ICEL. The elements that compose the leftmost vertical column of the RIO/ICEL table (**I**nstruction, **C**urriculum, **E**nvironment, and **L**earner) are described below:

- **Instruction.** The purpose of investigating the 'instruction' domain is to uncover any instructional practices that either help the student to learn more effectively or interfere with that student's learning. More obvious instructional questions to investigate would be whether specific teaching strategies for activating prior knowledge better prepare the student to master new information or whether a student benefits optimally from the large-group lecture format that is often used in a classroom. A less obvious example of an instructional question would be whether a particular student learns better through teacher-delivered or self-directed, computer-administered instruction.

- **Curriculum.** 'Curriculum' represents the full set of academic skills that a student is expected to have mastered in a specific academic area at a given point in time. To adequately evaluate a student's acquisition of academic skills, of course, the educator must: (1) know the school's curriculum (and related state academic performance standards); (2) be able to inventory the specific academic skills that the student currently possesses; and then (3) identify gaps between curriculum expectations and actual student skills. (This process of uncovering student academic skill gaps is sometimes referred to as 'instructional' or 'analytic' assessment.) More obvious examples of curriculum questions include checking whether a student knows how to compute a multiplication problem with double-digit terms and regrouping or whether that student knows key facts about the Civil War. A less obvious curriculum-related question might be whether a student possesses the full range of essential academic vocabulary (e.g., terms such as 'hypothesis') required for success in the grade 10 curriculum.

- **Environment.** The 'environment' includes any factors in students' school, community, or home surroundings that can directly enable their academic success or hinder that success. Obvious questions about environmental factors that impact learning include whether a student's educational performance is better or worse in the presence of certain peers and whether having additional adult supervision during a study hall results in higher student work productivity. Less obvious questions about the learning environment include whether a student has a setting at home that is conducive to completing homework or whether chaotic hallway conditions are delaying that student's transitioning between classes and therefore reducing available learning time.

- **Learner.** While the student is at the center of any questions of instruction, curriculum, and [learning] environment, the 'learner' domain includes those qualities of the student that represent their unique capacities and traits. More obvious examples of questions that relate to the learner include investigating whether a student has stable and high rates of inattention across different classrooms or evaluating the efficiency of a student's study habits and test-taking skills. A less obvious example of a question that relates to the

Exhibit 5-B, continued

learner is whether a student harbors a low sense of self-efficacy in mathematics that is interfering with that learner's willingness to put appropriate effort into math courses.

Integrating the RIOT/ICEL Matrix into a Building's Problem-Solving. The power of the RIOT/ICEL matrix lies in its use as a cognitive strategy, one that helps educators to verify that they have asked the right questions and sampled from a sufficiently broad range of data sources to increase the probability that they will correctly understand the student's presenting concern(s). Viewed in this way, the matrix is not a rigid approach but rather serves as a flexible heuristic for exploratory problem-solving.

At the very least, RTI consultants should find that the RIOT/ICEL matrix serves as a helpful mental framework to guide their problem-solving efforts. And as teachers over time become more familiar with the RTI model, they also might be trained to use the RIOT/ICEL framework as they analyze student problems in their classrooms and prepare Tier 1 interventions. Form 2 provides space for using this model.

References

Christ, T. (2008). Best practices in problem analysis. In A. Thomas & J. Grimes (Eds.), *Best practices in school psychology V* (pp. 159-176). Bethesda, MD: National Association of School Psychologists.

Fuchs L. S., Fuchs, D., and Compton, D. L. (2010). Rethinking response to intervention at middle and high school. *School Psychology Review,* 39, 22-28.

Hosp, J. L. (2006, May) *Implementing RTI: Assessment practices and response to intervention.* NASP Communiqué, 34(7). Retrieved September 8, 2010, from: http://www.nasponline.org/publications/cq/cq347rti.aspx

Hosp, J. L. (2008). Best practices in aligning academic assessment with instruction. In A. Thomas & J. Grimes (Eds.), *Best practices in school psychology V* (pp.363-376). Bethesda, MD: National Association of School Psychologists.

Exhibit 5-B, Form 1

RIOT/ICEL Matrix Example: The matrix below is filled out with some possible sources of information on a student, Rick, whose mathematics teacher is concerned at his apparent *lack of academic engagement in large-group settings*. NOTE: The examples in the matrix are for purposes of illustration only. It is probably somewhat unlikely that all of these sources of information would be collected for a single student, unless his or her needs were intensive.

	Review	Interview	Observe	Test
Instruction	[Review-Instruction] **Review of past report cards:** The teacher searches for comments from former instructors about instructional techniques to which Rick did or did not respond.	[Interview-Instruction] **Teacher interview:** The instructor is asked by the guidance counselor which instructional elements help Rick to attend in large-group instruction and which are less effective.	[Observe-Instruction] **Classroom observation:** During large-group instruction, an observer calculates Rick's rate of on-task behavior (e.g., through momentary time-sampling).	[Test-Instruction] **Note-taking conditions:** The teacher structures two large-group instruction conditions—regular note-taking and guided note —and observes whether Rick's level of academic engagement improves with guided notes.
Curriculum	[Review-Curriculum] **Work products:** The teacher collects the student's math homework and examines it for evidence about whether Rick is able correctly to use the algorithms taught in class.	[Interview-Curriculum] **Student interview:** The guidance counselor meets with Rick to ask him a series of questions about his math skills.	[Observe-Curriculum] **Classroom observation:** The teacher pairs students, directs each to describe to the other his/her reasoning for solving a multi-step word problem with math graphic. Rick is observed during this exercise.	[Test-Curriculum] **Diagnostic test:** The teacher prepares and administers to the class a diagnostic test with problems that test essential foundation math knowledge required for success in the course. Rick's test results are carefully reviewed.
Environment	[Review-Environment] **Folder review:** Rick's cumulative folder is reviewed for past instructor comments about aspects of the instructional environment (e.g., presence or absence of peers, teacher proximity) that helped or hindered academic performance.	[Interview-Environment] **Parent interview:** At a parent conference, the teacher asks Rick's father to describe the student's nightly homework routine, as well as those factors in the homework setting that appear to help or hinder Rick's homework completion.	[Observe-Environment] **Classroom observation:** During observations of Rick in a large-group math setting, the observer looks for environmental factors—e.g., presence or absence of peers, teacher proximity—that help or hinder academic performance.	[Test-Environment] **Peer seating conditions:** On different occasions, the instructor (a) allows Rick to choose his own seat-mates and (b) seats Rick next to positive peer role models. The instructor observes whether Rick's level of academic engagement improves in the peer role-model condition.
Learner	[Review-Learner] **Math journal:** The math teacher collects Rick's math journal and reviews the entries for hints about the student's attitude and level of self-confidence toward mathematics [Learner characteristic: math self-efficacy].	[Interview-Learner] **Parent interview:** In an email exchange with the student's mother, the teacher asks her what her son's study habits [Learner characteristic: study & organizational skills]	[Observe-Learner] **Behavior rating based on observation:** For one week, the math teacher rates the student daily on a behavior report card. One of the several rating items is the student's 'time on task' [Learner characteristic: attentional focus].	[Test-Learner] **Reward conditions:** On different occasions, the teacher (a) has Rick participate in large-group instruction with no reward and (b) offers Rick an incentive (reward) if he requires no more than 1 teacher prompt per session to direct him back to task. The instructor observes whether Rick's engagement increases in the reward condition [Learner characteristic: attentional focus].

Exhibit 5-B, Form 2
RIOT/ICEL Assessment Worksheet

Student: _____ Person Completing Worksheet: _____

Date: _____ Statement of Student Problem: _____

Directions: Fill out the grid below to develop an assessment plan for the targeted student.

	Review	Interview	Observe	Test
Instruction				
Curriculum				
Environment				
Learner				

Exhibit 5-C
'Academic Enabler' Observational Checklists: Measuring Students' Ability to Manage Their Own Learning

Student academic success requires more than content knowledge or mastery of a collection of cognitive strategies. Academic accomplishment depends also on a set of ancillary skills and attributes called 'academic enablers' (DiPerna, 2006). Examples of academic enablers include:

- Study skills
- Homework completion
- Cooperative learning skills
- Organization
- Independent seatwork

Because academic enablers are often described as broad skill sets, however, they can be challenging to define in clear, specific, measureable terms. A useful method for defining a global academic enabling skill is to break it down into a checklist of component sub-skills-- a process known as 'discrete categorization' (Kazdin, 1989). An observer can then use the checklist to note whether a student successfully displays each of the sub-skills.

Observational checklists that define academic enabling skills have several uses in Response to Intervention:

- Classroom teachers can use these skills checklists as convenient tools to assess whether a student possesses the minimum 'starter set' of academic enabling skills needed for classroom success.

- Teachers or tutors can share examples of academic-enabler skills checklists with students, training them in each of the sub-skills and encouraging them to use the checklists independently to take greater responsibility for their own learning.

- Teachers or other observers can use the academic enabler checklists periodically to monitor student progress during interventions—assessing formatively whether the student is using more of the sub-skills.

A collection of the most common global 'academic enabler' skills in ready-made checklist format appear below.

Exhibit 5-C, continued

Study Skills. The student...		
☐ takes complete, organized class notes in legible form and maintains them in one accessible note book.	Poor Fair Good NA 1 2 3 —
☐ reviews class notes frequently (e.g., after each class) to ensure understanding.	Poor Fair Good NA 1 2 3 —
☐ when reviewing notes, uses highlighters, margin notes, or other strategies to note questions or areas of confusion for later review with teacher or tutor.	Poor Fair Good NA 1 2 3 —
☐ follows an efficient strategy to study for tests and quizzes.	Poor Fair Good NA 1 2 3 —
☐ allocates enough time to study for tests and quizzes.	Poor Fair Good NA 1 2 3 —
☐ is willing to seek help from the teacher to answer questions or clear up areas of confusion.	Poor Fair Good NA 1 2 3 —
☐ Other: _____	Poor Fair Good NA 1 2 3 —
Comments: _____	

Organization Skills. The student...		
☐ arrives to class on time.	Poor Fair Good NA 1 2 3 —
☐ maintains organization of locker to allow student to efficiently store and retrieve needed books/assignments/work materials/personal belongings.	Poor Fair Good NA 1 2 3 —
☐ maintains organization of backpack or book bag to allow student to efficiently store and retrieve needed books/assignments/work materials/personal belongings.	Poor Fair Good NA 1 2 3 —
☐ brings to class the necessary work materials expected for the course (e.g., pen, paper, calculator, etc.).	Poor Fair Good NA 1 2 3 —
☐ is efficient in switching work materials when transitioning from one in-class learning activity to another.	Poor Fair Good NA 1 2 3 —
☐ Other: _____	Poor Fair Good NA 1 2 3 —
Comments: _____	Poor Fair Good NA 1 2 3 —

Exhibit 5-C, continued

Homework Completion. The student...				
☐ writes down homework assignments accurately and completely.	Poor 1	Fair 2	Good 3	NA —
☐ makes use of available time in school (e.g., study halls, homeroom) to work on homework.	Poor 1	Fair 2	Good 3	NA —
☐ has an organized, non-distracting workspace available at home to do homework.	Poor 1	Fair 2	Good 3	NA —
☐ creates a work plan before starting homework (e.g., sequencing the order in which assignments are to be completed; selecting the most challenging assignment to start first when energy and concentration are highest).	Poor 1	Fair 2	Good 3	NA —
☐ when completing homework, uses highlighters, margin notes, or other strategies to note questions or areas of confusion for later review with teacher or tutor.	Poor 1	Fair 2	Good 3	NA —
☐ turns in homework on time.	Poor 1	Fair 2	Good 3	NA —
☐ Other: _____	Poor 1	Fair 2	Good 3	NA —
Comments: _____				

Cooperative Learning Skills. The student...				
☐ participates in class discussion.	Poor 1	Fair 2	Good 3	NA —
☐ gets along with others during group/pair activities.	Poor 1	Fair 2	Good 3	NA —
☐ participates fully in group/pair activities.	Poor 1	Fair 2	Good 3	NA —
☐ does his or her 'fair share' of work during group/pair activities.	Poor 1	Fair 2	Good 3	NA —
☐ is willing to take a leadership position during group/pair activities.	Poor 1	Fair 2	Good 3	NA —
☐ Other: _____	Poor 1	Fair 2	Good 3	NA —
Comments: _____				

Exhibit 5-C, continued

Independent Seat Work. The student...		
☐ has necessary work materials for the assignment.	Poor Fair Good NA 1 2 3 —
☐ is on-task during the assignment at a level typical for students in the class.	Poor Fair Good NA 1 2 3 —
☐ refrains from distracting behaviors (e.g., talking with peers without permission, pen tapping, vocalizations such as loud sighs or mumbling, etc.).	Poor Fair Good NA 1 2 3 —
☐ recognizes when he or she needs teacher assistance and is willing to that assistance.	Poor Fair Good NA 1 2 3 —
☐ requests teacher assistance in an appropriate manner.	Poor Fair Good NA 1 2 3 —
☐ requests assistance from the teacher only when really needed.	Poor Fair Good NA 1 2 3 —
☐ if finished with the independent assignment before time expires, uses remaining time to check work or engage in other academic activity allowed by teacher.	Poor Fair Good NA 1 2 3 —
☐ takes care in completing work—as evidenced by the quality of the finished assignment.	Poor Fair Good NA 1 2 3 —
☐ is reliable in turning in assignments done in class.	Poor Fair Good NA 1 2 3 —
☐ Other: _____	Poor Fair Good NA 1 2 3 —
Comments: _____	

Motivation. The student...	
☐ has a positive sense of 'self-efficacy' about the academic content area (self-efficacy can be defined as the confidence that one can be successful in the academic discipline or subject matter if one puts forth reasonable effort).	Poor Fair Good NA 1 2 3 —
☐ displays some apparent intrinsic motivation to engage in course work (e.g., is motivated by topics and subject matter discussed or covered in the course; finds the act of working on course assignments to be reinforcing in its own right).	Poor Fair Good NA 1 2 3 —
☐ displays apparent extrinsic motivation to engage in course work (e.g., is motivated by grades, praise, public recognition of achievement, access to privileges such as sports eligibility, or other rewarding outcomes).	Poor Fair Good NA 1 2 3 —
☐ Other: _____	Poor Fair Good NA 1 2 3 —
Comments: _____	

Exhibit 5-C, continued

Teacher-Defined Academic Enabling Skill:

Skill Name: _____

Essential Subskills: The student::

| ☐ _____ | Poor Fair Good NA |
| | 1   2   3   — |

| ☐ _____ | Poor Fair Good NA |
| | 1   2   3   — |

| ☐ _____ | Poor Fair Good NA |
| | 1   2   3   — |

| ☐ _____ | Poor Fair Good NA |
| | 1   2   3   — |

| ☐ _____ | Poor Fair Good NA |
| | 1   2   3   — |

| ☐ _____ | Poor Fair Good NA |
| | 1   2   3   — |

Comments:

References

DiPerna, J. C. (2006). Academic enablers and student achievement: Implications for assessment and intervention services in the schools. *Psychology in the Schools,* 43, 7-17.

Kazdin, A. E. (1989). *Behavior modification in applied settings* (4th ed.). Pacific Gove, CA: Brooks/Cole.

Exhibit 5-D
Teacher-Friendly Methods to Monitor Tier 1 (Classroom) Interventions

	NOTES
Teacher Directions: Review the methods below for collecting progress-monitoring data to evaluate Tier 1 (classroom) interventions. Select one or more of these methods to monitor your student.	
☐ *Existing data.* The teacher uses information already being collected in the classroom or school that is relevant to the identified student problem. Examples of existing data include grades, attendance/tardy records, office disciplinary referrals, homework completion. NOTE: Existing data is often not sufficient alone to monitor a student on intervention but can be a useful *supplemental* source of data on academic or behavioral performance.	
☐ *Global skill checklist.* The teacher selects a global skill (e.g., homework completion; independent seatwork). The teacher then breaks the global skill down into a checklist of component sub-skills--a process known as 'discrete categorization' (Kazdin, 1989). An observer (e.g., teacher, another adult, or even the student) can then use the checklist to note whether a student successfully displays each of the sub-skills on a given day. Classroom teachers can use these checklists as convenient tools to assess whether a student has the minimum required range of academic enabling skills for classroom success. Teachers or tutors may also want to review these checklists with students and encourage them to use the checklists independently to take greater responsibility for their own learning.	
☐ *Behavioral Frequency Count/Behavioral Rate.* In a behavioral frequency count, an observer (e.g., the teacher) watches a student's behavior and keeps a cumulative tally of the number of times that the behavior is observed during a given period. Behaviors that are best measured using frequency counts have clearly observable beginning and end points—and are of relatively short duration. Examples include student call-outs, requests for teacher help during independent seatwork, and raising one's hand to make a contribution to large-group discussion. Teachers can collect data on the frequency of observed student behaviors during a class period in several ways: (1) by keeping a cumulative mental tally of the behaviors; (2) by recording behaviors on paper (e.g., as tally marks) as they occur; or (3) using a golf counter or other simple mechanical device to record observed behaviors. When multiple observations are made of student behaviors, those observations often last for differing periods of time. One method to standardize the results of observations conducted over varying timespans is to convert the results of each observation to a behavioral rate (behaviors divided by the length of the observation). To compute a behavioral rate, the observer (1) sums the total number of behaviors observed and (2) divides the total number of behaviors observed by total minutes in the observation period. The resulting figure represents a standardized 'behaviors observed per minute' and can be compared directly to student behavior rates observed at other times. For example, an observer may have noted that a student engaged in 5 call-outs during a 10-minute observation period. The observer then divides the 5 callouts by the 10 minute observation timespan to compute a standardized behavior rate of 0.5 callouts per minute.	

Exhibit 5-D, continued

	NOTES
☐ **Rating scales.** A scale is developed with one or more items that a rater can use to complete a global rating of a behavior. Often the rating scale is completed at the conclusion of a fixed observation period (e.g., after each class period; at the end of the school day). Here is an example of a rating scale item: *Brian focused his attention on teacher instructions, classroom lessons and assigned work. 1=Poor; 2=Fair; 3=Good.* NOTE: One widely used example of rating scales routinely used in classrooms is the daily behavior report (DBR) (Chafouleas, Riley-Tillman & Sugai, 2007). The teacher completes a 3- to 4-item rating scale each day evaluating various target student behaviors. Teachers can also create their own customized Daily Behavior Reports online. The Behavior Reporter is a free web-based application that allows educators to select and edit existing behavior rating items from a database or to write their own. This application can be accessed at: http://www.interventioncentral.org.	
☐ **Academic Skills: Cumulative Mastery Log.** During academic interventions in which the student is presented with a specific and limited pool of items (e.g., vocabulary terms for a biology course or entries in the Periodic Table of the Elements for a chemistry course), the instructor can track the impact of the intervention by recording and dating mastered items in a cumulative log. First, the instructor defines the set of academic items to be taught or reviewed during the intervention. Next, the instructor sets criteria for judging when the student has mastered a particular item from the academic item set. (Example: "A biology vocabulary item is considered mastered when the student supplies the correct definition within 3 seconds of being shown the term on a flashcard."). To collect baseline information, the instructor reviews all items from the academic-item set with the student, recording items the student already knows. Then, throughout the intervention, the instructor logs and dates additional items as they are mastered by the student.	
☐ **Work Products.** Student work products can be collected and evaluated to judge whether the student is incorporating information taught in the course, applying cognitive strategies that they have been taught, or remediating academic delays. Examples of work products are math computation worksheets, journal entries, and written responses to end-of-chapter questions from the course textbook. Whenever teachers collect academic performance data on a student, it is recommended that they also assess the performance of typical peers in the classroom. Peer performance information allows the teacher directly to estimate and to track the skill gap that separates the target student from others in the class who are not having academic difficulties. Teachers should select students to serve as 'comparison peers' whose skills represent the class average. Work products can be assessed in several ways to yield objective numeric data, depending on the nature of the identified student problem. The teacher can estimate the percentage of work completed on an assignment, for example, as well as the accuracy of the work actually completed. Additionally, the instructor may decide to rate the student's work for quality, using a rubric or other qualitative evaluation approach.	

Exhibit 5-D, continued

	NOTES
☐ ***Behavior Log.*** Behavior logs are narrative 'incident reports' that the teacher records about problem student behaviors. Behavior logs are most useful for tracking problem behaviors that are serious but do not occur frequently. The teacher makes a log entry each time that a behavior is observed. An advantage of behavior logs is that they can provide information about the context within which a behavior occurs.(Disciplinary office referrals are a specialized example of a behavior log.) A behavior log would typically note the date, start time, and end time of a behavioral incident, a brief narrative of the incident (including people involved, the activity, possible triggers to the student problem behavior, a description of the student problem behavior, and the outcome of the incident).	
☐ ***Curriculum-Based Measurement.*** Curriculum-Based Measurement (CBM) is a family of brief, timed measures that assess basic academic skills. CBMs have been developed to assess a considerable number of academic competencies, including oral reading fluency, reading comprehension, math computation, and written expression. Among advantages of using CBM for classroom assessment are that these measures are quick and efficient to administer; align with the curriculum of most schools; have good 'technical adequacy' as academic assessments; and use standard procedures to prepare materials, administer, and score (Hosp, Hosp & Howell, 2007). NOTE: Schools can find a comprehensive web directory of free or low-cost Curriculum-Based Measurement resources on CBM Warehouse at: http://www.interventioncentral.org/index.php/cbm-warehouse	

References

Chafouleas, S., Riley-Tillman, T.C., & Sugai, G. (2007). *School-based behavioral assessment: Informing intervention and instruction.* New York: Guilford Press.

Hosp, M. K., Hosp, J. L., & Howell, K. W. (2007). *The ABCs of CBM.* New York: Guilford Press.

Kazdin, A. E. (1989). *Behavior modification in applied settings* (4th ed.). Pacific Gove, CA: Brooks/Cole.

Exhibit 5-E
RTI Classroom Progress-Monitoring Worksheet: Guidelines

Academic and behavioral interventions under RTI are incomplete without data being collected to document whether those interventions are actually benefiting students. Indeed, an RTI intervention can be viewed as 'fatally flawed' (Witt, VanDerHeyden & Gilbertson, 2004) if it lacks any one of these data elements: (1) clear definition of the presenting student problem(s); (2) calculation of the student's starting point, or baseline performance, in the identified area of concern; (3) setting of a specific goal for student improvement; or (4) selection of a method to monitor the student's progress formatively during the intervention to judge whether the intervention is successful in helping the student to attain the goal. Clearly defining the student problem and collecting data are essential to implementing any school-based intervention.

As general education teachers are often the 'first responders' who provide classroom interventions under RTI, they need to know how to set up a data collection plan that includes baseline, goal, and progress-monitoring. Instructors, however, can find the task of data collection to be daunting—unless they are provided with a step-by-step tutorial in how to do so.

How to Use the *RTI Classroom Progress-Monitoring Worksheet*

As teachers adopt the role of RTI classroom 'first responder' interventionist, they are likely to need assistance—at least initially—with the multi-step process of setting up and implementing data collection, as well as interpreting the resulting data. Form 1 of this exhibit, *RTI Classroom Progress-Monitoring Worksheet*, is designed to walk teachers through the data-collection process—The *Worksheet* includes a seven-step 'wizard' form to help teachers in structuring their progress-monitoring. Here are the essential steps from the *Worksheet* that teachers should follow to ensure that their data collection is adequate to the task of measuring the impact of their classroom interventions:

A. *Identify the student problem.* The teacher defines the student problem in clear, specific terms that allow the instructor to select an appropriate source of classroom assessment to measure and monitor the problem.

B. *Select a data collection method.* The teacher chooses a method for collecting data that can be managed in the classroom setting and that will provide useful information about the student problem. Examples of data collection methods are curriculum-based measurement (e.g., oral reading fluency; correct writing sequences), behavior-frequency counts, and direct behavior report cards. When selecting a data collection method, the teacher also decides how frequently that data will be collected during intervention progress-monitoring. In some cases, the method of data collection being used will dictate monitoring frequency. For example, if homework completion and accuracy is being tracked, the frequency of data collection will be equal to the frequency of homework assignments. In other cases, the level of severity of the student problem will dictate monitoring frequency. Students on Tier 2 (standard-protocol) interventions should be monitored 1-2 times per month, for example, while students on Tier 3 (inten-

Exhibit 5-E, continued

sive problem-solving protocol) interventions should be monitored at least weekly (Burns & Gibbons, 2008).

C. *Collect data to calculate baseline.* The teacher should collect 3-5 data-points prior to starting the intervention to calculate the student's baseline, or starting point, in the skill or behavior that is being targeted for intervention. The student's baseline performance serves as an initial marker against which to compare his or her outcome performance at the end of the intervention. (Also,--because baseline data points are collected prior to the start of the intervention--they collectively can serve as an indication of the trend, or rate of improvement, if the student's program remains unchanged and no additional interventions are attempted.). In calculating baseline, the teacher has the option of selecting the median, or middle, data-point, or calculating the mean baseline performance.

D. *Determine the timespan of the intervention.* The length of time reserved for the intervention should be sufficient to allow enough data to be collected to clearly demonstrate whether that intervention was successful. For example, it is recommended that a high-stakes intervention last at least 8 instructional weeks (e.g., Burns & Gibbons, 2008).

E. *Set a performance goal.* The teacher calculates a goal for the student that, if attained by the end of the intervention period, will indicate that the intervention was successful.

F. *Decide how student progress is to be summarized.* A decision that the teacher must make prior to the end of the intervention period is how he or she will summarize the actual progress-monitoring data. Because of the variability present in most data, the instructor will probably not elect simply to use the final data point as the best estimate of student progress. Better choices are to select several (e.g. 3) of the final data points and either select the median value or calculate a mean value. For charted data with trendline, the teacher may calculate the student's final performance level as the value of the trendline at the point at which it intercepts the intervention end-date.

G. *Evaluate the intervention outcome.* At the conclusion of the intervention, the teacher directly compares the actual student progress (summarized in the previous step) with the goal originally set. If actual student progress meets or exceeds the goal, the intervention is judged to be successful.

References

Burns, M. K., & Gibbons, K. A. (2008). *Implementing response-to-intervention in elementary and secondary schools.* Routledge: New York.

Witt, J. C., VanDerHeyden, A. M., & Gilbertson, D. (2004). Troubleshooting behavioral interventions. A systematic process for finding and eliminating problems. *School Psychology Review,* 33, 363-383.

Exhibit 5-E, Form 1
RTI Classroom Progress-Monitoring Worksheet

Student: _____ Teacher: _____ Classroom/Course: _____

SET-UP

A. **Identify the Student Problem:** Describe in clear, specific terms the student academic or behavioral problem: _____

B. **Select a Data Collection Method:** Choose a method of data collection to measure whether the classroom intervention actually improves the identified student problem (e.g., curriculum-based measurement, etc.). _____

How frequently will this data be collected?: _____ times per _____

BASELINE

C. **Collect Data to Calculate Baseline:** What method from the choices below will be used to estimate the student's baseline (starting) performance? (NOTE: Generally, at least 3-5 baseline data points are recommended.)

From a total of _____ observations, select the **median** value.
From a total of _____ observations, calculate the **mean** value.
Other: _____

Baseline	3. Date: __/__/__ Obsv: _____
1. Date: __/__/__ Obsv: _____	4. Date: __/__/__ Obsv: _____
2. Date: __/__/__ Obsv: _____	5. Date: __/__/__ Obsv: _____

Baseline Performance: Based on the method selected above, it is calculated that the student's baseline performance is: _____

D. **Determine Intervention Timespan:** The intervention will last _____ instructional weeks and end on __/__/__.

E. **Set a Performance Goal:** What goal is the student expected to achieve if the intervention is successful? At the end of the intervention, it is predicted that the student will reach this performance goal: _____

PROGRESS-MONITORING

F. **Decide How Student Progress is to Be Summarized:** Select a method for summarizing student progress ('outcome') attained when the intervention ends. Student progress at the end of the intervention is to be summarized by:
☐ Selecting the **median** value from the final ____ data-points (e.g., 3).
☐ Computing the **mean** value from the final ____ data-points (e.g., 3).
☐ [For time-series graphs]: Calculating the **value on the graph trend line** at the point that it intercepts the intervention end date.

G. **Evaluate the Intervention Outcome:**
At the end of the intervention, compare student progress to goal. If **actual progress** meets or exceeds **goal**, the intervention is judged successful.

The student's ACTUAL Progress (Step F) is:	
The PERFORMANCE GOAL for improvement (Step E) is:	

Progress-Monitoring	5. Date: __/__/__ Obsv: _____
1. Date: __/__/__ Obsv: _____	6. Date: __/__/__ Obsv: _____
2. Date: __/__/__ Obsv: _____	7. Date: __/__/__ Obsv: _____
3. Date: __/__/__ Obsv: _____	8. Date: __/__/__ Obsv: _____
4. Date: __/__/__ Obsv: _____	9. Date: __/__/__ Obsv: _____

Exhibit 5-E, Form 1, continued

Student: _____ Grade: _____

Teacher: _____ School Year: _____

Progress-Monitoring (cont.)	**Progress-Monitoring** (cont.)
10. Date: ___/___/___ Obsv: _____	30. Date: ___/___/___ Obsv: _____
11. Date: ___/___/___ Obsv: _____	31. Date: ___/___/___ Obsv: _____
12. Date: ___/___/___ Obsv: _____	32. Date: ___/___/___ Obsv: _____
13. Date: ___/___/___ Obsv: _____	33. Date: ___/___/___ Obsv: _____
14. Date: ___/___/___ Obsv: _____	34. Date: ___/___/___ Obsv: _____
15. Date: ___/___/___ Obsv: _____	35. Date: ___/___/___ Obsv: _____
16. Date: ___/___/___ Obsv: _____	36. Date: ___/___/___ Obsv: _____
17. Date: ___/___/___ Obsv: _____	37. Date: ___/___/___ Obsv: _____
18. Date: ___/___/___ Obsv: _____	38. Date: ___/___/___ Obsv: _____
19. Date: ___/___/___ Obsv: _____	39. Date: ___/___/___ Obsv: _____
20. Date: ___/___/___ Obsv: _____	40. Date: ___/___/___ Obsv: _____
21. Date: ___/___/___ Obsv: _____	41. Date: ___/___/___ Obsv: _____
22. Date: ___/___/___ Obsv: _____	42. Date: ___/___/___ Obsv: _____
23. Date: ___/___/___ Obsv: _____	43. Date: ___/___/___ Obsv: _____
24. Date: ___/___/___ Obsv: _____	44. Date: ___/___/___ Obsv: _____
25. Date: ___/___/___ Obsv: _____	45. Date: ___/___/___ Obsv: _____
26. Date: ___/___/___ Obsv: _____	46. Date: ___/___/___ Obsv: _____
27. Date: ___/___/___ Obsv: _____	47. Date: ___/___/___ Obsv: _____
28. Date: ___/___/___ Obsv: _____	48. Date: ___/___/___ Obsv: _____
29. Date: ___/___/___ Obsv: _____	49. Date: ___/___/___ Obsv: _____

Chapter 6
The 'RTI Tipping Point': Making the First Positive Steps Toward Systems-Level Change

Middle and high schools implementing Response to Intervention quickly discover that the RTI model is complex and contains a large number of interlinked components. In the RTI-ready school, for example, 'evidence-based' interventions for struggling students are arranged in a multi-tier continuum; students are matched to intervention services based on profile of need; the integrity of interventions are routinely measured to ensure that they are carried out correctly; data are collected on each intervention to assess baseline levels, set goals for expected improvement, and measure actual student progress; and the school's RTI model is designed to be attainable using existing resources and to be scalable and sustainable over time (Glover & DiPerna, 2007).

As earlier chapters of this book illustrate, full implementation of the RTI represents nothing short of comprehensive schoolwide reform. Yet educators in any building or district charged with rolling out RTI can become so caught up in the thicket of details required to implement the model that they may lose sight of whether they are in fact accomplishing their global objective: to reengineer the school culture and teacher attitudes and realign resources to better support struggling learners. A concept from the social sciences that proves helpful to schools as they push system-wide change through RTI is the *'tipping point'*.

In a social system, a *tipping point* is reached when an attitude or practice that was previously rare in a social system becomes much more widespread—often within a very short period of time (Tipping Point, 2010). A popular recent work on the subject states that "the tipping point is the moment of critical mass, the threshold, the boiling point." (Gladwell, 2000; p. 12).

It is important to note that a tipping point can send a school attempting to implement RTI in either a positive or negative direction. A positive tipping point is reached when the majority of school staff—including administration, teachers, and support personnel—are knowledgeable about the RTI model, understand the specific role that they will play in supporting that model, and believe that RTI can help them to address chronic and stubborn challenges such as raising student academic achievement levels and increasing graduation rates. When this positive tipping point occurs, the school may still have much work to do to implement RTI but can count on staff to work together to overcome all obstacles. Progress toward RTI usually moves much more quickly after the positive tipping point than before.

However, a negative RTI tipping point is also a possible outcome—one that schools should strive at all costs to avoid. Examples of schools at risk of experiencing a negative RTI tipping point are those that do not regularly share RTI information with teachers or seek their input in shaping RTI, continually postpone implementing the most challenging elements of the RTI model, or are run by administrators who show little RTI leadership. When a school reaches a negative tipping point, it may suddenly discover that staff has responded to the vacuum of information, leadership, or meaningful progress toward RTI by withdrawing their support. In buildings where attitudes have crystallized in rejection of RTI, schools have a much, much more difficult task in undoing the damage and enlisting staff to take the responsibility for student interventions and problem-solving that RTI requires.

What follows are five recommendations summarized from earlier sections of this book that can help to nudge the school culture toward a positive RTI tipping point:

1. **Identify a collection of non-negotiable RTI core values.** When schools define a set of core values to support RTI, those values provide a shared reference point for all staff to guide their day-to-day professional conduct. The RTI core values can be thought of as self-evident statements. Below is a starter set of 3 core values that schools will want to adopt to promote acceptance of RTI:

   - *Students who begin to struggle in general education are 'typical'.* When general education students show emerging problems in academic skills or behavior, educators should respond as if these students are typical learners, accepting responsibility to find the instructional or behavior management strategies to unlock the students' potential. When general education teachers see struggling students as teachable, these instructors are more willing to explore various intervention strategies—thus increasing the probability of achieving a good student outcome. They also avoid falling into the trap of believing that common learning problems are inevitably evidence of a special education condition and thus are beyond the ability of the general education teacher to address (Martens, 1993).

   - *Interventions target factors that are 'alterable'.* When engaged in RTI problem-solving, schools can easily become distracted by factors that cannot be changed—such as presumed cognitive ability or factors in that student's home life—that can actually cause well-meaning educators to assume that classroom interventions will not be effective (Howell, Hosp, & Kurns, 2008). A central axiom of RTI is that educators should instead focus their intervention efforts on those factors that can be changed in a school setting, such as instructional materials, elements and pacing of instruction, and student motivation (Burns, VanDerHeyden, & Boice, 2008).

   - *Teacher intervention efforts provide crucial 'protective factors' for at-risk learners.* It is easy for teachers to be discouraged by the many 'risk factors' (e.g., difficult family situation, poverty) that may confront at-risk learners outside of school. Educators should keep in mind, however, that risk factors are only that—factors that can heighten the possibility of student failure but do not guarantee it. An important RTI core belief is that the efforts that teachers make in school to remediate academic or behavioral deficits represent 'protective factors' (Hosp, 2008) that can counterbalance a student's risk factors. In other words, RTI expects that an educator with significant concerns about the potential negative factors that a student faces outside of school is willing to apply correspondingly intensive intervention efforts on behalf of the student during the school day.

2. **Build teacher understanding and support for RTI.** For RTI to be a success, teachers must understand and support the model. It is surprising, however, that many schools seem to treat the task of presenting RTI information to teachers as an afterthought. In fact, communication with teachers about RTI should be a carefully plotted, ongoing campaign (McDougal, Graney, Wright & Ardoin, 2009). The school first defines the essential RTI information that faculty need to know, including specifics about how the general education teacher's role will change under RTI. The school then creates a plan to communicate with teachers about RTI at several points across the school year in both large- and small-group settings to allow participants ample opportunity to ask questions and offer their views and suggestions.

3. **Inventory existing district and school RTI resources.** A central fact about RTI for most school districts is that it must be implemented using existing resources. To establish positive RTI momentum, all resources available to support RTI should be inventoried at the district level and within each school. (Examples of potential RTI resources include published instructional and intervention materials; personnel with flexible schedules who can be tapped to assist with intervention planning or data collection; time during professional

development days to provide RTI training, etc.) When an RTI resource list is developed, the RTI Leadership Team (described below) can consult it to ensure that it is appropriately rolled out and to develop an RTI plan that conforms to the strengths and constraints of the district's educational resources.

4. **Ensure administrative buy-in.** Perhaps the strongest predictor of whether a district will successfully reach a positive RTI tipping point is the presence or absence of administrative support. When a district's leadership supports RTI across all schools, every obstacle can be overcome. When leadership is divided about or does not truly support RTI, the smallest challenge is enough to derail its implementation. Building administrators demonstrate understanding and support for RTI in highly visible ways, such as presenting knowledgeably about RTI to faculty, using job performance reviews as an opportunity to help teachers expand their classroom RTI skill set, and preventing referrals to special education that have not yet gone through all of the expected levels of general education problem-solving. District administrators show that they support RTI by establishing and serving on an RTI Leadership Team that speaks with one voice in designing an RTI model for schools across the district, holding principals accountable for the success of RTI in their respective buildings, and channeling to schools any available district resources such as professional development time or funds for intervention materials.

5. **Create a comprehensive district RTI plan.** Because RTI requires comprehensive change in educational practice at all tiers, there is a risk either that schools may keep postponing implementation as they ponder which elements to put into place first or that they will hastily implement elements of the RTI model piece-meal in a confused and uncoordinated manner. Either of these possible responses is likely to result in poor outcomes and erosion of staff confidence. To ensure a well-choreographed RTI roll-out, it is recommended that districts draft a multi-year RTI plan—one that maps out an RTI roadmap over 3-5 years and is updated yearly

(McDougal, Graney, Wright & Ardoin, 2009). The RTI Plan identifies essential RTI components (e.g., adoption of a schoolwide screening plan; creation of a menu of evidence-based interventions for the use of classroom teachers.) and affixes them to a timeline. The RTI Plan encourages districts and schools to be realistic in their rollout efforts and to move forward at a sustainable pace (Glover & DiPerna, 2007) that is ambitious but also works with the district's actual resources. The multi-year RTI Plan also provides at least some assurance to teachers that the district is serious about RTI and that this initiative will have a shelf life beyond a single year.

In the rush to develop and field their own version of the RTI model, administrative leaders at middle and high schools should not forget that staff understanding and support are paramount to the success of RTI. As a complex social system, a school district or building embarking on an RTI initiative can suddenly 'tip' – with staff deciding to support or resist the significant changes that RTI requires. However, districts can tilt their odds in favor of reaching a positive tipping point if they adopt a core set of RTI principles or axioms to guide staff RTI behavior, build teacher understanding and support for RTI, inventory available resources that can be committed to the RTI rollout, promote strong RTI administrative leadership, and develop a multi-year implementation plan that introduces RTI at an ambitious but sustainable pace.

Two exhibits follow that can assist schools as they move their staff toward a positive 'tipping point' with RTI.

- To help with the crucial first steps in planning (including promoting staff support for RTI), schools can use the forms from Exhibit 6-A, *RTI and Secondary Schools: Planning to Implement 5 Key Elements.*

- In some instances, general education students who fail to make expected academic progress under RTI may be referred for a Special Education evaluation. The use of RTI information to determine Special Education eligibility is beyond the scope of this book. However, a convenient checklist to certify that a student is indeed a 'non-responder' under RTI can be found in Exhibit 6-B,

Evaluating a Student's 'Non-Responder' Status: An RTI Checklist. Districts may wish to use this checklist as one tool to certify that their schools have the necessary RTI infrastructure and decision rules in place to identify reliably students who appear to need more academic assistance than can be provided through general education alone.

References

Burns, M. K., VanDerHeyden, A. M., & Boice, C. H. (2008). Best practices in intensive academic interventions. In A. Thomas & J. Grimes (Eds.), *Best practices in school psychology V* (pp.1151-1162). Bethesda, MD: National Association of School Psychologists.

Gladwell, M. (2000). *The tipping point: How little things can make a big difference.* New York: Little, Brown and Company.

Glover, T. A., & DiPerna, J. C. (2007). Service delivery for response to intervention: Core components and directions for future research. *School Psychology Review,* 36, 526-540.

Hosp, J. L. (2008). Best practices in aligning academic assessment with instruction. In A. Thomas & J. Grimes (Eds.), *Best practices in school psychology V* (pp.363-376). Bethesda, MD: National Association of School Psychologists.

Howell, K. W., Hosp, J. L., & Kurns, S. (2008). Best practices in curriculum-based evaluation. In A. Thomas & J. Grimes (Eds.), *Best practices in school psychology V* (pp.349-362). Bethesda, MD: National Association of School Psychologists.

Martens, B. K. (1993). A case against magical thinking in school-based intervention. *Journal of Educational and Psychological Consultation,* 4(2), 185-189.

McDougal, J. L., Graney, S. B., Wright, J. A., & Ardoin, S. P. (2009). *RTI in practice: A practical guide to implementing effective evidence-based interventions in your school.* New York: John Wiley & Sons.

Tipping point (sociology). (2010, May 24). In *Wikipedia, The Free Encyclopedia.* Retrieved 16:53, June 13, 2010, from http://en.wikipedia.org/w/index.php?title=Tipping_point_(sociology)&oldid=363959671

Exhibit 6-A
RTI and Secondary Schools: Planning to Implement 5 Key Elements

Response to Intervention has a number of interrelated components. This exhibit presents simple forms that highlight five key RTI elements and offer guiding questions that can assist schools as they frame a plan to implement RTI. These five elements can be viewed as important RTI first steps:

Form 1: Build classroom teacher understanding and support for RTI

Form 2: Create teacher capacity to deliver effective classroom (Tier 1) interventions

Form 3: Inventory evidence-based supplemental intervention programs available at Tiers 2 and 3

Form 4: Establish an RTI Problem Solving Team at Tier 3

Form 5: Select measures for universal screening and progress monitoring to evaluate student response to intervention

Use the attached planning forms as one tool to assist in drafting a school or district-wide plan for rolling out RTI.

Exhibit 6-A, Form 1
RTI Plan: Element 1...
Build Classroom Teacher Understanding & Support for RTI

Directions: Read the quote and goal statement below. Then develop an implementation plan for this goal.

> *"Significant and sustained investments in professional development programs [are required] to provide teachers with the array of skills required to effectively implement RTI as well as to deal with ongoing staff turnover."*
> *(Fuchs & Deshler, 2007; p. 131)*

RTI Goal: The district has determined what teachers need to know about RTI and has defined what changes in teacher practice are needed under RTI. The district then creates a professional development plan (to be updated yearly) to share information about RTI and to dialog with teachers about ongoing implementation of the model.

Questions: Here are key questions to consider when developing a plan to building teacher understanding and support for RTI: For the coming school year:

What is the grade range of classroom teachers that will be targeted for RTI professional development?

_____

How will your district determine the minimum essential information that classroom teachers must know about RTI?:

_____

_____

How does your district expect to see the practice of classroom teachers change as they learn more about RTI?:

_____

_____

_____

How will your district create a calendar of large- and small-group opportunities to provide training and promote dialog about RTI for teachers and other staff?

_____

_____

Fuchs, D., & Deshler, D. D. (2007). What we need to know about Response to Intervention (and shouldn't be afraid to ask). *Learning Disabilities Research & Practice,* 22(2), 129–136.

Exhibit 6-A, Form 2

RTI Plan: Element 2…
Create Teacher Capacity to Deliver Effective Classroom (Tier 1) Interventions

Directions: Read the quote and goal statement below. Then develop an implementation plan for this goal.

> *"…intervention and management approaches that are universal in nature and that involve a standard dosage that is easy to deliver (e.g., classwide social skills training) have a higher likelihood of making it into routine or standard school practice." (Walker, 2004; pp. 400-401)*

RTI Goal: Classroom teachers are trained as RTI 'first responders'. They are able to clearly define student academic or behavioral problems, select and implement evidence-based intervention ideas, and evaluate whether those interventions result in significant student improvements.

Questions: Here are questions to consider when developing a plan to create teacher capacity to deliver effective classroom (Tier 1) interventions:

Interventions are likely to be effective only if appropriately matched to student needs. How does your district train classroom teachers to write clear, specific, measureable 'problem identification' statements?

_____

_____

How does your district identify effective, evidence-based Tier 1 intervention ideas and put them into the hands of teachers?

_____

_____

In what manner does your district expect teachers to document their Tier 1 intervention efforts?

_____

_____

How long are teachers expected to attempt Tier 1 interventions before deciding to seek additional assistance with a struggling student?

_____

_____

Walker, H. M. (2004). Use of evidence-based interventions in schools: Where we've been, where we are, and where we need to go. *School Psychology Review,* 33, 398-407. pp. 400-401.

Exhibit 6-A, Form 3
RTI Plan: Element 3...
Inventory Evidence-Based Supplemental Intervention Programs Available at Tiers 2 & 3

Directions: Read the quote and goal statement below. Then develop an implementation plan for this goal.

> "...Because RTI practices target all students, rather than only those identified as at risk, services are provided along a continuum, with all students receiving class- or schoolwide instructional or behavioral supports and select individuals participating in need-based intervention of varying levels of intensity."
> (Glover & DiPerna, 2007; p. 527)

RTI Goal: The district has inventoried its supplemental intervention programs and verified that these programs are evidence-based. Furthermore, the district has organized its supplemental intervention programs into levels or tiers—with objective, data-based guidelines for entry and exit. The district has identified any current gaps in supplemental programs (e.g., in math computation skills) and is working to locate programs to fill those gaps. NOTE: Tier 2 programs are typically group-based (limited to 6-7 students) and students are placed in these groups based on school-wide screening data. Tier 3 programs are the most intensive levels of support available in a general education setting (small group or individual student services). It is recommended that students be referred to Tier 3 programs through the RTI Problem-Solving Team.

Questions: Here are questions to consider when inventorying evidence-based supplemental intervention programs:

What standards has your school adopted to validate specific programs as 'evidence-based'? Note: Here are two websites that can help to provide guidance on the evidence supporting specific programs:

- What Works Clearinghouse: http://ies.ed.gov/ncee/wwc/
- Florida Center for Reading Research: http://www.fcrr.org/FCRRReports/LReports.aspx

_____

_____

_____

What are the existing supplemental intervention programs in place in your district (use attached inventory form)?

What gaps in programming are revealed by the Tier 2/3 intervention inventory?

_____

_____

_____

Glover, T. A., & DiPerna, J. C. (2007). Service delivery for Response to Intervention: Core components and directions for future research. *School Psychology Review, 36,* 526-540.

Exhibit 6-A, Form 3, continued

Tier 2/Tier 3 Supplemental Evidence-Based Intervention Programs: Inventory

Directions: Inventory all current programs in place in your school or district to provide supplemental evidence-based interventions to students at Tiers 2 and 3.

Program Name	Grade(s) Served	Specific Academic Skill Area(s) Targeted	Tier
			☐ Tier 2 ☐ Tier 3
			☐ Tier 2 ☐ Tier 3
			☐ Tier 2 ☐ Tier 3
			☐ Tier 2 ☐ Tier 3
			☐ Tier 2 ☐ Tier 3
			☐ Tier 2 ☐ Tier 3
			☐ Tier 2 ☐ Tier 3
			☐ Tier 2 ☐ Tier 3
			☐ Tier 2 ☐ Tier 3
			☐ Tier 2 ☐ Tier 3
			☐ Tier 2 ☐ Tier 3
			☐ Tier 2 ☐ Tier 3
			☐ Tier 2 ☐ Tier 3
			☐ Tier 2 ☐ Tier 3
			☐ Tier 2 ☐ Tier 3
			☐ Tier 2 ☐ Tier 3
			☐ Tier 2 ☐ Tier 3
			☐ Tier 2 ☐ Tier 3

Exhibit 6-A, Form 4
RTI Plan: Element 4…
Establish an RTI Problem Solving Team at Tier 3

Directions: Read the quote and goal statement below. Then develop an implementation plan for this goal.

> "…Students who do not adequately respond to interventions provided in tiers 1 or 2 receive daily individualized interventions for at least 30 minutes per day with at least weekly progress monitoring in tier 3. These interventions are usually developed from a problem-analysis procedure often involving a problem-solving team and are delivered via general education.." (Burns & Gibbons, 2008; p. 6)

RTI Goal: The district has established an effective RTI Problem-Solving Team ('RTI Team') to meet on the most intensive student cases at Tier 3 to design customized intervention plans. The RTI Team is multi-disciplinary, follows a structured problem-solving approach at each meeting, uses data to guide its decision-making, and ensures that all interventions included on its student plans are evidence-based.

Questions: Here are questions to consider when establishing an RTI Problem-Solving Team:

In what schools are RTI Teams to be set up and on what timeline?

School	Yr to Begin	School	Yr to Begin

Who serves on the multi-disciplinary RTI Team? _____

_____

How frequently does the RTI Team meet? How much time is reserved each meeting day for the RTI Team? _____

What structured problem-solving process does the RTI Team follow to ensure that its meetings are efficient, productive, and result in effective intervention plans matched to the needs of the student? _____

_____

What initial training does the RTI Team require? _____

_____

Burns, M. K., & Gibbons, K. A. (2008). *Implementing response-to-intervention in elementary and secondary schools.* Routledge: New York.

Exhibit 6-A, Form 5
RTI Plan: Element 5...
Select Measures for Universal Screening and Progress Monitoring to Evaluate Student Response to Intervention

Directions: Read the quote and goal statement below. Then develop an implementation plan for this goal.

> *"Local norm data in many schools are collected three or four times per year every year and are used for universal screening, instructional planning, resource allocation, and program evaluation in addition to their use as the comparison group for a particular identified student.."* (Steward & Silberglit, 2008; p. 225)

RTI Goal: The district has determined a range of grades at which universal academic screenings will be done at least 3 times per year, has selected specific measures to be included in the academic screening battery for each grade, and has established a plan to share updated screening information in a timely manner with each participating grade level at 'data team' meetings.

Questions: Here are questions to consider when selecting measures for universal screening and student progress-monitoring:

What are the student skills, grade ranges, and specific measures that will be selected for the universal academic screening plan?

_____

_____

How does your district convene 'Data Team' meetings after each screening (consisting of grade-level classroom teachers, administration, and Tier 2 service providers) to select students for supplemental intervention groups?

_____

_____

What objective data is to be used at Data Team meetings to select students for Tier 2 services?

_____

_____

_____

Stewart, L. H. & Silberglit, B. (2008). Best practices in developing academic local norms. In A. Thomas & J. Grimes (Eds.), *Best practices in school psychology V* (pp. 225-242). Bethesda, MD: National Association of School Psychologists.

Exhibit 6-B
Evaluating a Student's 'Non-Responder' Status: An RTI Checklist

When a school attempts to determine whether a particular general education student has responded adequately to an academic RTI plan, it must conduct a kind of 'intervention audit'—reviewing documentation of the full range of interventions attempted.

The intervention-audit process is complex. After all, before a school can decide whether a struggling student has truly failed to respond to intervention, it must first have confidence that in fact each link in the chain of RTI general education support was in place for the student and was implemented with quality.

Presented below are the most crucial links in the RTI chain. This listing summarizes important RTI components to support intervention, assessment, and data analysis. A school must ensure that all of these elements are in place in the general education setting before that school can have decide with confidence whether a particular student is a 'non-responder' to intervention. Schools can use this RTI 'non-responder' checklist both to evaluate whether general education has yet done all that it can to support a struggling student and whether that student should be considered for possible special education services.

Interventions: Evidence-Based & Implemented With Integrity		
Tier 1: Classroom Interventions. The classroom teacher is the 'first responder' for students with academic delays. Classroom efforts to instruct and individually support the student should be documented.		
Adequately Documented?	**RTI Component**	**If this element is incomplete, missing, or undocumented…**
☐ YES ☐ NO	**Tier 1: High-Quality Core Instruction.** The student receives high-quality core instruction in the area of academic concern. 'High quality' is defined as at least 80% of students in the classroom or grade level performing at or above gradewide academic screening benchmarks through classroom instructional support alone (Christ, 2008).	Inadequate or incorrectly focused core instruction may be an explanation for the student's academic delays.
☐ YES ☐ NO	**Tier 1: Classroom Intervention.** The classroom teacher gives additional individualized academic support to the student beyond that provided in core instruction. • The teacher documents those strategies on a Tier 1 intervention plan. • Intervention ideas contained in the plan meet the district's criteria as 'evidence-based'. • Student academic baseline and goals are calculated, and progress-monitoring data are collected to measure the impact of the plan. • The classroom intervention is attempted for a period sufficiently long (e.g., 4-8 instructional weeks) to fully assess its effectiveness.	An absence of individualized classroom support or a poorly focused classroom intervention plan may contribute to the student's academic delays.

Exhibit 6-B, continued

Tiers 2 & 3: Supplemental Interventions. Interventions at Tiers 2 & 3 supplement core instruction and specifically target the student's academic deficits.		
Adequately Documented?	**RTI Component**	**If this element is incomplete, missing, or undocumented…**
☐ YES ☐ NO	**Tier 2 & 3 Interventions: Minimum Number & Length.** The student's cumulative RTI information indicates that an adequate effort in the general education setting has been made to provide supplemental interventions at Tiers 2 & 3. The term 'sufficient effort' includes the expectation that within the student's general education setting: • A minimum number of separate Tier 2/3 intervention trials (e.g., three) are attempted. • Each intervention trial lasts a minimum period of time (e.g., 6-8 instructional weeks).	A foundation assumption of RTI is that a general-education student with academic difficulties is typical and simply needs targeted instructional support to be successful. Therefore, strong evidence (i.e., several documented, 'good-faith' intervention attempts) is needed before the school can move beyond the assumption that the student is typical to consider whether there are possible 'within-child' factors such as a learning disability that best explain the student's academic difficulties.
☐ YES ☐ NO	**Tier 2 & 3 Interventions: Essential Elements.** Each Tier 2/3 intervention plan shows evidence that: • Instructional programs or practices used in the intervention meet the district's criteria of evidence-based. • The intervention has been selected because it logically addressed the area(s) of academic deficit for the target student (e.g., an intervention to address reading fluency was chosen for a student whose primary deficit was in reading fluency). • If the intervention is group-based, all students enrolled in the Tier 2/3 intervention group have a shared intervention need that could reasonably be addressed through the group instruction provided. • The student-teacher ratio in the group-based intervention provides adequate student support. NOTE: For Tier 2, group sizes should be capped at 7 students. Tier 3 interventions may be delivered in smaller groups (e.g., 3 students or fewer) or individually. • The intervention provides contact time adequate to the student academic deficit. NOTE: Tier 2 interventions should take place a minimum of 3-5 times per week in sessions of 30 minutes or more; Tier 3 interventions should take place daily in sessions of 30 minutes or more (Burns & Gibbons, 2008).	Supplemental intervention programs are compromised if they are not based on research, are too large, or include students with very discrepant intervention needs. Schools cannot have confidence in the impact of such potentially compromised supplemental intervention programs.

Exhibit 6-B, continued

Adequately Documented?	RTI Component	If this element is incomplete, missing, or undocumented…
☐ YES ☐ NO	**Tier 1, 2, & 3 Interventions: Intervention Integrity.** Data are collected to verify that the intervention is carried out with integrity (Gansle & Noell, 2007; Roach & Elliott, 2008). Relevant intervention-integrity data include information about: • Frequency and length of intervention sessions. • Ratings by the interventionist or an independent observer about whether all steps of the intervention are being conducted correctly.	Without intervention-integrity data, it is impossible to discern whether academic underperformance is due to the student's 'non-response' to intervention or due to an intervention that was poorly or inconsistently carried out.

Academic Screenings: General Outcome Measures and Skill-Based Measures

Peer Norms: The school selects efficient measures with good technical adequacy to be used to screen all students at a grade level in targeted academic areas.

Adequately Documented?	RTI Component	If this element is incomplete, missing, or undocumented…
☐ YES ☐ NO	**Selection of Academic Screening Measures.** The school has selected appropriate grade-level screening measures for the academic skill area(s) in which the target student struggles (Hosp, Hosp & Howell, 2007). The selected screening measure(s): • Have 'technical adequacy' as grade-level screeners—and have been researched and shown to predict future student success in the academic skill(s) targeted. • Are general enough to give useful information for at least a full school year of the developing academic skill (e.g., General Outcome Measure or Skill-Based Mastery Measure). • Include research norms, proprietary norms developed as part of a reputable commercial assessment product, or benchmarks to guide the school in evaluating the risk level for each student screened.	Academic screening measures provide a shared standard for assessing student academic risk. If appropriate gradewide academic screening measure(s) are not in place, the school cannot efficiently identify struggling students who need additional intervention support or calculate the relative probability of academic success for each student.
☐ YES ☐ NO	**Local Norms Collected via Gradewide Academic Screenings at Least 3 Times Per Year.** All students at each grade level are administered the relevant academic screening measures at least three times per school year. The results are compiled to provide local norms of academic performance.	In the absence of regularly updated local screening norms, the school cannot easily judge whether a particular student's skills are substantially delayed from those of peers in the same educational setting.

Exhibit 6-B, continued

Dual Discrepancy Cut-Offs: Academic Skill Level & Student Rate of Improvement

Establishment of Guidelines for Determining Student 'Non-Response' to Intervention as a Dual Discrepancy: The school has developed definitions for 'severely discrepant' academic performance and student growth.

Adequately Documented?	RTI Component	If this element is incomplete, missing, or undocumented...
☐ YES ☐ NO	**Cut-point Established to Define 'Severely Discrepant' Academic Performance.** Using local norms, research norms, proprietary norms developed as part of a reputable commercial assessment product, or benchmarks, the school sets a 'cut-point' below which a student's academic performance is defined as 'severely discrepant' from that of peers in the enrolled grade. For example, a school conducts a winter screening in Oral Reading Fluency for 6th grade and finds based on local norms that 10 percent of students in that grade read 82 words correctly read per minute (wcpm) or less. The school therefore sets 82 wcpm as the winter screening cut-point for reading fluency at 6th grade, defining any student whose performance falls below that level as 'severely discrepant' in the skill.	The RTI model uses a 'dual discrepancy' approach to identify a student as a 'non-responder' to academic intervention (Fuchs, 2003)--to include (1) a severe discrepancy in academic performance and (2) a discrepancy in rate of student growth during intervention. Demonstration that the student continues to lag severely behind peers in academic skills despite intensive intervention is a key requirement in certifying RTI 'non-responder' status.
☐ YES ☐ NO	**Cut-Off Criterion Selected to Define Discrepant Slope.** The school has selected a formula for determining when a student's rate of improvement (slope) is severely discrepant from that of peers. Here are two options for generating slope cut-off values: • Slope Cut-Off Option 1 (for use with external and local norm slopes): The student's slope is divided by the comparison peer slope (derived from external or local norms). If the quotient falls below 1.0, the student's rate of improvement is less than that of the comparison peer slope. A quotient greater than 1.0 indicates that the student's rate of improvement exceeds that of the comparison peer slope. The school can set a fixed cut-off value (e.g., 0.75 or below) as a threshold for defining a student slope as discrepant from the comparison peer slope. • Slope Cut-Off Option 2 (for use with local screening data only): To derive a slope cut-off value from local norms, the school uses data collected during its schoolwide academic screening. Because each student included in the screening will have three screening data points on a given measure—e.g., in oral reading fluency—by the end of the year, the school can use those successive data points to generate slopes for each student. Once slopes for each student have been calculated, the school can compute a mean and standard deviation for the entire collection of student slopes at a grade level. Any student found to have a slope that is at least one standard deviation below the mean slope would be considered to be 'discrepant' (Burns & Gibbons, 2008).	A clear formula is needed for determining whether a student slope reaches the threshold of 'discrepancy' to ensure consistency across all student cases.

Exhibit 6-B, continued

Data Collection

Intervention Outcome Data: Student baseline level and goals are calculated for each intervention, and a sufficient number of data points are collected during progress-monitoring to judge accurately whether the intervention is successful.

Adequately Documented?	RTI Component	If this element is incomplete, missing, or undocumented…
☐ YES ☐ NO	**Use of Both 'Off-Level' and Enrolled Grade-Level Benchmarks & Progress-Monitoring Measures to Assess Student Skills and Growth.** For students with substantial skill deficits (e.g., a 3-year delay in reading fluency), any Tier 2/3 intervention is likely to be off-level to match the student's actual skills. Here are data-collection guidelines for off-level interventions (Shapiro, 2008): • Benchmarks and progress-monitoring should generally match the intervention level. So if a 7th-grade student receives a supplemental reading fluency intervention using grade 5 texts, the school would use grade 5 reading fluency benchmarks and progress-monitoring measures to track student growth and to determine when the student has reached mastery at this off-level intervention point. • It is also recommended that the school occasionally (e.g., once per month) assess an off-level student using benchmarks and progress-monitoring measures from his or her enrolled grade level as a means to assess the student's abilities relative to same-grade peers.	If an off-level student is tracked using *only* unrealistically difficult progress-monitoring measures from his or her enrolled-grade level, any actual evidence of student progress may be masked by the challenging nature of the assessment materials. This intervention-assessment mismatch could lead the school erroneously to judge the student a 'non-responder' to an off-level intervention when in fact the student is actually making substantial academic progress.
☐ YES ☐ NO	Student Baseline Calculated. For each Tier 2/3 intervention being reviewed, the school calculates the student's baseline level, or starting point, in the academic skill before starting the intervention (Witt, VanDerHeyden, & Gilbertson, 2004).. Baseline is calculated in either of the following ways: • If no previous Tier 2/3 interventions had been attempted, baseline is calculated by assessing the student on at least three separate dates in close proximity using the appropriate the General Outcome Measure or Skill-Based Measure (e.g., CBM Oral Reading Fluency). The median value from this baseline assessment comprises the calculation of 'baseline'. • If a previous Tier 2/3 intervention has been recently attempted, baseline can be assessed by taking the three final (that is, most recent) data points from that progress-monitoring data series and selecting the median value from the three points as a calculation of baseline.	Without information about baseline student performance prior to an intervention, it is difficult to estimate the actual progress that the student made during the intervention. Lack of baseline data therefore comprises a 'fatal flaw' (Witt, VanDerHeyden, & Gilbertson, 2004) that invalidates any RTI intervention.

Exhibit 6-B, continued

Adequately Documented?	RTI Component	If this element is incomplete, missing, or undocumented…
☐ YES ☐ NO	**Student Goal Calculated.** For each Tier 2/3 intervention being reviewed, the school calculates a 'predicted' goal for student progress to be attained by the end of the intervention period. The goal: • Is based on acceptable norms for student growth (i.e., research-based growth norms, proprietary growth norms developed as part of a reputable commercial assessment product, or growth norms derived from the local student population). • Represents a realistic prediction of student growth that is sufficiently ambitious—assuming that the intervention is successful—to eventually close the gap between the student and grade-level peers.	If no clear goal for student progress is established prior to the start of a Tier 2/3 intervention, the school cannot know at the conclusion of that intervention whether it was successful. Lack of a specific criterion or goal for student improvement, therefore comprises a 'fatal flaw' (Witt, VanDerHeyden, & Gilbertson, 2004) that invalidates any RTI intervention.
☐ YES ☐ NO	**Regular Progress-Monitoring Conducted.** Each Tier 2/3 intervention is monitored on a regular basis. • If Tier 2, the intervention is monitored at least 1-2 times per month (Burns & Gibbons, 2008). • If Tier 3, the intervention is monitored at least 1-2 times per week (Burns & Gibbons, 2008; Howell, Hosp, & Kurns, 2008).	A student's observed rate of improvement, or slope, during an intervention is calculated from the total progress-monitoring data points collected. The greater the number of data points, the greater the confidence that the observed slope is a good approximation of the student's actual progress. If, however, the data collected during the intervention are too sparse, the school cannot have confidence that the few data points collected are an accurate representation of actual student progress.

Exhibit 6-B, continued

	Application of RTI Decision Rules to a Particular Student Case	
	RTI Data Analysis. The student's individual RTI data is analyzed to determine if that student is a 'non-responder' despite the best efforts to provide evidence-based interventions in the general-education setting.	
Adequately Documented?	**RTI Component**	**The importance of this element...**
☐ YES ☐ NO	**Despite the Tier 2/3 Interventions Attempted, the Student's Skills Continue to Fall Below the Boundary of 'Severely Discrepant' Academic Performance.** Using the school's definition for calculating 'severely discrepant academic performance' (above), it is determined that the student's current academic performance is discrepant from that of peers.	A discrepant student performance level is the first element of a 'dual discrepancy' needed under RTI to define a student as a 'non-responder' to general-education interventions.
☐ YES ☐ NO	**Despite the Tier 2/3 Interventions Attempted, the Student's Rate of Improvement (Slope) Continues to Be Discrepant.** Applying the school's formula for calculating discrepant slope (above), it is determined that the student's slope (growth during the intervention) is discrepant from that of peers.	A discrepant student slope is the second element of a 'dual discrepancy' needed under RTI to define a student as a 'non-responder' to general-education interventions.

References

Burns, M. K., & Gibbons, K. A. (2008). *Implementing response-to-intervention in elementary and secondary schools.* Routledge: New York.

Christ, T. (2008). Best practices in problem analysis. In A. Thomas & J. Grimes (Eds.), *Best practices in school psychology V* (pp. 159-176). Bethesda, MD: National Association of School Psychologists.

Fuchs, L. (2003). Assessing intervention responsiveness: Conceptual and technical issues. *Learning Disabilities Research & Practice,* 18(3), 172-186.

Gansle, K. A., & Noell, G. H. (2007). The fundamental role of intervention implementation in assessing response to intervention. In S. R. Jimerson, M. K. Burns, & A. M. VanDerHeyden (Eds.), *Response to intervention: The science and practice of assessment and intervention* (pp. 244-251). New York: Springer Publishing.

Hosp, M. K., Hosp, J. L., & Howell, K. W. (2007). *The ABCs of CBM: A practical guide to curriculum-based measurement.* New York: Guilford Press.

Howell, K. W., Hosp, J. L., & Kurns, S. (2008). Best practices in curriculum-based evaluation. In A. Thomas & J. Grimes (Eds.), *Best practices in school psychology V* (pp.349-362). Bethesda, MD: National Association of School Psychologists.

Exhibit 6-B, continued

Roach, A. T., & Elliott, S. N. (2008). Best practices in facilitating and evaluating intervention integrity. In A. Thomas & J. Grimes (Eds.), *Best practices in school psychology V* (pp.195-208).

Shapiro, E. S. (2008). Best practices in setting progress-monitoring monitoring goals for academic skill improvement. In A. Thomas & J. Grimes (Eds.), *Best practices in school psychology V* (pp. 141-157). Bethesda, MD: National Association of School Psychologists.

Witt, J. C., VanDerHeyden, A. M., & Gilbertson, D. (2004). Troubleshooting behavioral interventions. A systematic process for finding and eliminating problems. *School Psychology Review,* 33, 363-383.

Addendum

Core Instructional Ideas to Promote Literacy Skills in Secondary Classrooms

Middle and high school teachers can incorporate activities into their instruction that both promote learning of course content and also strengthen students' literacy skills. The guides below offer classwide ideas for: (1) boosting vocabulary knowledge; (2) modeling critical thinking skills through extended discussion; and (3) reinforcing reading comprehension skills.

Classroom Literacy Strategies: Academic & Content-Area Vocabulary
Why This Instructional Goal is Important
The explicit teaching of instructional vocabulary is a central literacy-building goal in secondary classrooms. As vocabulary terms become more specialized in content area courses, students are less able to derive the meaning of unfamiliar words incidentally simply by relying on the context in which they appear. Students must instead learn vocabulary through more direct means, including having opportunities to explicitly memorize words and their definitions. On average, students expand their reading vocabularies by 2000 to 3000 new words per year (Texas Reading Initiative, 2002). While the typical student can master a new word after about 12 meaningful exposures to the term, some students may require as many as 17 exposures to learn a word. (Kamil, et al., 2008). In secondary courses with a substantial number of specialized terms, time should be set aside each period to explicitly teach and review vocabulary. There are two general approaches to vocabulary instruction: 'additive' and 'generative' (Kamil et al., 2008). Additive strategies are the range of techniques used to teach specific words. For example, having students create flashcards to review vocabulary with the term on one side and its definition on the other would be one additive strategy. Generative strategies are those that teach students how to derive the meaning of words independently. Teaching students to identify word roots and affixes is one generative approach to vocabulary instruction.
Strategies to Promote This Instructional Goal
Provide Dictionary Training. The student is trained to use an Internet lookup strategy to better understand dictionary or glossary definitions of key vocabulary items. The student first looks up the word and its meaning(s) in the dictionary/glossary. If necessary, the student isolates the specific word meaning that appears to be the appropriate match for the term as it appears in course texts and discussion. The student goes to an Internet search engine (e.g., Google) and locates at least five text samples in which the term is used in context and appears to match the selected dictionary definition. Optional: Have students meet in pairs or cooperative groups to review their written definitions and context examples of target vocabulary.

Enhance Vocabulary Instruction Through Use of Graphic Organizers or Displays: A Sampling. Teachers can use graphic displays to structure their vocabulary discussions and activities (Boardman et al., 2008; Fisher, 2007; Texas Reading Initiative, 2002). Four graphic display formats are described briefly below—and examples of each appear in the next few pages of this handout:

- *4-Square Word Activity, Form 1.* The student divides a page into four quadrants. In the upper left section, the student writes the target word. In the lower left section, the student writes the word definition. In the upper right section, the student generates a list of examples that illustrate the term, and in the lower right section, the student writes 'non-examples' (e.g., terms that are the opposite of the target vocabulary word).

- *Semantic/Word Definition Map, Form 2.* The graphic display contains sections in which the student writes the word, its definition ('what is this?'), additional details that extend its meaning ('What is it like?'), as well as a listing of examples and 'non-examples' (e.g., terms that are the opposite of the target vocabulary word).

- *Semantic Feature Analysis, Form 3.* A target vocabulary term is selected for analysis in this grid-like graphic display. Possible features or properties of the term appear along the top margin, while examples of the term are listed in the left margin. The student considers the vocabulary term and its definition. Then the student evaluates each example of the term to determine whether it does or does not match each possible term property or element.

- *Comparison/Contrast (Venn) Diagram, Form 4.* Two terms are listed and defined. For each term, the student brainstorms qualities or properties or examples that illustrate the term's meaning. Then the student groups those qualities, properties, and examples into 3 sections: items unique to Term 1; items unique to Term 2; and items shared by both terms.

Promote 'Wide Reading' (Fisher, 2007). Students are encouraged to read widely in the content area, using texts that supplement and extend information supplied by the textbook. 'Wide reading' results in substantial increases in student vocabulary over time due to incidental learning. The effects of wide reading accumulate over time and result in increases in general academic vocabulary as well as vocabulary in specific content areas. Wide reading should be encouraged at the earliest possible grades, so that students can benefit from their expanded vocabulary knowledge 'downstream' (in later, higher grade levels). To strengthen the positive impact of wide reading on vocabulary development, have student texts available that vary in difficulty and are of high interest. Discuss readings in class. Experiment with ways to document student independent reading and integrate that 'wide reading' into an effort grade for the course. If needed, build time into the student's school schedule for supervised 'wide reading' time.

Hold 'Read-Alouds' (Fisher, 2008). The teacher selects texts that supplement the course textbook, illustrate central concepts, and contain important vocabulary covered in the course. The instructor or another accomplished reader reads aloud selections from those texts for 3 to 5 minutes per class session--while students follow along silently. Read-alouds provide students with additional exposure to vocabulary items in context. They can also lower the threshold of difficulty: Students may be more likely to attempt to read an assigned text independently if they have already gotten a start in the text by listening to a more advanced reader read the first few pages aloud. Read-alouds can support other vocabulary-building activities such as guided discussion, vocabulary review, and wide reading.

Provide Regular In-Class Instruction and Review of Vocabulary Terms, Definitions (Texas Reading Initiative, 2002). The teacher presents important new vocabulary terms in class, along with student-friendly definitions. The instructor also provides 'example sentences' to illustrate the use of each term. Students are then assigned to write example sentences employing new vocabulary to illustrate their mastery of the terms.

Generate 'Possible Sentences' (Texas Reading Initiative, 2002). The teacher selects vocabulary that applies to the day's text selection, including 6 to 8 challenging new vocabulary terms and 4 to 6 easier, more familiar vocabulary items. First, the instructor introduces the vocabulary terms to the class. Then, the teacher provides definitions of the words (or better yet elicits those definitions from students if possible). Then students are directed individually, in pairs, or in small groups to write sentences that contain at least two words from the posted vocabulary list. Next, in large group, students share their composed sentences, which are written on the board. This report-out continues until all words from the original list have been put into sentences. NOTE: Students and the instructor refrain from evaluating sentences as being 'correct' or 'incorrect' during this stage.

Next, students are directed to read the text selection. After students have completed their reading, they review the 'possible sentences' that were previously generated and written on the board. For each sentence, the class evaluates whether, based on the passage just read, the sentence is 'possible' (true) in its current form. If a sentence is found to be untrue ('not possible'), the group recommends how to change the sentence to make it 'possible'.

Troubleshooting Tips

Students Lack Basic Academic Vocabulary. Some students may have deficits in their grasp of more general academic terms, such as *discourse* or *hypothesis*. The school may want to develop a list of the most crucial of these more general academic terms and make this shared list available to all teachers to better allow those instructors to regularly use and model this more general academic vocabulary. As a starting point, teachers can view a comprehensive list of academic words and the frequency with which they are used in English at: http://language.massey.ac.nz/staff/awl/

Building Capacity

Develop Content-Area Vocabulary Lists for Each Course. Whether working alone or with their instructional departments, secondary teachers should develop a list of the most important vocabulary items that students should master in each content-area course. When teachers have identified essential vocabulary in advance, they can more easily integrate vocabulary instruction into their lessons.

Measure Student Acquisition of Target Vocabulary. Teachers can informally track student vocabulary acquisition by listening to student use of vocabulary during guided discussions and monitoring vocabulary terms that appear in student journal entries.

More formally, teachers can track student acquisition of specialized vocabulary by using brief, timed vocabulary matching probes (Espin, Shin, & Busch, 2005). The student is given a worksheet with vocabulary items appearing on the left side of the page. Definitions that correspond to each of the terms appear on the right side of the page, in scrambled order. The student matches terms to their correct definitions.

References

Boardman, A. G., Roberts, G., Vaughn, S., Wexler, J., Murray, C. S., & Kosanovich, M. (2008). *Effective instruction for adolescent struggling readers: A practice brief.* Portsmouth, NH: RMC Research Corporation, Center on Instruction.

Carnine, L., & Carnine, D. (2004). The interaction of reading skills and science content knowledge when teaching struggling secondary students. *Reading & Writing Quarterly,* 20, 203-218.

Espin, C. A., Shin, J., & Busch, T. W. (2005). Curriculum-based measurement in the content areas: Vocabulary matching as an indicator of progress in social studies learning. *Journal of Learning Disabilities,* 38, 353-363.

Fisher, D. (2007). Creating a schoolwide vocabulary initiative in an urban high school. Journal of Education for Students Placed at Risk, 12, 337-351.

Kamil, M. L., Borman, G. D., Dole, J., Kral, C. C., Salinger, T., & Torgesen, J. (2008). *Improving adolescent literacy: Effective classroom and intervention practices: A practice guide* (NCEE #2008-4027). Washington, DC: National Center for Education Evaluation and Regional Assistance, Institute of Education Sciences, U.S. Department of Education. Retrieved from http://ies.ed.gov/ncee/wwc.

Texas Reading Initiative. (2002). *Promoting vocabulary development: Components of effective vocabulary instruction.* Austin, TX: Author. Retrieved November 15, 2008, from http://www.tea.state.tx.us/reading/practices/redbk5.pdf

Addendum, Form 1

This Word	Examples of This Word
Definition of This Word	**Non-Examples of This Word**

4-Square Word Activity

Adapted from: Texas Reading Initiative. (2002). *Promoting vocabulary development: Components of effective vocabulary instruction.* Austin, TX: Author. Retrieved November 15, 2008, from http://www.tea.state.tx.us/reading/practices/redbk5.pdf.

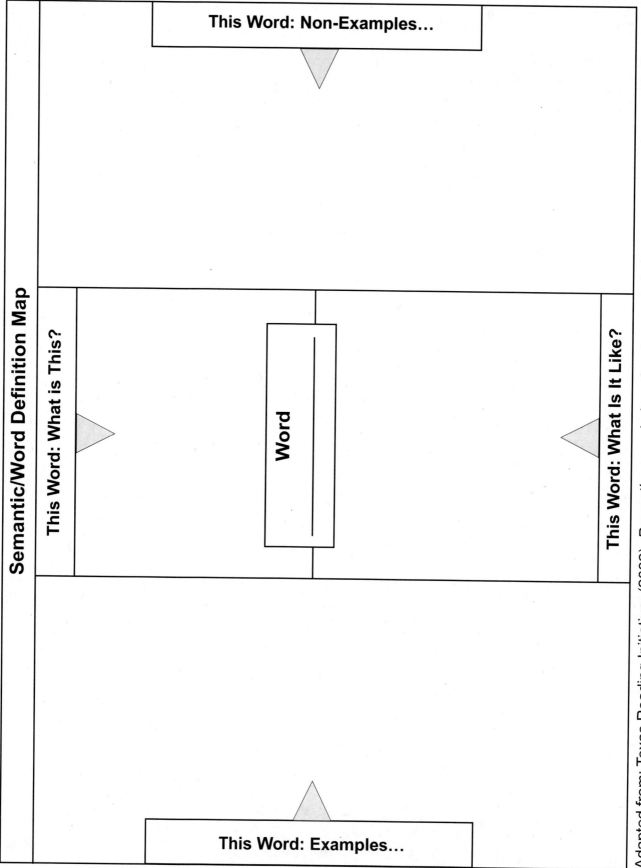

Semantic Feature Analysis: ___

Possible Features of This Term

Examples of This Term

Adapted from: Fisher, D. (2007). Creating a schoolwide vocabulary initiative in an urban high school. *Journal of Education for Students Placed at Risk, 12,* 337–351.

Texas Reading Initiative. (2002). *Promoting vocabulary development: Components of effective vocabulary instruction.* Austin, TX: Author. Retrieved November 15, 2008, from http://www.tea.state.tx.us/reading/practices/redbk5.pdf

Addendum, Form 2
Comparison/Contrast/Venn Diagram Display

Term 1 & Definition: _____

Term 2 & Definition: _____

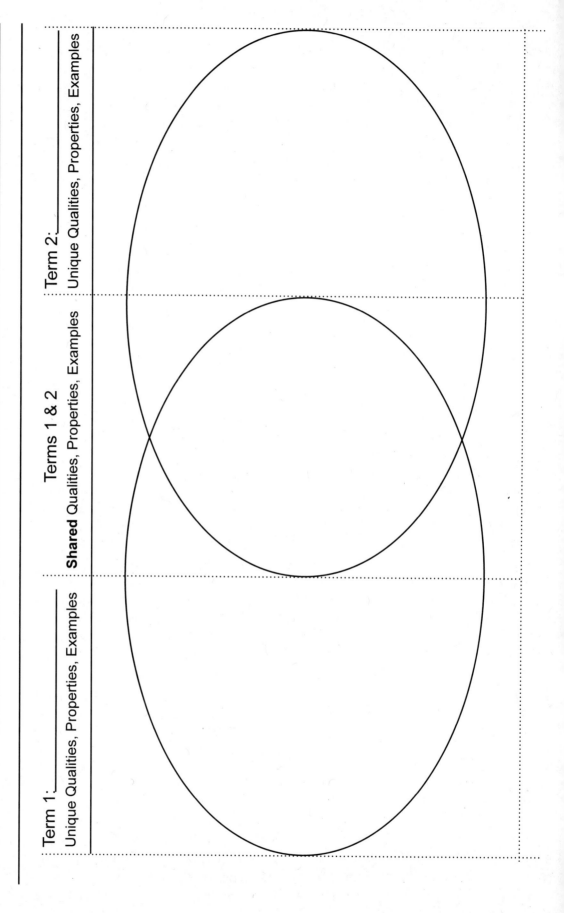

Term 2: _____
Unique Qualities, Properties, Examples

Terms 1 & 2
Shared Qualities, Properties, Examples

Term 1: _____
Unique Qualities, Properties, Examples

Classroom Literacy Strategies: Extended Discussions

Why This Instructional Goal is Important

Extended, guided group discussion is a powerful means to help students to learn vocabulary and advanced concepts. Discussion can also model for students various 'thinking processes' and cognitive strategies(Kamil et al. 2008, p. 22). To be effective, guided discussion should go beyond students answering a series of factual questions posed by the teacher: Quality discussions are typically open-ended and exploratory in nature, allowing for multiple points of view (Kamil et al., 2008).

When group discussion is used regularly and well in instruction, students show increased growth in literacy skills. However, discussion is often underused as an instructional method. In one large research study of middle and high school language arts classes, for example, teachers were found on average to devote less than 2 minutes per class period to discussion activities (Kamil et al., 2008). Guided discussion holds an additional benefit: Content-area teachers can use it to demonstrate the 'habits of mind' and patterns of thinking of experts in various their discipline: e.g., historians, mathematicians, chemists, engineers, literacy critics, etc.

Strategies to Promote This Instructional Goal

Use a 'Standard Protocol' to Structure Guided Discussions (Kamil et al., 2008). Good guided classwide discussions elicit a wide range of student opinions, subject individual viewpoints to critical scrutiny in a supportive manner, put forth alternative views, and bring closure by summarizing the main points of the discussion. Teachers can use a simple structure to effectively and reliably organize their discussions:

A. Pose questions to the class that require students to explain their positions and the reasoning to support those positions.

B. When needed, 'think aloud' as the discussion leader to model good reasoning practices such as taking a clear stand on a topic or providing an explanation of why one supports a particular position.

C. Supportively challenge student views by offering possible counter arguments that students must attempt to answer.

D. Single out and mention examples of effective student reasoning.

E. Avoid being overly directive; the purpose of extended discussions is to more fully investigate and think about complex topics, not to push students toward a pre-determined viewpoint or finding.

F. At the conclusion of the discussion, sum up the general ground covered in the discussion and highlight the main ideas covered.

Teachers can train students to lead discussions (with teacher coaching as needed) and have those students moderate extended discussions in whole-group or cooperative learning format. Teachers can use the standard discussion protocol provided here as a starting point for training students as discussion leaders.

Troubleshooting Tips

Students Are Reluctant to Participate in Discussions (Kamil et al., 2008). As the discussion leader, be sure to make the discussion activity a 'safe' one in which all students feel that their thoughts are valued. The teacher should provide sufficient structure to the activity so that students know clearly what is expected of them. If necessary when first training students to participate in extended discussions, the instructor can use texts that will elicit student interest—even if those texts are only marginally related to course content. As students are drawn into discussion by those high-interest texts and class participation increases, the teacher can start to use texts for future discussions that overlap more with the curriculum.

Teachers Lack the Time for Frequent Use of Extended Discussion. Guided discussion is an effective method for enhancing and verifying student understanding of course content (Kamil et al., 2008). If class time is limited, the instructor should reserve discussion time at least for those course topics and concepts that are potentially most complex, challenging, ambiguous, or open to misinterpretation.

Teachers Require Behavior Management Training to Manage Discussions. Extended discussions can require flexible behavior management strategies to both promote student involvement and maintain classroom order. Some teachers may be reluctant to engage in sustained discussions in their classrooms because of behavior management concerns. One solution is for the school to offer staff development to teachers on how to effectively manage a classroom during large-group or small-group discussion activities (Kamil et al., 2008).

Building Capacity

Provide 'Discussion Coaches'. The school can identify teachers in the school who have the formal training and/or experience to run effective discussion groups. These teachers might then be available to coach other instructors in how to integrate discussion into classroom instruction. The school may consider having these 'discussion coaches' visit classrooms to actually demonstrate discussion techniques with students, as well as to observe and provide feedback to other teachers on those educators' use of discussion strategies.

Allow Teachers Opportunities to Share Their Successes in Using Extended Discussion. Adopting new classroom practices is not easy. Schools can assist teachers to make the transition to using discussion more creatively and widely by allowing them opportunities to communicate regularly with their colleagues (perhaps by content area) to share ideas for discussion topics, formats, etc.

References

Kamil, M. L., Borman, G. D., Dole, J., Kral, C. C., Salinger, T., & Torgesen, J. (2008). *Improving adolescent literacy: Effective classroom and intervention practices: A practice guide (NCEE #2008-4027).* Washington, DC: National Center for Education Evaluation and Regional Assistance, Institute of Education Sciences, U.S. Department of Education. Retrieved from http://ies.ed.gov/ncee/wwc.

Classroom Literacy Strategies: Reading Comprehension

Why This Instructional Goal is Important

Teachers have a wide degree of latitude in selecting reading comprehension strategies to use in their classrooms. At present, there is no clear evidence that any one instructional technique to promote reading comprehension is clearly superior to others. In fact, it appears that students benefit from being taught **any** self-directed practice that prompts them to engage more actively in understanding the meaning of text (Kamil et al., 2008). Reading comprehension interventions vary: Some (e.g., Oral Retell) are whole-group or cooperative learning strategies that promote a better understanding of specific reading assignments, while others (e.g., Question Generation) are designed to teach specific reading comprehension skills such as the ability to formulate a main idea sentence to capture essential ideas from an informational passage.

Strategies to Promote This Instructional Goal

Assist Students to Set 'Content Goals' for Reading (Boardman et al., 2008). Students are more likely to be motivated to read--and to read more closely—if they have specific content-related reading goals in mind. At the start of a reading assignment, for example, the instructor has students state what questions they might seek to answer or what topics they would like to learn more about in their reading. The student or teacher writes down these questions. After students have completed the assignee reading, they review their original questions and share what they have learned (e.g., through discussion in large group or cooperative learning group, or even as a written assignment).

Have Students Monitor Their Own Comprehension and Apply 'Fix-Up' Skills (Boardman et al., 2008). Teachers can teach students specific strategies to monitor their understanding of text and independently use 'fix-up' skills as needed. Examples of student monitoring and repair skills for reading comprehension include encouraging them to:

- Stop after every paragraph to summarize its main idea;
- Reread the sentence or paragraph again if necessary;
- Generate and write down questions that arise during reading;
- Restate challenging or confusing ideas or concepts from the text in the student's own words.

Teach Question-Answer Relationships (QARs) (Raphael, 1982; Raphael, 1986). Students are taught to identify 'question-answer relationships', matching the appropriate strategy to comprehension questions based on whether a question is based on fact, requires inferential thinking, or draws upon the reader's own experience. Students learn that answers to RIGHT THERE questions are fact-based and can be found in a single sentence, often accompanied by 'clue' words that also appear in the question. Students are informed that they will also find answers to THINK AND SEARCH questions in the text--but must piece those answers together by scanning the text and making connections between different pieces of factual information. AUTHOR AND YOU questions require that students take information or opinions that appear in the text and combine them with the reader's own experiences or opinions to formulate an answer. ON MY OWN questions are based on the students' own experiences and do not require knowledge of the text to answer. Students are taught to identify question-answer relationships in class discussion and demonstration. They are then given specific questions and directed to identify the question type and to use the appropriate strategy to answer.

Use a Pre-Reading Questionnaire to Tap Prior Knowledge (Duffelmeyer, 1994; Merkley, 1996). To activate their prior knowledge of a topic, students complete a brief questionnaire on which they must express agreement or disagreement with 'opinion' questions tied to the selection to be read; students then engage in a class discussion of their responses. The instructor first constructs the questionnaire. Each item on the questionnaire is linked to the content of the article or story that the students will read. All questionnaire items use a 'forced-choice' format in which the student must simply agree or disagree with the item. After students have completed the questionnaire, the teacher reviews responses with the class, allowing students an opportunity to explain their rationale for their answers. Then students read the article or story.

Troubleshooting Tips

Content-area Teachers Are Intimidated by the Request to Teach 'Reading Comprehension'. A busy teacher may feel overwhelmed at the thought of having to teach so global a skill as 'reading comprehension' to struggling students. Instead, the school can acknowledge that classroom teachers are 'content experts' and encourage them to generate ideas for helping students to better those comprehend specialized course texts and readings in which the teacher is highly knowledgeable.

Building Capacity

Allow Instructional Departments to Develop Their Own Set of Comprehension Ideas. Each academic subject presents unique reading comprehension challenges. For example, social studies often requires that students be able to read and understand historical documents from different time periods, while advanced math courses expect that students can comprehend and solve word problems with advanced math graphics. Build in regular opportunities for teachers within the various instructional departments to communicate with each other about reading comprehension strategies that work best within their discipline.

References

Boardman, A. G., Roberts, G., Vaughn, S., Wexler, J., Murray, C. S., & Kosanovich, M. (2008). *Effective instruction for adolescent struggling readers: A practice brief.* Portsmouth, NH: RMC Research Corporation, Center on Instruction.

Duffelmeyer, F.A. (1994). Effective anticipation guide statements for learning from expository prose. *Journal of Reading,* 37, 452 - 457.

Kamil, M. L., Borman, G. D., Dole, J., Kral, C. C., Salinger, T., & Torgesen, J. (2008). Improving adolescent literacy: Effective classroom and intervention practices: A practice guide (NCEE #2008-4027). Washington, DC: National Center for Education Evaluation and Regional Assistance, Institute of Education Sciences, U.S. Department of Education. Retrieved from http://ies.ed.gov/ncee/wwc.

Merkley, D.J. (1996). Modified anticipation guide. Reading Teacher, 50, 365-368.

Raphael, T. (1982). Question-answering strategies for children. *The Reading Teacher,* 36, 186-190.

Raphael, T. (1986). Teaching question answer relationships, revisited. *The Reading Teacher,* 39, 516-522.

RESOURCES Available from:
National Professional Resources, Inc.
1-800-453-7461 — www.NPRinc.com

Books

Appelbaum, Maryln. (2008). *The One-Stop Guide to Implementing RTI (K-12).* Thousand Oaks, CA: Corwin Press.

Bean, Thomas. (2010). *Multimodal Learning for the 21st Century Adolescent.* Huntington Beach, CA: Shell Education.

Bender, William. (2009). *Beyond the RTI Pyramid: Solutions for the First Years of Implementation.* Bloomington, IN: Solution Tree.

Bender, William & Cara Shores. (2007). *Response to Intervention: A Practical Guide for Every Teacher.* Thousand Oaks, CA: Corwin Press.

Bongolan, Ellen Moir, and Wendy Baron. (2009). *Keys to the Secondary Classroom: A Teacher's Guide to the First Months of School.* Thousand Oaks, CA: Corwin Press.

Brown-Chidsey, Rachel, Louise Bronaugh & Kelly McGraw. (2009). *RTI in the Classroom: Guidelines and Recipes for Success.* New York, NY: Guilford Publications, Inc.

Brozo, William G. (2011). *RTI and the Adolescent Reader: Responsive Literacy Instruction in Secondary Schools.* New York, NY: Teacher's College Press.

Buffam, Austin, Mike Mattos & Chris Weber. (2009). *Pyramid Response to Intervention.* Bloomington, IN: Solution Tree.

Campbell, Pam, et al. (2009). *55 Tactics for Implementing RTI in Inclusive Settings.* Thousand Oaks, CA: Corwin Press.

Collier, Catherine. (2010). *RTI for Diverse Learners: More Than 200 Instructional Interventions.* Thousand Oaks, CA: Corwin Press.

Donnelly, Mark & Julie Donnelly. (2011). *Guiding Adolescent Readers to Success.* Huntington Beach, CA: Shell Education.

Esquivel, G.B., Lopez, E.C. & Nahari, S. *Handbook of Multicultural School Psychology: An Interdisciplinary Perspective* (pp29-46). Mahwah, NJ: Lawrence Erlbaum Associates.

Feinstein, Sheryl (2009) *Secrets of the Teenage Brain: Research-Based Strategies for Reaching and Teaching Today's Adolescent, Second Edition.* Thousand Oaks, CA: Corwin Press.

Fisher, Douglas & Nancy Frey. (2010). *Enhancing RTI: How to Ensure Success with Effective Classroom Instruction and Intervention.* Baltimore, MD: ASCD.

Fitzell, Susan A. Gingras. (2011). *RTI Strategies for Secondary Teachers.* Thousand Oaks, CA: Corwin Press.

Gore, M.C. (2010). *Inclusion Strategies for Secondary Classrooms: Keys for Struggling Learners, Second Edition.* Thousand Oaks, CA: Corwin Press.

Haager, Diane, Janette Klingner & Sharon Vaughn. (2007). *Evidence-Based Reading Practices for Response to Intervention.* Baltimore, Maryland: Paul H. Brookes Publishing Co.

Hall, Susan L. (2008). *Implementing Response to Intervention: A Principal's Guide.* Thousand Oaks, CA: Corwin Press.

Honos-Webb, Lara. (2011) .*The ADHD Workbook for Teens: Activities to Help You Gain Motivation and Confidence.* Oakland, CA: Instant Help Books-New Harbinger Publications, Inc.

Hosp, Michelle K., John L. Hosp & Kenneth W. Howell. (2007). *The ABCs of CBM: A Practical Guide to Curriculum-Based Measurement.* New York, NY: Guilford Publications, Inc.

Howell, Robert, Sandra Patton & Margaret Deiotte. (2008). *Understanding Response to Intervention.* Bloomington, IN: Solution Tree.

Hunley, Sawyer, et al. (2009). Tier 3 of the RTI Model: *Problem Solving Through a Case Study Approach.* Thousand Oaks, CA: Corwin Press.

Jennings, Matthew. (2008). *Before the Special Education Referral.* Thousand Oaks, CA: Corwin Press.

Johnson, Evelyn S., et al. (2009). *How RTI Works in Secondary Schools.* Thousand Oaks, CA: Corwin Press.

Johnson, LouAnne. (2011). *Teaching Outside the Box: How to Grab Your Students By Their Brains, Second Edition.* Somerset, NJ: Jossey Bass-John Wiley & Sons, Inc.

Kemp, Karen & Mary Ann Eaton. (2007). *RTI: The Classroom Connection for Literacy—Reading Intervention and Measurement.* Port Chester, NY: Dude Publishing-National Professional Resources, Inc.

Kemp, Karen, et al. (2009). *RTI & Math: The Classroom Connection.* Port Chester, NY: Dude Publishing-National Professional Resources, Inc.

Lasater, Mary. (2009). *RTI and the Paraeducator's Roles: Effective Teaming.* Port Chester, NY: Dude Publishing-National Professional Resources, Inc.

Little, Mary E. (2008). *Response to Intervention for Teachers: Classroom Instructional Problem Solving.* Denver, CO: Love Publishing Company.

McDougal, James L. (2009). *RTI in Practice: A Practical Guide to Implementing Effective Evidence-Based Interventions in Your School.* Somerset, NJ: Jossey Bass-John Wiley & Sons, Inc.

Mellard, Daryl E. & Evelyn Johnson. (2008). *RTI: A Practitioner's Guide to Implementing Response to Intervention.* Thousand Oaks, CA: Corwin Press.

Ogonosky, A. (2009). *Response to Intervention for Secondary School Administrators: How to Implement RTI in Middle and High Schools.* Austin, TX: Legal Digest.

Ogonosky, A. (2008). *Response to Intervention Handbook: Moving from Theory to Practice.* Austin, TX: Legal Digest.

Rooney, K. (2009). *Strategies for Learning: Empowering Students for Success, Grades 9-12.* Thousand Oaks, CA: Corwin Press.

Russo, C., et al. (2009). *RTI Guide: Making it Work—Strategies = Solutions.* Port Chester, NY: Dude Publishing-National Professional Resources, Inc.

Sailor, Wayne. (2009). *Making RTI Work: How Smart Schools are Reforming Education Through Schoolwide Response-to-Intervention.* Somerset, NJ: Jossey-Bass/John Wiley & Sons, Inc.

Shapiro, Edward S. (2010). *Academic Skills Problems: Direct Assessment and Intervention, Fourth Edition.* New York, NY: The Guilford Press.

Shores, Cara & Kim Chester. (2008). *Using RTI for School Improvement.* Thousand Oaks, CA: Corwin Press.

Smith, L., et al. (2009). *How RTI Works in Secondary Schools.* Thousand Oaks, CA: Corwin Press.

Stone, Randi. (2010). *More Best Practices for High School Classrooms: What Award-Winning Teachers Do.* Thousand Oaks, CA: Corwin Press.

Strichart, Stephen & Charles T. Magnum II (2009). *Study Skills for Learning Disabled and Struggling Students Grades 6-12, Fourth Edition.* Upper Saddle River, NJ: Prentice Hall.

Thomas, Edward J., John R. Brunsting, Pam L Warrick. (2010). *Styles and Strategies for Teaching High School Mathematics: 21 Techniques for Differentiating Instruction and Assessment.* Thousand Oaks, CA: Corwin Press.

Whitten, Elizabeth, Kelli J. Esteves & Alice Woodrow. (2009). *RTI Success: Proven Tools & Strategies for Schools & Classrooms.* Minneapolis, MN: Free Spirit Publishing.

Wilcox, Kristen C. & Janet I. Angelis. (2009). *Best Practices from High-Performing Middle Schools: How Successful Schools Remove Obstacles and Create Pathways to Learning.* New York, NY: Teacher's College Press.

Wright, J. (2007). *RTI Data Collection Forms & Organizer: Middle/Secondary Schools.* Port Chester, NY: Dude Publishing- National Professional Resources, Inc.

Wright, J. (2007). *RTI Toolkit: A Practical Guide for Schools.* Port Chester, NY: Dude Publishing-National Professional Resources, Inc.

Young, Ellie L., et al. (2011) *Positive Behavior Support in Secondary Schools: A Practical Guide.* New York, NY: The Guilford Press.

Laminated Reference Guides

Aldrich, Seth. (2010). *RTI & ELL: Response to Intervention & English Language Learners (Laminated Reference Guide).* Port Chester, NY: Dude Publishing-National Professional Resources, Inc.

Casbarro, Joseph. (2011). *RTI for Middle Schools (Laminated Reference Guide).* Port Chester, NY: Dude Publishing-National Professional Resources, Inc.

Casbarro, Joseph. (2011). *RTI—Response to Intervention (Laminated Reference Guide).* Port Chester, NY: Dude Publishing- National Professional Resources, Inc.

Casbarro, Joseph. (2010). *Test Preparation: A Teacher's Guide (Laminated Reference Guide).* Port Chester, NY: Dude Publishing-National Professional Resources, Inc.

Ditrano, Christine. (2010). *FBA and BIP: Functional Behavioral Assessments and Behavioral Intervention Plans (Laminated Reference Guide).* Port Chester, NY: Dude Publishing-National Professional Resources, Inc.

Hanson, Helene. (2009). *RTI & DI: Response to Intervention & Differentiated Instruction: Optimizing Teaching & Learning (Laminated Reference Guide).* Port Chester, NY: Dude Publishing-National Professional Resources, Inc.

Hoerr, Thomas R. (2010). *Multiple Intelligences (MI): Pathways to Success (Laminated Reference Guide).* Port Chester, NY: Dude Publishing- National Professional Resources, Inc.

Kemp, Karen. (2010). *RTI and Reading: The Middle School Classroom Connection (Laminated Reference Guide).* Port Chester, NY: Dude Publishing- National Professional Resources, Inc.

Love, Nancy. (2011). *Data Literacy for Teachers (Laminated Reference Guide).* Port Chester, NY: Dude Publishing-National Professional Resources, Inc.

Villa, Rich & Jacqueline Thousand. (2010). *RTI: Co-Teaching and Differentiated Instruction (Laminated Reference Guide).* Port Chester, NY: Dude Publishing-National Professional Resources, Inc.

Wright, J. (2010). *RTI & Classroom Behaviors (Laminated Reference Guide).* Port Chester, NY: Dude Publishing-National Professional Resources, Inc.

DVDs

ASCD. (2010). *Implementing RTI in Secondary Schools. (DVD)*. Baltimore, MD: ASCD.

Heintzman, Lynn & Helene Hanson. (2009). *RTI & DI: The Dynamic Duo (DVD)*. Port Chester, NY. National Professional Resources, Inc.

Kemp, Karen. (2007). *RTI Tackles Reading (DVD)*. Port Chester, NY: National Professional Resources, Inc.

About the Author

Jim Wright, M.S., is a certified school psychologist and school administrator who worked for 17 years in schools in central New York State. Jim now works full-time as a regional and national RTI consultant and trainer. He has also written or contributed to several recent books on Response to Intervention. Of major significance, Jim is the creator of Intervention Central (www.interventioncentral.org), a popular web site featuring free student intervention ideas and assessment resources.